OECD Tax Policy Studies

Taxation and Philanthropy

No. 27

OECD
BETTER POLICIES FOR BETTER LIVES

This document, as well as any data and map included herein, are without prejudice to the status of or sovereignty over any territory, to the delimitation of international frontiers and boundaries and to the name of any territory, city or area.

The statistical data for Israel are supplied by and under the responsibility of the relevant Israeli authorities. The use of such data by the OECD is without prejudice to the status of the Golan Heights, East Jerusalem and Israeli settlements in the West Bank under the terms of international law.

Please cite this publication as:
OECD (2020), *Taxation and Philanthropy*, OECD Tax Policy Studies, No. 27, OECD Publishing, Paris, *https://doi.org/10.1787/df434a77-en*.

ISBN 978-92-64-63114-4 (print)
ISBN 978-92-64-40619-3 (pdf)

OECD Tax Policy Studies
ISSN 1990-0546 (print)
ISSN 1990-0538 (online)

Photo credits: Cover © selensergen/Thinkstock.

Corrigenda to publications may be found on line at: *www.oecd.org/about/publishing/corrigenda.htm*.

Foreword

Philanthropy plays an important role in most countries, providing private support to a range of activities for the public good. This differentiates the sector from government initiatives (i.e., public action for the public good) and profit-based initiatives (i.e., private action for the private good). Almost all OECD countries provide some form of preferential tax treatment for philanthropy. Entities with a philanthropic status typically receive tax relief directly in relation to their activities, while both individual and corporate donors to these entities are often able to receive tax incentives that lower the cost of giving. This report represents one of the most comprehensive attempts to catalogue the tax treatment of philanthropic entities and philanthropic giving across 40 OECD member and participating countries.

In many countries these tax preferences have been in place, unaltered, for many years despite changing social conditions. For example, when income tax exemptions for philanthropic entities were introduced in many countries around the beginning of the 20th century, there were relatively few eligible entities and most of their income was in the form of donations. Over time, the philanthropic sector has grown and many philanthropic entities now rely significantly on self-generated income, including business and investment income. Large philanthropic foundations have also become more prevalent, placing greater focus on the degree of influence of large donors on the use of taxpayer funds. Meanwhile, the increasingly global nature of many policy challenges – such as environmental and public health concerns (including the COVID-19 pandemic) – raises questions regarding the appropriate tax treatment of cross-border giving. These developments suggest that a review of the tax rules in place in many countries may be warranted.

This report provides a detailed review of the tax treatment of philanthropic entities and philanthropic giving in 40 OECD member and participating countries. The report first examines the various arguments for and against the provision of preferential tax treatment for philanthropy. It then reviews the tax treatment of philanthropic entities and giving in the 40 participating countries, in both a domestic and cross-border context. Drawing on this analysis, the report then highlights a range of potential tax policy options for countries to consider.

The report, which has been carried out as part of a collaboration between the OECD and the Geneva Centre for Philanthropy, draws heavily on country responses to a questionnaire on *Taxation and Philanthropy* by country delegates to Working Party No. 2 on Tax Policy Analysis and Tax Statistics of the OECD's Committee on Fiscal Affairs.

Acknowledgements

This study was produced by the Tax Policy and Statistics Division of the OECD Centre for Tax Policy and Administration (CTPA) in collaboration with the Geneva Centre for Philanthropy (GCP).

The study was led by Alastair Thomas, under the supervision of David Bradbury and Bert Brys. The main authors of the report were Daniel Fichmann and Alastair Thomas of the CTPA. Chapters 1, 2 and 5 were co-authored by Professor Ann O'Connell of the University of Melbourne. Chapter 5 was co-authored by Alexandre Jutand of the CTPA. The study draws heavily on information gathered from a questionnaire issued to OECD and participating countries in December 2019. This questionnaire was developed, and country responses collated, by Daniel Fichmann and Alexandre Jutand.

The study draws on the questionnaire responses and additional comments received from delegates to Working Party No. 2 on Tax Policy Analysis and Tax Statistics of the OECD Committee on Fiscal Affairs. The study has also benefitted from significant input and guidance provided by Pascal Saint-Amans, Director of the CTPA, as well as Dr Giedre Lideikyte-Huber and Professor Henry Peter, Head of the GCP. Karena Garnier and Carrie Tyler assisted with the publication process. Violet Sochay provided administrative assistance.

Table of contents

Tables

Figures

Boxes

Executive Summary

Most countries provide some form of preferential tax treatment for philanthropy. Entities with a philanthropic status typically receive tax relief directly in relation to their activities, while both individual and corporate donors to these entities are typically able to receive tax incentives that lower the cost of giving. This report provides a detailed review of the taxation of philanthropic entities and philanthropic giving in 40 OECD member and participating countries, and draws on this analysis to highlight a range of potential policy options for countries to consider.

The report first examines the various arguments for and against tax concessions, highlighting that there is no single generally accepted rationale for the preferential tax treatment of philanthropy. Economic theory, for example, provides a limited rationale for preferential tax treatment of philanthropy where there is under-provision of a public good or where there are positive externalities associated with the philanthropic activity. Additional arguments include that the surplus of a philanthropic entity is different in nature to income (and therefore beyond the scope of the income tax base), and that philanthropic giving strengthens civil society and so should be encouraged. Arguments against tax concessions for philanthropy highlight, for example, their fiscal cost, as well as potential distributional and democratic concerns. In particular, richer taxpayers often receive larger tax incentives than poorer taxpayers. Meanwhile, as a tax incentive effectively reallocates tax revenue towards the favoured philanthropic entity, richer taxpayers who make larger donations may gain a disproportionate influence over how public resources are allocated.

The report then considers, in turn, the tax treatment of philanthropic entities and of giving to philanthropic entities, before considering cross-border issues. For an entity to receive philanthropic status and the associated tax benefits, it typically must meet "not-for-profit", "worthy purpose", and "public benefit" requirements, as well as being subject to other administrative and oversight requirements. Not-for-profit requirements prevent any form of profit distribution. Worthy purpose requirements specify the types of activities eligible for support – most commonly welfare, education, scientific research, and healthcare. Public benefit requirements typically stipulate that the benefit must be open to a sufficiently broad section of the public.

Most countries surveyed provide concessionary income tax treatment for approved philanthropic entities. The report identifies two approaches commonly taken: the first is to exempt all (or specific) income, and the second is to consider all forms of income taxable, but to allow the entity to reduce its taxable income through current or future reinvestments towards the fulfilment of its worthy purpose. Countries following the first approach generally exclude non-commercial income (received gifts or grants) from the tax base. Approaches to dealing with commercial activities and the income generated from those activities, diverge. A common approach is to exempt commercial income that is related to the worthy purpose and tax unrelated commercial income. A number of countries also provide preferential VAT treatment to philanthropic entities, and concessions regarding various other taxes (e.g. property taxes).

All the countries surveyed also provide some form of tax incentive to encourage philanthropic giving to eligible entities, although the generosity and design of the incentives vary. In the large majority of countries surveyed, donations are deductible from an individual's taxable income. Other countries offer tax credits instead and, in some cases, the donations of individuals are matched by government. Furthermore, as long as there is a sufficient nexus with earning income, most countries consider corporate sponsoring of philanthropic entities a deductible business expense. Additionally, most countries that levy inheritance or estate taxes generally provide preferential tax relief for philanthropic bequests. Restrictions on the size of tax incentives for giving are common and vary across countries. Some countries limit the size of the tax incentive by adopting a cap of a fixed amount, while others adopt caps based on a percentage of the donor's income or tax liability, and some adopt a combination of both. To limit the cost of matching schemes, countries set the rate at which the relief may be claimed by the receiving philanthropic entity. Lastly, the majority of countries that incentivise cash donations of individuals also incentivise non-monetary donations.

Regarding cross-border philanthropy, the report finds that, beyond the European Union, there is little tax support provided by countries for cross-border giving. With regard to philanthropic entities that operate across borders, beyond the European Union, most countries do not provide tax relief for foreign philanthropic entities operating domestically. However, many countries do allow domestic entities to operate abroad without losing their tax-favoured status, though they are potentially subject to additional restrictions or reporting requirements.

Drawing on the preceding analysis, the report highlights a number of key issues that countries face in the design of their tax rules for philanthropy. First, the report highlights that countries need to ensure that the design of their tax incentives for philanthropic giving is consistent with their underlying policy goals. For example, countries that are particularly concerned about restricting support to areas prioritised by government may wish to consider limiting the breadth of their eligibility criteria. Countries particularly concerned about the distributional impact of the tax incentive, may wish to provide a tax credit, which will ensure that the same proportionate tax benefit is provided to taxpayers irrespective of their income level. Conversely, countries with a progressive personal income tax system wishing to provide a greater incentive to richer donors in order to maximise total giving, may wish to provide a tax deduction.

Second, countries should reassess the merits of providing tax exemptions for the commercial income of philanthropic entities, at least insofar as this income is unrelated to the entity's worthy purpose. In undertaking such a reassessment, countries will need to consider the added complexities associated with distinguishing between taxable (i.e. unrelated commercial income) and exempt income and weigh the additional compliance and administrative costs against the pursuit of competitive neutrality. Furthermore, countries that currently provide an exemption should consider fully subjecting philanthropic entities to the VAT.

Third, the report identifies a number of ways countries can look to both reduce the complexity and improve the oversight of the concessionary tax regimes for philanthropy. These include: applying the same eligibility tests for both philanthropic entities and philanthropic giving; imposing a minimum value threshold for a non-monetary donation to receive a tax incentive; establishing a publicly available register of approved philanthropic entities; introducing an annual reporting requirement; implementing a combined oversight approach (e.g. tax administration and independent commission); clearly differentiating between corporate donations and sponsorship; improving data collection and tax expenditure reports; implementing limits to fundraising expenditures; implementing rules that limit certain types of operating expenses of philanthropic entities; and limiting the remuneration of staff, managers, and board members of philanthropic entities.

Finally, the increasingly global nature of many policy challenges – such as environmental and public health concerns (including the COVID-19 pandemic) – may require countries and institutions to cooperate across borders. In this context, there is merit in countries reassessing whether there may be some instances where equivalent tax treatment should be provided to domestic and cross-border philanthropy. To address concerns regarding oversight, countries could impose equivalent requirements as apply in the domestic philanthropy context, or require additional checks before providing tax-favoured status.

1 Introduction

This introductory chapter provides background information on the characteristics of the philanthropic sector, to set the scene for the detailed analysis of the taxation of philanthropy that follows in the report. It also provides an outline of the overall structure of the report.

Philanthropy plays an important role in most countries, providing support for a wide range of private activities and initiatives in support of the public good. This differentiates the sector from government initiatives (i.e., public action for the public good) and profit-based initiatives (i.e., private action for the private good). The use of the tax system as a means of supporting philanthropy is widespread. In addition to government grants and the contracting of services to philanthropic entities ("direct support"), governments typically support philanthropy ("indirectly") in two ways, by providing: tax incentives for giving to philanthropic entities; and (full or partial) exemptions of philanthropic entities from various taxes.

In many cases these tax preferences have been in place, unaltered, for many years despite changing social conditions. For example, when income tax exemptions for philanthropic entities were introduced in many countries around the beginning of the 20th century, there were relatively few eligible entities and most of their income was in the form of donations. Over time, the sector has grown, often in response to out-sourcing by governments of welfare and other services, and many philanthropic entities now rely significantly on self-generated income, including business and investment income. There have also been significant developments in research on the optimal design of tax incentives for giving that highlight, for example, a range of efficiency and distributional concerns. Furthermore, the increasing prevalence of large philanthropic foundations has placed greater focus on the degree of influence of large donors on the use of taxpayer funds. Finally, the global nature of many of the challenges facing the world such as environmental, medical research, and public health concerns (such as the COVID-19 pandemic), raises questions regarding the appropriate tax treatment of cross-border giving.

In light of these developments, a reassessment of the tax rules in place in many countries may be warranted. To aid such reassessment, this report provides a detailed review of the taxation of philanthropic entities and philanthropic giving in 40 OECD member and participating countries, and highlights potential reform options for countries to consider. The report draws heavily on country responses to a questionnaire on *Taxation and Philanthropy* ("the questionnaire") by country delegates to Working Party No. 2 on Tax Policy Analysis and Tax Statistics of the OECD's Committee on Fiscal Affairs.

This introductory chapter provides a range of background information on the philanthropic sector to aid the analysis to follow. It first discusses the exact meaning of philanthropy adopted in this report. It then highlights a number of key aspects of the philanthropic sector, before discussing the size of the philanthropic sector both in terms of the number of philanthropic entities and the total amount of giving to the philanthropic sector. Finally, the chapter provides an outline of the structure of the report to follow.

1.1. Defining philanthropy

The term "philanthropy" does not have a universally accepted meaning. The term derives from the Greek "philanthropia" meaning "love of humanity" or "love of gods for humanity". Various attempts have been made to define the term. Dictionary definitions include "the gratuitous transfer of funds or other property for altruistic purposes".[1]

Scholars from different disciplines have also sought to define the term, referencing various concepts such as the "voluntary" aspect of philanthropy, the notion of "generosity" or concern for others, or the application of private resources for public purposes. For example, philanthropy has been described as:

- voluntary giving, and voluntary association, primarily for the benefit of others; (Payton, 1988[1]) or
- the voluntary giving and receiving of time and money, aimed (however imperfectly) towards the needs of charity and the interests of all in a better quality of life; (Van Til, 1990[2]) or
- the use of personal wealth and skills to benefit specific public causes. (Anheier, 2005[3])

All of these 'definitions' are concerned with the act of giving, but the term philanthropy is also used in other contexts. For example, philanthropy has been defined as being 'one form of income of non-profit entities' (Salamon and Anheier, 1992[4]), equating philanthropy with donations and moving the focus from the act of giving to the recipient entities. The term is also sometimes used to refer to the entities themselves, with one researcher noting that the term 'typically applies to philanthropic foundations and similar institutions' (Anheier, 2005[3]).

Another definition is: 'The planned and structured giving of money, time, information, goods and services, influence and voice to improve the wellbeing of humanity and the community' (Philanthropy Australia[5]). This definition is narrower in that it emphasises planned and structured giving, but also notes different types of gifts and includes the notion of community. It has also been said that 'being a philanthropist is synonymous with the largesse of rich individual donors' (Anheier and Leat, 2006[6]). But generally the term is considered broad enough to cover all giving.

Despite the divergent uses of the term, there are some common threads: philanthropy is concerned with 'giving', and with 'worthy' and 'public', rather than private, causes. Several definitions refer to giving time as well as money. There is also a reference to 'altruism' or concern for others in some of the definitions, but this is not generally part of any definition that specifies which entities or activities qualify for tax relief. Indeed, some entities exist for the benefit of their members rather than for the broader public benefit e.g. a disability support group. The focus then, is on 'gifting' – the making of voluntary contributions without expectation of return; and on identification of appropriate worthy causes or purposes. This identification of 'worthy purposes' is likely to differ between jurisdictions and is an important part of the tax framework in this area.

In some common law countries, the term 'charity' is often used to refer to the act of giving or to the entities that either enable or carry out activities. Although the terms charity and philanthropy are sometimes used interchangeably, they do not necessarily have the same meaning. While charity and philanthropy both seek to accomplish the same outcome – to address needs and make the world a better place – the method that philanthropic entities and charitable entities each use to reach that outcome is different. Whereas charity refers to the direct relief of suffering and social problems, philanthropy systematically seeks out root causes of these issues and endeavours to find a solution (Anheier and Toepler, 2010[7]). This distinction has been significant in the emergence of modern philanthropic foundations, particularly in the United States.

This report will use the terms philanthropic giving and philanthropic entities, respectively, to refer to:

- the act of giving by individuals and corporations, to philanthropic entities with worthy purposes, and
- entities that are engaged in activities in pursuit of those purposes, including by providing funds to other entities.

1.2. The philanthropic sector

Although philanthropy has a long history, the idea of a philanthropic sector or 'third sector' beyond the realms of the state and the market is of fairly recent origin, certainly post-World War 2. This relatively recent recognition of the sector as having an economic and political presence may explain why there is limited research into the sector as such, with the notable exception being in the United States.[2] More recently other countries have undertaken research, and there have been a number of comparative world-wide studies[3] that have identified common characteristics and helped to inform decision-makers. The notion of a distinct sector remains a perplexing concept in modern political and social discourse, as it covers a tremendous diversity of institutions and behaviours.

It is difficult to compare philanthropic sectors across countries for a number of reasons. First, each country will have its own historical, economic and political background that will influence the size and scope of the sector. This has been described as the 'social origins' theory that considers inter alia, how and why welfare states took on different forms (Anheier and Salamon, 1996[8]). The theory suggests an inverse relationship between the extent of government social welfare spending and the size of the non-profit sector. This research identifies countries as having one of four characterisations:

- **'liberal states'** – where democratic government developed before the welfare state. The welfare state may be limited but available to the 'deserving poor'. These countries are likely to have a larger philanthropic sector;
- **'social-democratic states'** – where the working class gained power and pushed for a universal welfare state. As a result of the high level of welfare, these countries tend to have smaller philanthropic sectors;
- **'corporatist states'** – where the welfare state developed under the control of non-democratic states that later became democratic. These countries tend to have low welfare and large philanthropic sectors;
- **'statist states'** – where a country's elites are in control of the public good provision, and this leads to both low government spending on social welfare and a small philanthropic sector.[4]

The theory also suggests that there will be differences across countries in the predominant types of non-profits, shaped by historical development and class relations. Other country specific issues may include the role of religion in the development of the country, including in the development of philanthropic traditions. Economic development may also be significant both in terms of needy recipients and in the accumulation of the financial ability to provide welfare and for citizens to be able to contribute by way of philanthropy.

Other factors that may make comparisons difficult include notions of 'legal families', that is whether the country has a common law or civil law tradition. Common law countries tend to adopt the notion of 'charity' that dates from the Preamble to a Statute of Elizabeth of 1601,[5] as the basis for identifying worthy purposes and activities. Civil law countries will not be constrained by these notions but may have strong traditions of freedom of association and organising for workers' rights. The German non-profit sector has, for example, been influenced by the principle of 'subsidiarity' that gives priority to private over public action in many areas such as health and social services. The principle of 'self-administration' also gives independence to many public institutions and both of these features make it difficult to identify the non-profit or philanthropic sector as such. (Salamon and Anheier, 1992[4])

Given this diversity, identifying the philanthropic sector in a country for the purposes of comparison means identifying characteristics that are essential. The Johns Hopkins University Comparative Non-profit Sector Project (JHU Project) (Salamon, Sokolowski and List, 2003[9])[6] developed a set of factors to identify non-profit entities that they suggested could be applied across jurisdictions for the purpose of carrying out comparisons of the 'non-profit sector':

- **voluntary** – the voluntariness of those participating and of the entity acting is one of the factors that sets these activities apart from government;
- **self-governing** – not directed by government or others as to how to act;
- **private** – that is, not part of government. The Project notes that in some countries there may a blurring of the line between private and public activity;
- **non-profit distributing** – although these entities may make profits or generate a surplus, they are not formed for the purpose of profit making. The non-distribution requirement distinguishes these entities from for-profit entities;
- **formal**, that is institutionalised to some extent. This would preclude individual acts of philanthropy or assistance to another individual.[7]

1.2.1. Philanthropic activity

This report separates **philanthropic activity** into three dimensions: Giving; funds; and Public Benefit Organisations (PBOs). Each of these activities has different tax implications.

Giving

An important source of funds for philanthropic entities is donations. Philanthropic giving occurs at an individual or corporate level, typically in the form of gifts to funds or PBOs directly, and in the case of individual giving, it may also be in the form of bequests. Individuals may also contribute time or services i.e. volunteering. Businesses may also provide services on a pro bono basis.

Funds

Funds are entities such as grant-making foundations (or 'fundaçions') and trusts that hold assets with which they provide support in the form of grants to PBOs to advance a worthy purpose. This report uses the term 'funds' to refer to intermediaries that provide support to PBOs.

Public Benefit Organisations (PBOs)

Public Benefit Organisation or 'PBO' is the term used in this report to refer to entities that carry out the worthy purposes. However, the distinction between funds and PBOs is not always clear cut, for example, in some countries PBOs do not exclusively work directly with beneficiaries. Many jurisdictions use the term 'charity' to refer to these types of entities. PBOs can be distinguished from funds as they work directly with beneficiaries. There are two matters that are specific to PBOs – the fact that they obtain monies to carry out their worthy purpose from philanthropy – both directly and in the form of grants from funds, but also from government and from self-funded sources, including commercial activities. Secondly, PBOs can take a variety of legal forms. This may have significance for tax purposes e.g. if it is a condition of relief that an entity take a particular form.

In general, philanthropic entities may adopt, or be regarded as having, various legal forms. Some jurisdictions may exclude some legal forms from eligibility such as partnerships, political parties or government entities. Forms that may be adopted include:

- unincorporated associations – a number of people coming together to pursue a common purpose. Generally, these associations are not treated as having legal personality, although some form of registration process may confer legal status in certain jurisdictions. In civil law countries, the right to form associations is often enshrined in the Constitution;
- incorporated entities – the adoption of separate legal form e.g. corporations. Some jurisdictions also offer a special form of incorporation for charitable or philanthropic entities. Some jurisdictions may offer a modified form of incorporation to allow for the non-distribution requirement;
- foundations – may be either grant-making or operating foundations. This report uses the term 'funds' to refer to grant-making foundations. Foundations may take a variety of legal forms;
- trusts – a legal device used in common law countries to denote the separation of the legal rights to the (trust) property from the enjoyment of that property. The holding of trust property in this way ensures that the holder (the trustee) must comply with high standards in dealing with the property. The trust is commonly used for establishing foundations or other funds and denotes a setting aside of monies for the philanthropic purpose;
- co-operatives or mutual entities – are also associations of persons that come together for a common purpose, although they may also have a special form of incorporation. A non-profit co-operative e.g. a child-care co-operative, where the parents run a child care centre but do not distribute any surplus (a 'non-distributing co-operative'), may qualify as part of the philanthropic sector in some countries. Other countries may consider such co-operatives or mutual entities as providing more than an insubstantial benefit to private interests (e.g. the parents of the children being cared for) and therefore would not consider them a philanthropic entity. Co-operatives that distribute profits to members ('distributing co-operatives') will typically be taxed under special provisions. Generally, non-distributing co-operatives will not be taxed under specialist co-operative tax provisions;
- other – there may be other types of entities e.g. religious orders that do not fit into the other categories.

Whatever legal form is adopted; most jurisdictions will treat the entity as a corporation for tax purposes. The legal form may however be relevant for matters such as regulation and for other legal obligations.

1.2.2. The size of the philanthropic sector

The results of the *Taxation and Philanthropy* questionnaire highlight significant variety in terms of the size and scope of the philanthropic sector. Table 1.1 presents the approximate number of philanthropic entities that were eligible for some form of preferential tax treatment in 2018 (for the 27 countries that provided data).[8] The Table also contains the respective populations, expressed in millions.

What these numbers show is that there are a significant number of entities that are eligible for tax concessions, although the number of entities varies widely between countries.

The number of philanthropic entities in a country is, of course, only one measure of the size and significance of the sector in a country. Other measures include the economic contribution, the size of the workforce and, uniquely to the sector, the number of people volunteering. Reliable data on these measures across countries is notoriously difficult to estimate. Despite the limitations of measuring the contribution of the philanthropic sector, the JHU Project surveyed 35 countries in the period 1995 to 2002 and found that using expenditures as a proxy for economic contribution, the sector accounted for USD 1.3 trillion, or 5.1%

of combined Gross Domestic Product (GDP) (Salamon, Sokolowski and List, 2003[9]). The JHU Project also looked at the size of the workforce and found that there were 39.5 million full-time equivalent (FTE) workers, including 21.8 million paid workers and 12.6 FTE volunteers representing 4.4% of the economically active population. Further, they found that 190 million people were volunteers across the 35 countries surveyed. More recently, in 2013 the JHU project estimated for a smaller sample of 15 countries (drawing on data from 2002-2009) that the sector's economic contribution was 4.5% of GDP (Salamon et al., 2013[10]).

Table 1.1. Number of philanthropic entities across countries

Country	Approximate number of entities	Population in 2018 (million)
Argentina	17 756	44.5
Australia	188 000[1]	25.0
Austria	1 230	8.8
Belgium	2241[2]	11.4
Canada	86 000	37.1
Chile	311 319[3]	18.8
Colombia	44 000	49.8
Czech Republic	130 000[4]	10.6
Estonia	2 474	1.3
France	4 188[12]	66.9
Germany	600 000	82.9
Ireland	9 781[5]	4.9
Israel	40 000[6]	8.9
Italy	98 231[13]	60.4
Latvia	2 000	1.9
Lithuania	11 400	2.8
Mexico	8 763[7]	125.3
Netherlands	43 000[8]	17.2
New Zealand	27 000	4.9
Portugal	8 148	10.3
Romania	144	19.5
Singapore	2 277[9]	4.0
Slovak Republic	8 687	5.4
Slovenia	28 524	2.1
Sweden	99 300[10]	10.2
Switzerland	10 000	8.5
United States	1 682 091[11]	327.2

Notes:

1. Includes income tax exempt and gift deductible recipients.
2. Registered since 2018.
3. This is the total number of taxpayers registered as non-profit organizations, however it may include inactive entities. Additionally, it may include organizations that do not fit within the PBO definition.
4. Total number of not-for-profit entities
5. Tax exempt entities.
6. Not-for-profit, but not necessarily eligible for tax concessions.
7. Authorised donees.
8. PBOs; number of funds not available.
9. In Singapore, registered charities are eligible for income tax relief. Of these registered charities, 666 are Institutions of Public Character (IPCs) which receive 250% tax deductions on qualifying donations.
10. Registered as not-for-profit but not necessarily eligible for all concessions.
11. Recognised entities under s 501(c) Internal Revenue Code (this does not include churches).
12. 2 537 foundations and 1 651 active endowment funds (no data on total PBOs).
13. Data refer to ONLUS (Non-profit organisation of social utility) from data from tax returns and other fiscal-related administrative information.

Source: OECD Taxation and Philanthropy Questionnaire and OECD Labour Force Statistics 2020

1.2.3. Total amount of giving to funds and PBOs

The significance of philanthropy can also be seen in the level of donations to philanthropic entities, which is presented in Table 1.2. Data availability, and comparability, is however imperfect. In particular, not all countries were able to provide the total annual amount of donations to PBOs and funds in 2018, and, in some countries, only the amount of donations eligible for preferential tax treatment is available. Nevertheless, the questionnaire responses highlight that the amount of philanthropic giving varies widely across countries and that there is a significant amount of giving to philanthropic entities that gets the benefit of preferential tax treatment.

Table 1.2. Total amount of giving to funds and PBOs

Country	Total amount of giving to funds and PBOs	USD million
Argentina	ARS 5 019 million (2018)	72.0
Austria	EUR 630 million (2017)	704.0
Belgium	EUR 263.2 million (PIT donations) (2017)	294.0
Canada	CAD 9.6 billion (individuals) (2017)	7 100.0
	CAD 3.8 billion approx. (corporations) (2017)	2 790.0
Chile	CLP 276 479 million donations (2018)	358.1
	CLP 10 052 million inheritances (2018)	13.0
Czech Republic	CZK 5.9 billion (2017)	249.0
Estonia	EUR 9.4 million (2018).	10.5
France	EUR 2 545 million (PIT donations) (2018)	2 968.9
	EUR 112 million in donations reported by the real estate and wealth tax (2018)	130.6
	Between EUR 2.3 billion and EUR 2.5 billion in corporate donations (2015)	2 683.0 – 2 916.1
Germany	EUR 5.3 billion (2018)	5 920.0
Ireland	EUR 83.7 million 2018	93.5
Italy	EUR 705.5 million (2017)	788.4
Latvia	EUR 28 million (2017)	32.1
Lithuania	EUR 12.2 million (individuals) (2018)	13.6
	EUR 68 million (companies) (2018)	76.0
Mexico	MXN 47 659 million (2018)	2 477.0
Netherlands	EUR 845 million (including EUR 20 million from businesses) (yearly average from 2008-2014)	944.5
New Zealand	NZD 900 million approx. (2018)	577.0
Portugal	EUR 372 million, including EUR 59 million in goods in kind	415.0
Romania	RON 115.5 million in 2014-2017	26.0
Singapore	SGD 1 billion (2018)	715.0
Slovak Republic	EUR 14 million (2018)	15.6
Slovenia	EUR 29.6 million (2018)	33.0
United States	USD 180.5 billion in cash donations, USD 88.1 billion in non-cash donations, and USD 35.4 billion carried over from prior periods (individuals) (2017) C corporations USD 18.6 billion (2017), charitable bequests of USD 22.8 billion (2018)	345 400.0

Source: OECD Taxation and Philanthropy Questionnaire

The data provided does not, of course, reveal the total amount of giving in a country. It does not reflect, for example, giving to entities that are not eligible recipients. In Australia, giving to religious entities is not deductible, but nevertheless approximately 30% of annual giving is to a religious entity (Charities Aid Foundation, 2019[11]). The data will also not include giving where the donor has not claimed the tax relief. This may be inadvertent, or where giving falls below relevant thresholds, but there are also cases where donors choose not to access tax relief as a means of retaining greater control of the spending.[9]

Research by the Charities Aid Foundation in 2016, compared giving as a percentage of GDP for 24 countries using surveys and publicly available data. Table 1.3 shows the results for countries that are included in the questionnaire. It should be noted however that the results are not necessarily confined to giving that received subsidies and preferential tax treatment.

Table 1.3. Giving as a percentage of GDP

Country	Giving as a percentage of GDP
Australia	0.23
Austria	0.14
Canada	0.77
Czech Republic	0.04
Finland	0.13
France	0.11
Germany	0.17
India	0.37
Ireland	0.22
Italy	0.30
Japan	0.12
Korea	0.50
Netherlands	0.30
New Zealand	0.79
Norway	0.11
Singapore	0.39
Sweden	0.16
Switzerland	0.09
United Kingdom	0.54
United States	1.40

Source: Derived from Charities Aid Foundation, Gross Domestic Philanthropy: An international analysis of GDP, tax and giving, January 2016, https://www.cafonline.org/docs/default-source/about-us-policy-and-campaigns/gross-domestic-philanthropy-feb-2016.pdf

1.2.4. Sources of revenue for philanthropic entities

Another finding of the JHU Project is that philanthropic giving is significant but not the main source of revenue for philanthropic entities. The composition of the sources of revenue, namely which proportion of revenue is from philanthropy, from fee income and from government, also varies widely. According to the JHU Project, the classification they adopted refers to *philanthropic giving*, which includes individual giving, corporate giving and foundation giving (grants); *fees*, which includes private payments for goods and services, membership dues, and investment income; and *government* or public sector support, which includes grants, contracts, and payments from all levels of government. The results for countries in our survey are in Table 1.4.

The data shows that philanthropic giving is not the most significant source of funding for any country. Beyond that, it is not possible to say whether self-funding or government support is the most significant as the results vary substantially by type of philanthropic entity and country. Furthermore, averages can be misleading. In the United States, for example, non-profit schools, colleges and hospitals receive substantial revenues from tuition, fees and some government grants, reducing the average percentage from donations. Other types of philanthropic entities, however, such as food banks and other social welfare organisations depend much more on donations. It is also not possible to say whether there is any causal relationship – that is, whether entities turn to self-funding because the other sources of revenue are in decline, or whether the receipt of government funding means the entity has less need to generate its own income or to engage in fundraising. One issue that has generated significant literature is whether the receipt of government grants by non-profits has a crowding-out effect i.e. whether the receipt of such funding means that philanthropy is discouraged. This is considered in Chapter 2.

Table 1.4. Not-for-profit revenue sources across countries

Country	% Philanthropic giving	% Fees	% Government
Argentina	7	73	19
Australia	6	63	31
Austria	6	44	50
Belgium	5	19	77
Colombia	15	70	15
Czech Republic	14	47	39
Germany	3	32	64
Finland	7	58	58
Hungary	18	55	27
Japan	3	52	45
Korea	4	71	24
Ireland	7	16	77
Israel	10	26	64
Italy	3	61	37
Mexico	6	85	9
Netherlands	2	39	59
Norway	7	58	35
Romania	27	29	45
Slovak Republic	23	55	22
Sweden	9	62	29
United Kingdom	9	45	47
United States	13	57	31
South Africa	24	31	44

Source: Derived from Salamon, Sokolowski and List (2003[9]) Figure 11, p 32 and Salamon, Sokolowski and Anheiner (2000[12]) Figure 3, p 6, The Johns Hopkins Comparative Non-profit Sector Project.

1.3. Outline of the report

The rest of this report is structured as follows. Chapter 2 investigates the various arguments both for and against the provision of tax concessions for philanthropic entities, and the provision of tax incentives for philanthropic giving.

Chapter 3 examines the tax treatment of philanthropic entities across OECD member and selected participating countries, starting with the qualification process for entities to become recognised PBOs or funds, including worthy purpose, public benefit, and not-for-profit requirements, followed by an overview of the administrative application and regulatory process. The chapter then analyses the different forms of tax relief that philanthropic entities benefit from. Finally, the chapter highlights the potential risk of tax avoidance and evasion schemes involving philanthropic entities and the anti-abuse policies countries have put in place as a result.

Chapter 4 examines the tax treatment of donors and philanthropic giving across OECD member and selected participating countries. It first considers the tax design of incentives for giving by individuals, and then countries' tax incentives for corporate giving. It also highlights the potential risk of tax avoidance and evasion and the anti-abuse policies countries have put in place as a result.

Chapter 5 considers the taxation of cross-border philanthropy. It first considers tax incentives for giving: both donations and bequests; and also considers how gift and inheritance taxes apply and how capital gains tax might apply where the gift is non-cash. It then considers the tax treatment of philanthropic entities that operate across borders, examining whether tax relief is extended to foreign philanthropic entities operating domestically, and the tax treatment of domestic PBOs operating across borders. Finally, it considers the tax treatment of international grant-making by funds.

Chapter 6 brings together the key insights from the preceding chapters and discusses their tax policy implications. It highlights the importance of countries ensuring that the design of their tax incentives for philanthropic giving are consistent with their underlying policy goals. It also suggests that countries reassess the merits of providing tax exemptions for the commercial income of philanthropic entities, at least insofar as this income is unrelated to the entity's worthy purpose. More broadly, the chapter finds scope for countries to both reduce the complexity and improve the oversight of their concessionary regimes for philanthropic entities and philanthropic giving. Finally, in light of the increasingly global nature of many policy challenges – such as environmental and public health concerns (including the COVID-19 pandemic) – it suggests countries reassess the restrictions commonly imposed on access to tax concessions for cross-border philanthropy.

References

Anheier et al. (2020), *The Non-profit Sector: A Research Handbook*, Yale University Press, London. [13]

Anheier, H. (2005), *A Dictionary of Civil Society, Philanthropy and the Non-profit Sector*, Routledge, London. [3]

Anheier, H. and D. Leat (2006), *Creative Philanthropy: Toward a New Philanthropy for the Twenty-First Century*, Routledge, London. [6]

Anheier, H. and L. Salamon (1996), "The Social Origin of Civil Society: Explaining the Non-profit Sector Cross-Nationally", *International Journal of Voluntary and Nonprofit Organizations*, Vol. 9, pp. 213–248. [8]

Anheier, H. and S. Toepler (2010), *International Encyclopedia of Civil Society*, Springer Publishing, New York. [7]

Charities Aid Foundation (2019), *Australia Giving 2019*, https://www.cafonline.org/docs/default-source/about-us-publications/caf-australia-giving-report-2019-16master.pdf?sfvrsn=65e49940_2. [11]

Philanthropy Australia (n.d.), "Glossary", https://www.philanthropy.org.au/tools-resources/glossary/#P. [5]

Payton, R. (1988), *Philanthropy: Voluntary action for the public good*, Macmillan Publishing, London. [1]

Salamon, L. and H. Anheier (1992), "In search of the non-profit sector I: The question of definitions", *International Journal of Voluntary and Non-profit Organisations*, Vol. 3, pp. 125–151. [4]

Salamon, L., S. Sokolowski and H. Anheiner (2000), *Social Origins of Civil Society: An Overview*, Johns Hopkins Comparative Nonprofit Sector Project, Johns Hopkins University, Baltimore. [12]

Salamon, L., S. Sokolowski and R. List (2003), *Global Civil Society: An Overview*, Johns Hopkins Comparative Nonprofit Sector Project, Johns Hopkins University, Baltimore. [9]

Salamon, L. S. Sokolowski, M. Haddock and H.Tice (2013), "The State of Global Civil Society and Volunteering: Latest findings from the implementation of the UN Nonprofit Handbook", *Comparative Nonprofit Sector Working Papers*, No. 49, Johns Hopkins University. [10]

Van Til, J. (1990), *Defining Philanthropy*, Jossey Bass, San Francisco. [2]

Notes

[1] Merriam-Webster Dictionary (online).

[2] See, for example, the work of the Johns Hopkins University Comparative Non-profit Sector Project and the University of Indiana's Lilly Family School of Philanthropy.

[3] See for example, the Comparative Non-profit Sector Project at The Johns Hopkins University: http://ccss.jhu.edu/research-projects/comparative-nonprofit-sector-project/

[4] More recently one of the original authors has questioned the utility of the theory (Anheier et al., 2020[13]).

[5] The Preamble set out a range of (mostly) secular purposes that could be supported. The classification of 'charity' into four heads arises from the case of Commissioners for Special Purposes of Income Tax v Pemsel (1891) AC 531.

[6] JHU launched this project in the 1990s to gather systematically a body of internationally comparative data on community service organisations (CSOs), philanthropy, and volunteerism. The Project operates in more than 45 countries, spanning all of the world's continents and most of its major religious and cultural traditions. The Project has produced a rich body of comparative data, the Johns Hopkins Global Civil Society Index, several books, and more than 60 published working papers written or edited by Project staff, mostly with indigenous authors. More information about the JHU Project is available at: http://ccss.jhu.edu/research-projects/comparative-nonprofit-sector-project/

[7] Ibid.

[8] In the last years, the Italian philanthropic sector has been involved in a wide reform that aims to simplify philanthropic businesses and encourage public giving. The reform, approved by the Italian Parliament in 2017 (legislative decree 117/2017), is not yet entirely in force, because some technical ministerial decrees are still missing. In particular, as regards the fiscal aspects of the reform, an authorisation of the European Commission is necessary to allow the implementation of a preferential regime, according to the European Union State-aid rules.

[9] See, for example, the Chan Zuckerberg Initiative which is structured as an LLC rather than a traditional foundation: https://chanzuckerberg.com

2 The case for providing tax concessions for philanthropy

The chapter provides an overview of the different rationales for tax incentives for philanthropy domestically and internationally and some of the arguments against providing incentives. It starts by providing a brief overview of the different rationales for tax incentives for philanthropic entities and the case for tax incentives for giving to philanthropic entities. It then summarises the arguments against these tax incentives. Finally, the chapter also discusses the rationales for incentivising cross-border giving.

2.1. Introduction

While philanthropy plays an important role in most countries, this does not automatically mean that it justifies support through the tax system.[1] This chapter examines the different rationales for and against providing tax incentives for philanthropy[2] domestically and internationally. It considers both: (1) tax concessions for philanthropic entities; and (2) tax incentives for giving to philanthropic entities. The chapter highlights that there is no single generally accepted rationale for preferential tax treatment of philanthropic entities. Economic theory provides a limited rationale for providing tax concessions for philanthropy (potentially both for entities and giving) where there is under-provision of a public good or where there are positive externalities associated with philanthropic activity. In this regard, tax concessions will be justified if they result in a larger increase in social welfare than that which government could have otherwise achieved through direct spending. Legal scholars frequently refer to this as the subsidy rationale.

Another often articulated argument for exempting philanthropic entities from income tax is the "base defining" rationale which argues that the surplus of a philanthropic entity is different in nature to income and therefore beyond the scope of the income tax base. Additional arguments include that philanthropic giving, as well as the institutions it develops, strengthen civil society, and decentralise decision-making, and are thus an important feature of a democratic society and worth supporting.

A number of arguments have been raised against the provision of tax preferences for philanthropic entities and/or giving. The cost of providing concessions is often highlighted as a concern. By reducing government revenue, tax concessions for philanthropy require other taxpayers to bear an increased tax burden (or alternatively result in less government expenditure on other policy priorities). A concern regarding exemption of commercial income of philanthropic entities is that this may create an unfair competitive advantage for philanthropic entities over for-profit businesses.

Two related concerns that are raised regarding tax incentives for giving are that they may be regressive and undemocratic. Tax incentives may be regressive in that higher income taxpayers benefit from a larger tax incentive than lower income taxpayers. This can be the case in both aggregate terms, but also in proportionate terns as a tax deduction will provide a greater benefit to higher income taxpayers where they are subject to higher marginal tax rates than lower income taxpayers. The democratic argument highlights the concern that, as a tax incentive effectively reallocates tax revenue towards the favoured philanthropic entity, higher income taxpayers that make larger donations benefit from a disproportionate influence in the determination of how tax revenue is spent. This may be of particular concern where the priorities of donors are not consistent with those of society in general.

Irrespective of the arguments for and against tax concessions, most countries do provide tax incentives for giving, and in general provide exemptions from some taxes for philanthropic entities. The design of these tax concessions are examined in detail in the subsequent chapters of this report.

This chapter is organised as follows: Section 2.2 and 2.3 provide, respectively, an overview of the rationales for and against the provision of tax concessions for philanthropy in a domestic context. Section 2.4 then considers arguments for and against tax concessions for cross-border philanthropy.

2.2. Arguments for tax concessions for domestic philanthropy

A range of arguments can be made in favour of the provision of tax concessions for philanthropic entities and for tax incentives for giving to such entities. This section first considers arguments from economic theory that point to a potential market failure rationale for the subsidisation of both philanthropic entities and philanthropic giving. It then summarises a number of broader arguments drawing on legal, accounting and philosophical perspectives.

2.2.1. Economic theory

The section first outlines two economic theory-based rationales for government intervention to subsidise philanthropy: the under-provision of a public good; and the presence of positive externalities. It then considers whether such a subsidy, if warranted, should be provided via direct grants or via tax concessions (to philanthropic entities and/or philanthropic giving). Finally, it discusses the various trade-offs that must be made in determining the optimal level of a tax incentive for philanthropic giving.

Under-provision of public goods

The under-provision of public goods rationale requires three "failures" to occur to justify government subsidisation of philanthropy: "market failure", "government failure", and "voluntary failure" (Hansmann (1987[1]), Weisbrod (1975[2]) and Salamon (1987[3]) (2016[4]). A "market failure" case will exist for government to intervene and provide public goods that would be welfare improving, but that, due to their non-rival non-excludable nature, are not provided by the market. However, in some cases "government failure" may also occur where the government does not, or is unable to, provide (or unable to provide at a welfare maximising level) the public good. In such cases, philanthropic entities can play an important role in providing these public goods. However, "voluntary failure" may also occur in the sense that philanthropic entities provide an inefficiently low level of the public good, for example, due to insufficient resourcing.

In the presence of these three failures, there is a case for the government to subsidise the philanthropic activity in order to increase supply of the public good to the social optimal level. This subsidisation could occur via a tax incentive for giving, tax concessions to the philanthropic entities themselves, or direct grants to these entities.

Positive externalities

While not providing a public good in the technical sense of a non-rival non-excludable good, a philanthropic entity may provide goods and services that produce positive externalities that are not fully captured by the entity itself or by those contributing to the entity. The presence of externalities may justify government intervention to correct the market failure. In the case of negative externalities, the intervention generally consists of a tax. In the case of positive externalities, on the other hand, the intervention may consist of a subsidy which could take the form of a tax incentive for giving, a tax concession for the entity itself, or a government grant.

It is often argued that philanthropic activity may be viewed as having consumption externalities. To the extent that the private marginal benefit of a gift to a philanthropic entity (i.e. the donor's "warm glow" – see Box 2.1) is below the social marginal benefit of that gift, philanthropic giving has positive consumption externalities and may be 'under-consumed.' Although views in the literature differ to which extent this argument could justify tax subsidies for giving to philanthropic entities (in particular because the argument would provide a justification to subsidise giving to, for instance, other family members, but tax systems typically do not provide a tax subsidy for this type of giving).'

Therefore, to internalise the externality and correct the market failure, there may be a case for government to intervene. This intervention could occur via tax concessions or direct grants to the philanthropic entity. In the case of tax concessions to philanthropic entities, reducing the taxes borne will (directly or indirectly) lower the private marginal cost of producing the goods and services, which can increase the provision of these goods towards the social optimal level. In the case of philanthropic giving, a tax incentive lowers the price of giving so that the private marginal benefit of the donor increases towards the social marginal benefit, thereby increasing the level of giving towards the social optimal level.

Box 2.1. The drivers of philanthropic giving

Overview

Noting the importance of philanthropic giving has led researchers in various fields and the sector itself to consider what drives philanthropy. Such analysis is important in the context of tax policy because it may indicate whether tax policy is efficient in increasing philanthropy i.e. whether tax is a driver of philanthropy. Bekkers and Wiepking (2011[5]) have identified eight mechanisms that they say are key mechanisms determinants of philanthropy. They are (i) awareness of need; (ii) solicitation; (iii) costs and benefits; (iv) altruism; (v) reputation; (vi) psychological benefits; (vii) values; (viii) efficacy. The Charities Aid Foundation (2014[6]) carried out a survey of donors in 2012 and the top 5 factors identified for the decision to giver were: (i) personal values; (ii) sense of morality/ethics; (iii) particular belief in cause; (iv) faith and (v) personal experience. Other factors, including societal factor may also be relevant. Classifications of this kind are complex and rarely clear-cut. Research into the drivers of philanthropy can be seen as identifying three types of factors: personal; societal and 'other factors'.

Personal factors

Various researchers have identified that personal values; personal experience; belief in specific causes; faith and religion are likely to influence the decision to give. The notion of 'altruism' – the desire to help others, is likely to be part of an individuals' personal values. Individuals and social entities are said to have an altruistic view if they value positively what is good for others. Such an altruistic view leads to giving when the donor views the value of such a gift as greater than the cost to them. This is why a number of tax incentives are aimed at either lowering the price of giving (in the case of tax deductions and credits) or increasing its value (in the case of matching schemes such as Gift Aid). Altruism is, of course, not the only driver of giving, self-esteem as well as social norms and status are examples of other causes of philanthropy that have been identified.

Economic models of philanthropic giving have also identified 'warm glow' (or the 'joy of giving') as a key driver of private giving to philanthropy. Warm glow models suggest that donors receive some positive utility from giving to philanthropy. Andreoni (1990[7]) for example, models philanthropic giving with what he calls 'impure altruistic' motives. In the model, individuals have wealth which they can allocate between consuming a private good and a donation towards a public good. In a purely altruistic model, the donor does not get any utility from their gift and only receives utility from the level of the public good as well as their consumption of the private good. In a purely warm glow model, the donor only receives utility from their gift and their consumption of the private good. In the impurely altruistic model, individuals receive utility from both the level of the public good as well as the gift itself.

Personal experience, such as knowing someone assisted by the philanthropic entity or having some other connection to the entity or cause may also increase the likelihood of giving. Religious faith may also reinforce the sense of moral obligation. Other personal factors may include feeling good about oneself by giving or demonstrating virtue to others. Signalling virtue may be demonstrated by requesting acknowledgement, particularly for large donations, but this of itself may lead others to give. While these personal factors are generally related to individual giving, they may also translate into corporate philanthropy. Of course, it may not be possible to know whether a business gives money because they care or because they believe it will be good for business. Personal wealth will also be important in determining ability to donate to various causes, and much work has been done on the types of entities or causes that are likely to attract high wealth individuals. Several studies show that high end philanthropy is likely to be attracted to arts and cultural entities, with lower end donors favouring religion and welfare.

Societal factors

Some countries appear to have a stronger giving culture than others. This might be influenced by historical factors as well as cultural factors. The Johns Hopkins University Comparative Non-profit Project ('JHU Project') has carried out significant research on the 'social origins' of philanthropy. This theory posits that the political and economic history of a country will be a strong indicator of the size and scope of the non-profit sector. This theory has been considered in Chapter 1. Broader cultural and political factors may also be important e.g. whether the sector is regulated may impact on perceptions of the transparency and reliability of the sector and whether entities are viewed as trustworthy. The way in which the government supports the sector e.g. by making grants may also be significant, although researchers are divided as to whether government support will 'crowd-out' private giving or in fact have the effect of 'crowding-in', that is signalling to private donors that the worthy purpose and/or the entity engaged in carrying out the worthy purpose should be supported.

Government grants vs. tax concessions

The public good and positive externality arguments provide a case for government subsidisation of philanthropic entities and giving. However, as alluded to in the preceding discussion, an alternative to providing tax concessions to subsidise philanthropic activities, is for government to provide direct grants to a philanthropic entity. A grant may be preferable to a tax concession where the government wants greater control regarding the destination of the government support, where the level of "crowding out" of private contributions is low, or where a tax concession is not "treasury efficient" – that is, where it would result in a smaller increase in funding of the philanthropic entity than the tax revenue forgone. Equally, when government grants largely crowd out philanthropic giving, tax concessions may be preferable to government grants, even when tax incentives for philanthropic giving are not treasury efficient. More generally, a tax incentive may still be welfare increasing even if it is not treasury efficient if the benefit to society of the activity funded by the giving is sufficiently large.

The economic literature has focused on two key factors that may influence whether government grants or tax concessions are preferable: crowding out of private contributions and the treasury efficiency of a tax incentive. For the crowding out effect, the hypothesis is that since government grants are financed through taxes, taxpayers will be less inclined to donate to a philanthropic entity that has already received their tax dollars (Andreoni and Payne, 2003[8]). Research suggests that although government support for a non-profit entity might influence private donations, it is unlikely to fully 'crowd-out' private giving (references). There is, in fact, some support for the opposite conclusion, namely that government support for a philanthropic entity may be a signal of the entity's quality, resulting in a crowding-in effect. A variation on the notion of crowding-out is that government grants may discourage an entity from fundraising and that this might then lead to a decline in private support (Andreoni and Payne, 2003[8]).

Whether a tax incentive for philanthropic giving is "treasury efficient" is typically examined by empirical estimation of the price elasticity of philanthropic giving – with an elasticity greater than one indicating the tax incentive is treasury efficient.[3] More generally, the issue of whether philanthropic giving is responsive to tax incentives lowering the price of giving, has prompted significant debate in the econometric literature, mostly based on data from the United States, but more recently also on European data.

A major review by Clotfelter in 1985 found a notable consistency in the findings, with the consensus being that the price elasticity for the population of taxpayers was probably greater than -1, with a range of -0.9 to -1.4. As well, it was observed that the price elasticity appeared to rise with income; there are substantial lags in giving behaviour; and there is little effect of 'crowding out' individual contributions through government contributions (Clotfelter, 1985[9]). While there were tax effects on corporate giving, this appeared to be less than for individual contributions, and there was also evidence that corporations time-shift their donations (Clotfelter, 1985[9]).

The literature has examined both the 'price effects' (including tax rates), which influence the cost of giving, and the 'income effects', such as inflation or economic growth, that affect the income available for philanthropic giving (Clotfelter and Salamon, 1982[10]). Different methodologies used in other studies reported much lower price elasticities (e.g. Steinberg (1990[11]) and Randolph (1995[12])). Nevertheless, an analysis in 2005 of 40 years of research in this field concluded that tax deductions were treasury efficient, and (surprisingly) that the price elasticity was not significantly higher for high-income earners (Peloza and Steel, 2005[13]).

A more recent paper by Backus and Grant (Backus and Grant, 2019[14]) noted that results varied depending on whether studies were based on tax return data of individuals who itemise their deductions (a group substantially wealthier than the average taxpayer), or were based on general population survey data. Backus and Grant concluded that the top 10% of income earners had an elasticity of at least -1, but middle-income taxpayers were less sensitive (see also Fack and Landais (2010[15]), Bönke et. al. (2013[16]), and Bönke and Werdt (2015[17])).[4]

Determining the size of the tax concession

When there is a rationale for government intervention in the form of a tax concession for philanthropic entities or a tax incentive for philanthropic giving to these entities, determining the optimal subsidy level for philanthropic giving is complicated and involves various trade-offs. On the one hand, there are the welfare gains from increasing the provision of the public good or the externality generating activity. On the other, there is the opportunity cost in terms of what the tax revenue that would have otherwise been collected could have been used for (acknowledging the distortionary impact of taxation). Consideration must also be given to the distributional impact of the tax concession. In particular, if the benefit (e.g. the additional warm glow, or the reduced cost of generating the same warm glow) of the tax concession is primarily enjoyed by individuals at the top of the income distribution, this may conflict with the underlying redistributive preferences of government. That said, if the resulting increase in the philanthropic activity primarily benefits lower-income households this will aid redistribution goals. Moreover, tax concessions can only be enjoyed if individuals give away part of their income or wealth to a philanthropic activity, and the mere fact of giving by the rich will reduce income and wealth inequality, irrespective of the design of the tax concession.

The optimal tax literature has attempted to incorporate these trade-offs into a single welfare-maximising framework (see Box 2.2 for more detail on optimal taxation of philanthropic giving). In this regard, Saez (2004[18]) models the optimal tax rate for private contributions to a public good in the presence of warm-glow effects, externalities, crowding out, and the redistributive preferences of government. Subject to a number of strong assumptions, the model suggests that the optimal tax subsidy for philanthropic giving:

- increases with the size of the external effect of a marginal increase in the level of contributions;
- increases with the responsiveness of the donor to the subsidy;
- increases with the level at which public contributions crowd out private contributions;
- and decreases with the proportion of giving made by high-income individuals (assuming government values redistribution).

The optimal tax subsidy itself will depend on the interaction of all these factors. In the model, the optimal subsidy rate is found to decrease with the proportion of giving made by high-income individuals because government is placing a lower weight on the utility that higher income individuals derive from contributing as compared to lower income individuals. The model also suggests that the optimal tax subsidy for philanthropic activity does not necessarily have to be linked to the personal income tax rate schedule, which is the case in countries where contributions are deductible from the personal income tax base.

Box 2.2. Optimal taxation in the presence of externalities

The optimal taxation literature essentially formalises the equity-efficiency trade-off inherent in tax design. Saez (2004[18]) incorporates tax expenditures into the standard optimal tax model of Diamond and Mirrlees (1971[19]). Previous work in the area has considered the presence of externalities (Sandmo, 1975[20]) or public goods (Atkinson and Stern, (1974[21]); Boadway and Keen, (1993[22])).

In Saez's (2004[18]) model there are three goods: private consumption *c*, earnings *z* and a contribution good *g*. A lump sum payment, *R*, is made to all individuals to achieve the government's redistributional goals. The public good nature of charitable contributions or tax expenditures is reflected in the level of contributions per capita G. The model assumes that individuals derive utility from giving through what is often referred to as warm glow (discussed in more detail in Box 2.1). Therefore, the utility function of each individual, $u(c, z, g, G)$, is non-decreasing in c, g, and G and decreasing in z. The government's problem is to set

- the flat tax rate on earnings (τ),

- the tax rate on contributions (t),
- the level of the lump sum payment to all individuals (R),
- and possibly the amount G^0 of the contribution good that it finances directly (i.e. government grants),

in a way that maximises social welfare subject to the requirement that it collects enough tax revenues to finance R, G^0, and government consumption E. Welfare is measured by the weighted sum of individual utilities, where the weights β^h reflect the level at which government values redistribution. For example, if government values redistribution, $\beta^h$is higher for low-income individuals than for high-income individuals.

With a few simplifying assumptions[5], the model produces two sets of expressions for the optimal tax rate t on contributions in a setting where government cannot contribute to the public good, and in a setting where it can. In the first setting, the optimal tax rate t on contributions is given by:

$$t = -e + \frac{1}{\rho}[1 - \beta(G)], \quad [1]$$

where e denotes the external effect of a marginal increase in the level of the contribution good, ρ is a measure of the price response of private contributions, and $\beta(G)$ denotes the average social welfare weight, weighted by contribution levels. Equation [1] shows that the optimal subsidy rate for contributions is larger when the external effect of a marginal increase in the level of the contribution good is larger. The optimal subsidy rate is lower if the price response of the contribution is small. If on the other hand contributions are perfectly elastic, the optimal subsidy rate would equal the external effect. Finally, if high-income individuals contribute disproportionately to the rest of the population, $\beta(G)$ is assumed to be low (meaning the utility derived from, for example, warm glow is weighted less because it is disproportionately experienced by high-income individuals) and thus the optimal subsidy rate for contributions is lower.

In a setting where the government can contribute directly to the public good (i.e. where crowding out is possible), the optimal tax rate on contributions is given by:

$$t = -1 + \frac{1}{\rho}(1 + \bar{G}_{G^0})[1 - \beta(G)], \quad [2]$$

where public contributions crowd out private contributions when $\bar{G}_{G^0} < 0$. Equation [2] shows that the optimal subsidy rate increases in $\beta(G)$, the size of the price response, and in the absolute value of crowding out.

A weakness of the model may be that it assumes that private contributions are equally as efficient as direct government contributions. This is likely not the case, due to the fundraising activities that philanthropic entities frequently have to engage in to receive private contributions. On the other hand, the collection of taxes is not without inefficiencies either.

2.2.2. Base-defining rationale

Base-defining theories aim to identify what is properly taxable e.g. as income or profit. This approach recognises that some revenue of philanthropic entities may not be appropriately included in the tax base. These theories assert that income tax can only logically be levied on activities undertaken for profit (see for example, Bittker and Rahdert (1976[23])). For example, for many philanthropic entities, a not insignificant portion of revenue will comprise contributions or membership payments which may not fall within notions of 'income'. Similarly, many expenses incurred in operating the philanthropic entity e.g. the Red Cross providing relief after a disaster, may not fit within notions of deductible expenditure as ordinary and necessary business expenses. There will, of course be some philanthropic entities that derive most of their income from 'business' activities, e.g. hospitals or universities, and it would be relatively easy to calculate taxable income.

Brody (1999[24]) proposes what she describes as a 'sovereignty view' as a variation on the base defining approach. She argues that charities go untaxed because 'Caesar should not tax god' (or its modern secular equivalent). Brody acknowledges that although this might have something to do with the role of religion in early charity, its continued existence can be justified based on the independence of the sector. She argues that a sovereignty view also explains why a subsidy would take the form of tax exemption rather than more logical form of direct grants: for all its imperfections, tax exemption keeps governments out of charities day to day business and keeps charities out of the business of petitioning government for subvention.

Another variation on the tax base theory is that taxation of corporations is sometimes viewed as a proxy for taxation of shareholders, and the philanthropic entity will generally not have shareholders (Rushton, 2007[25]) (Buckles, 2005[26]). Rather those who are beneficiaries of the activities of the philanthropic entity, would not be viewed as appropriate subjects of taxation.

2.2.3. Distributive justice theory

Fleischer (2018[27]) has put forward an alternative to the traditional theories. She argues that support for philanthropy can be justified based on what she terms 'two bedrock principles of Western liberal democracies' namely: limited government and equal opportunity. She argues that the charitable tax subsidies reflect these principles, as expressed in the two theories of distributive justice respectively associated with them, libertarianism and resource egalitarianism. However, she acknowledges problems that may need to be tempered. In her view, the tax subsidies may undermine the principle of limited government by coercing taxpayers to subsidise activities that are not the legitimate purview of government. The subsidies' relation to resource egalitarianism is more complex: she argues that tax subsidies may undermine basic equality of opportunity notions both by subsidising activities that increase the head-start of the wealthy and by giving wealthy taxpayers more say over government resources than poorer taxpayers.

2.3. Arguments against tax concessions for domestic philanthropy

Although there were earlier critics of the tax concessions,[6] the case against the tax concessions was put most powerfully in the 1960s and 1970s by US scholars, most notably Kahn (1960[28]), and Rabin (1966[29]), in the context of the charitable contribution deduction. The arguments of the critics are considered below. Some, but not all of these arguments can be used to critique all tax concessions for philanthropic entities.

2.3.1. Cost of providing the concessions and tax expenditure analysis

The starting point is that tax concessions have a 'cost', that is, they reduce government revenue, and therefore shift the tax burden to other taxpayers. This is relatively uncontroversial. More controversial, however, is a second related argument that the loss in revenue amounts to a 'tax expenditure'. Tax expenditure analysis distinguishes between tax measures which seek to achieve the primary goal of income taxation and those ('tax expenditures') which reduce tax liability to support social or economic objectives. Tax expenditure analysis treats tax exemptions and concessions as government subsidies and evaluates them in the same way as direct expenditures. Tax expenditure analysis has its modern genesis in a seminal US Treasury analysis in 1968 (1968[30]) and subsequent explanations of its implications by Assistant Secretary of the United States Treasury, Stanley Surrey (1970[31])

It is necessary to consider whether tax concessions for philanthropy are, in fact, tax expenditures. This is likely to be the case for property tax exemptions. It is also relatively, although not universally, accepted in the case of the charitable contribution deduction or credit, since the outgoing does not fall into either the recognised category of expenses in the production of income, or expenses that are in a legal or moral sense necessary or involuntary. There has been significantly more contest over whether the income tax exemption (or other relief) is a tax expenditure or could be justified by principles of income taxation ('base-defining theories') (Brody, 1999[24]) as discussed above.

There are a number of issues relating to the notion of tax expenditure analysis in relation to the philanthropic sector:

- Tax expenditure analysis compares the current or prospective tax treatment of taxpayers who receive the concession to a 'benchmark' treatment. (Andrews, 1972[32]) For example, in relation to the gift concession it assumes that the same amount would be donated even without the concession. That is, it assumes that taxpayer behaviour is unchanged and for that reason may not accurately reflect revenue foregone.
- There is some debate about whether the tax exemptions for non-profits are, in fact, tax expenditures. For example, much of the revenue received by philanthropic entities would not be income in most countries, such as donations and government grants. In that sense the exemption may not be a concession in relation to that revenue (Krever, 1991[33]) . There is also an argument, discussed above, that philanthropic entities may be 'outside' the system for taxing corporations.
- There are also concerns about the reliability and accuracy of the tax expenditure statements. For example, tax expenditure estimates are only concerned with statutory provisions and do not take into account situations where income is not taxed for some other reason e.g. because of the common law principle of 'mutuality' or because of the exercise of an administrative discretion (Burton and Sadiq, 2013[34]).
- Perhaps most significantly, there is simply insufficient data available to quantify the tax expenditures in relation to the philanthropic sector across jurisdictions. There are a number of reasons for this: many countries do not calculate tax expenditures – of the countries responding to the survey, less than half were able to provide estimates of revenue foregone in relation to either gift concessions or exemptions from other taxes. In addition, information to estimate the amount of tax that might be payable is often not available e.g. if the philanthropic entity is not required to lodge a tax return, it will not be possible to quantify the amount of revenue foregone. Several countries that did provide responses to the questions relating to the cost of concessions, were only able to provide estimates, suggesting either that it is too soon to provide the data or that the data cannot be accurately identified.

What does appear from the responses provided to our survey is that there is an amount of tax revenue foregone, and hence the tax treatment of philanthropy is an important topic that needs to be considered in detail to ensure that the concessions are justified and well designed.

2.3.2. Inequality and the regressive nature of tax incentives for giving

The pluralism argument considered as part of the subsidy rationale carries with it the importance of a heterogeneous and large number of donors. However, the design of tax-subsidies may lead to incentivising large donations from a small number of wealthy donors rather than smaller donations from a large number of donors.

In this regard, it has been argued that one of the main objections to the philanthropic gift concessions is the inequity that results from its regressive nature (Rabin, 1966[29]). This arises because the deduction is tied to progressive tax brackets. A progressive income tax system results in all deductions 'benefiting' higher income taxpayers more, and the philanthropic contribution deduction has a similar effect of reducing the 'price of giving' more for higher income earners. This is said to conflict with the basic premise of a progressive income tax. It is also said to be inequitable because the evidence is that higher income taxpayers favour different types of charities, typically higher education and arts and culture, than lower income taxpayers which tend to favour religion and welfare (Rabin, 1966[29]) (Atkinson, 1997[35]). This may have implications for the potentially undemocratic nature of tax concessions for giving (discussed below). Incentivising the wealthy more may increase the treasury efficiency of the tax subsidies, that is, if those with higher income levels are more responsive to tax incentives for donations, a tax-subsidy would be more efficient if it focused on big donors[7]

Some authors have observed that this is the effect of all tax deductions and not peculiar to the charitable contribution (Bittker, 1972[36]) Most of the proposals that seek to redesign the philanthropic gift concession attempt to minimise this regressive effect by proposing tax credits or matching schemes (Duff, 2014[37]).

2.3.3. Competitive neutrality

It is often claimed that commercial operations run by non-profit entities have an unfair advantage when competing with for-profit organisations offering the same or similar goods and services (Brody and Cordes (2001[38]); Sharpe (1996[39])). A competitive advantage may result from tax concessions that apply to the income, inputs, or outputs of philanthropic entities, including when they operate businesses. In this context it is argued that philanthropic entities can undercut the competition. The notion of unfair competition underpinned the introduction of the unrelated business income tax ('UBIT') in the United States in the 1950s. Before that time, the tax system followed a 'destination of income' approach under which income, whatever the source, could be earned tax-free if profits were dedicated to a charitable or philanthropic purpose. The introduction of the UBIT was also said to be about preserving the corporate income tax base, and to have been the result of the infamous ownership of Mueller Macaroni by New York University Law School (Brody and Cordes, 2001[38]). The UBIT operates so that to the extent that an activity is 'substantially related' to the entity's tax-exempt purpose, the income is tax-free (and the associated expenses are, essentially, not deductible). By contrast, net income from 'unrelated business activities', is subject to the UBIT, which generally taxes such income at ordinary corporate (or trust) tax rates. Congress, however, has exempted dividends, interest, rents, and royalties from the UBIT.

It has also been argued that an income tax exemption (on all income or on income from related activities) does not provide an unfair advantage to philanthropic entities (Henry et al. (2009[40]); Steuerle (1998[41])). An income-tax exemption is not a subsidy on the cost of inputs; it does not reduce the charities cost of purchasing goods. One commentator has argued that:

> *the zero rate for charity is no more 'unfair' to a [fully] taxed competitor than are the progressive income-tax rates on individuals who conduct business activities in a sole proprietorship or through a partnership, [or a corporation]..... Nor is a non-profit organisation likely to under-price its for-profit competitor (the 'unfair' part of the competition), just as it would not accept a lower return on an (untaxed) passive investment (Weisbrod, 1988[42]).*

The UBIT in the United States, and similar arrangements in other countries to impose tax on 'unrelated' commercial profits, suffer from the difficulty of trying to identify what is related and what is unrelated. It has been noted that very little revenue is in fact collected in the United States from the UBIT. However, the income tax concessions available to philanthropic entities may provide them with some advantages over for-profit firms, such as in relation to cash flow.

In response to these concerns, many countries do tax income or profits derived from commercial operations. A variety of terms are used to signify the types of income being taxed e.g., commercial, business or trading income; and a distinction is often made between commercial activities that are part of the philanthropic activities of the PBO, such as operating a school or hospital (commonly referred to as 'related commercial income') and activities that are not part of the philanthropic activities, other than as providing revenue to undertake those philanthropic activities (commonly referred to as 'unrelated commercial income'). These distinctions are often difficult to make and complex to administer. Some countries either prohibit, or at least tax, commercial activities that are undertaken by for-profit competitors (see Chapter 3).

It has also been argued that concessions related to the cost of inputs, e.g., employee-related tax concessions, do provide a competitive advantage for the commercial activities of philanthropic entities compared with for-profits and that they could be distortionary because they provided an incentive for non-profits to favour the use of the inputs that attracted the concessional taxation treatment.

Distortions from VAT concessions for philanthropic entities typically arise from the exemption from VAT of the output of these entities. The distortion can result in either a competitive advantage or a competitive disadvantage to the philanthropic entity, depending on who is the recipient of the supply and what the recipient uses it for.

A VAT exemption can provide a competitive advantage to a philanthropic supplier if the recipient is a consumer or an entity that uses it as an input to the production of its own exempt supplies. This is because the total price paid by the recipient is lower than the VAT-inclusive price they would pay to a for-profit supplier.

A VAT exemption can create a competitive disadvantage for a philanthropic supplier if the recipient is an entity, such as a for-profit business, that uses the good or service as an input to a taxable supply. This is because input tax credits would allow the purchaser to fully recover any VAT paid on inputs purchased on a non-exempt basis (e.g., from another for-profit business), and the suppliers of those inputs are entitled to input tax credits on their own inputs. In contrast, the philanthropic supplier of exempt goods and services cannot recover the VAT it pays on its inputs. This VAT gets embedded into the cost of the good or service itself and is not recoverable by the purchaser.

When the exemption of the entity's outputs causes a competitive disadvantage, input concessions may reduce the distortion. Either way, philanthropic entities that make VAT exempt supplies will tend to favour the use of inputs with VAT concessions. The VAT treatment of philanthropic entities in countries is discussed in more detail in Chapter 3.

2.3.4. Inflexibility (once introduced difficult to change)

A somewhat related argument is that tax subsidies are not subject to the same periodic review that spending programs receive. As a result, once enacted, there is no need for the recipients to justify the concession. Further, the operation of a tax concession can result in unexpected budgetary outcomes. Tax incentives are usually 'open-ended' – that is, they do not limit the tax benefits a taxpayer can receive. In the case of direct expenditures, if the legislator considers that certain programmed costs in a given year are too high, it can cap them in advance. However, it is often impossible to apply such restrictions to existing tax incentives: they do not require annual approval from the legislator and remain valid as long as the tax law remains unchanged (Lideikyte-Huber, 2020[43]).

Perhaps surprisingly it has been suggested that tax expenditure analysis, which aimed to highlight the 'cost' of providing various concessions has resulted in more 'tax expenditures' being included in tax legislation in many jurisdictions. One commentator has noted that the effect of producing tax expenditure statements, 'unintended by the advocates of tax expenditure analysis, has been to legitimate and expand tax expenditures (Zelinsky, 2012[44]).

2.3.5. Undemocratic (the power of large philanthropists)

Reich (2019[45]) argues that much philanthropy is undemocratic and unaccountable. His arguments are really concerned with 'big philanthropy' or large private foundations, and is focussed on the United States.

Reich notes that a fundamental commitment of a democratic society is that individuals have an equal opportunity to influence politics or public policy. This is enshrined in the constitutional protections for 'one person, one vote'. However, by operating through a private foundation, wealthy people are able to uniquely influence public policy. In other words, the power to spend money gives the philanthropist significant political power. This is not restricted to tax-preferred philanthropy e.g., Mark Zuckerberg and Priscilla Chan have established a limited liability company rather than a private foundation to undertake philanthropic activities. This means they will not be subject to IRS rules about disbursements or any reporting requirements. Furthermore, there is no guarantee that big philanthropy will relieve poverty or direct monies to reducing inequality.

Reich (2019[45]) also notes that large foundations are largely unaccountable – they do not have to account to customers or competitors and, unlike politicians, cannot be voted out of office. Reich notes that this was a matter of real concern in the 1880s when the first private foundations were mooted, and refers to the fact that Rockefeller had considerable trouble in setting up his private foundation – and that there were no tax concessions for doing so at the time. Moreover, he argues that instead of moderating the behaviour of big philanthropy, governments encourage it with tax concessions, and the charitable deduction in the US provides benefits that reinforce inequality. However, Reich does not argue that there should be no tax support, but rather that the contribution concession should be a credit rather than a deduction, so that the value of the concession does not give greater support to wealthy donors.

While not accountable to 'customers', foundations are accountable to the tax authorities in staying compliant with the tax rules including using funds for personal benefit and disposing of donated stock within a specified period. In the United States, for example, IRS audits periodically result in imposition of penalties, court cases or even the closing down of a foundation.

2.4. The rationale for incentivising cross-border philanthropy is distinct from that of domestic philanthropy

The discussion above has assumed that the donor and the recipient entity are located in the domestic or home jurisdiction and that the entity pursues its objectives domestically. The notion of cross-border philanthropy raises distinct issues for various stakeholders. Cross-border philanthropy has been defined as 'voluntary contributions from private donors in one country to a recipient in another country' (Moore and Rutzen, 2011[46]).

There is little comprehensive or comparable data on the extent of cross-border philanthropy, although the data that is available suggests that such giving is growing. In many cases, the discussion around cross-border philanthropy revolves around assistance for developing countries or in conflict situations. But potentially, cross-border philanthropy could relate to any of the worthy purposes identified previously. A philanthropic intermediary in Europe has reported that for the period 2010 to 2016 donations channelled related to education accounted for 42%, social matters 18%, heritage and culture 14%, health 11%, international development 11%, environment 3% and religion 1%. (European Foundation Centre, 2017[47]) There is some data on private philanthropy related to development. An OECD survey on private foundation giving for development found that the 147 foundations surveyed provided approximately USD7.96 billion per year to developing countries from 2013 to 2015, representing an average annual increase of 19% (OECD, 2018[48]). The OECD survey also noted that the sources of philanthropic giving for development are highly concentrated. Of the 143 foundations included in the data survey sample, the Bill & Melinda Gates Foundation was by far the most significant philanthropic donor, and 81% of the total philanthropic giving during 2013-15 was provided by only 20 foundations.

The increase in cross-border philanthropy has given rise to concerns in both donor and recipient countries. Donor countries are concerned that the money donated may be diverted for the purposes of terrorism and money-laundering. This was the view taken by the Financial Action Task Force ('FATF') – an intergovernmental body that promotes implementation of anti-money laundering and anti-terrorist financing measures through its recommendations and country evaluations – in its initial assessment of the terrorist financing vulnerabilities and threats faced by the non-profit sector (FATF, 2012[49]). Since 2012, FATF's Recommendation 8 has served as an international policy standard influencing the domestic regulation of cross-border philanthropy. FATF subsequently acknowledged that the non-profit sector's vulnerability to terrorist abuse in Recommendation 8 may have been overstated given that 'not all non-profit organisations are inherently high risk (and some may represent little or no risk at all)' (FATF, 2016[50]).

The initial view about the vulnerability of the non-profit sector has resulted in additional administrative and due diligence requirements being imposed on donors and philanthropic entities seeking to work abroad in many countries. It has also been put forward as one reason for imposing restrictions on tax deductibility of donations as revenue authorities refer to the lack of control over the recipient entity (Charities Aid Foundation, 2016[51]).

Some recipient countries have also viewed foreign funding or foreign activities as a threat to national sovereignty and have imposed restrictions that might include prohibiting foreign funding or requiring all funding to be channelled through the government or approved by government (Indiana University Lilly Family School of Philanthropy, 2018[52]). Concerns about cross-border philanthropy raise some of the same issues as official aid programs, although as noted, not all cross-border aid is concerned with humanitarian or development activities.

There are various ways that cross-border philanthropy can occur where:

- a donor in one country makes a donation directly to a philanthropic entity in another country ('direct cross-border philanthropy'); or
- the donation is made to a domestic philanthropic entity that pursues its programs abroad; or the donation is made to a domestic philanthropic entity that channels the funds to the foreign philanthropic entity ('indirect cross-border philanthropy').

2.4.1. Direct philanthropy

Most countries do not permit tax relief for donations to foreign philanthropic entities (direct cross-border philanthropy), subject to some exceptions that allow tax relief for donations within a geographic region.

The position in the European Union ('EU') is based on the fundamental freedoms of the *Treaty on the Functioning of the EU* ('TFEU') mandating the non-discrimination of philanthropic entities and their donors. This has been confirmed by the case law of the European Court of Justice ('ECJ'), which ensures that the tax autonomy of the Member States is exercised in accordance with the fundamental freedoms as enshrined in the TFEU. In the landmark judgement in *Stauffer* (Case C-386/04), the ECJ held that non-resident philanthropic entities should not be treated differently for tax purposes simply because they are resident in another Member State. Thus, if a Member State grants an income tax exemption to domestic philanthropic entities, it should extend such advantageous tax treatment to entities in other Member States which meet the same conditions as domestic philanthropic entities. In a subsequent judgement in *Persche* (Case C-318/07), which complements the Stauffer case with regard to the tax treatment of donors in respect of cross-border giving, the ECJ ruled that limiting the preferential tax treatment for donations to domestic philanthropic entities while excluding donations to comparable foreign entities is not compatible with the free movement of capital as guaranteed by the TFEU. This means that tax relief should be provided where the foreign charities in a Member State can be shown to be 'comparable' to domestic organisations holding charitable tax status. Practical difficulties remain in demonstrating comparability and the process for seeking tax incentives is complex and burdensome (European Foundation Centre, 2017[47]). The end result is that donors are more likely to use indirect channels (discussed below).

Another regional grouping that permits some cross-border donations to qualify for tax relief concerns the United States. The US permits deductions for philanthropic contributions in its treaties with Canada (USA-Canada DTA, Article XXI), Mexico (USA-Mexico DTA Article 22) and Israel (USA-Israel DTA Article 15A). Like the EU, the basis for the concession is 'comparability' with eligible domestic entities. The rationale for the philanthropic contribution provisions in the tax treaties with Canada and Mexico are close geographic and economic ties. In the case of Israel, the reasons for the preferential tax treatment appear to be the close political ties and the extensive funding of philanthropic activities in Israel by US citizens. There is however no equivalent provision in the Canada-Mexico DTA.

2.4.2. Indirect philanthropy

Some countries do permit domestic philanthropic entities to transfer funds or to operate overseas. There are various models that are used to facilitate this. Many international non-government organisations (NGOs) such as the Red Cross, Amnesty International, Greenpeace and World Vision, establish domestic entities in a large number of countries but essentially undertake all their activities offshore. There may also be a process for other domestic philanthropic entities to be approved so that they can undertake activities overseas. The approval processes for such entities tend to be quite onerous and may be restricted to entities that undertake humanitarian and/or development type of activities. In addition to an approval process, there may be a code of conduct imposed to ensure that entities operating overseas, that are eligible for tax preferred donations, meet certain standards. Some countries permit a wider group of domestic entities to be approved. One example is the proliferation of entities designated by the prefix 'friends of' which allows tax relief for donations that are to be used offshore. The need to go through an onerous approval process tends to penalise smaller philanthropic entities. However, a number of countries permit a 'work around' that is, entities can request an approved entity to act as a conduit and pass on donations to intended recipients overseas. The entity acting as a conduit will typically charge a fee of between 5% and 10% and will be responsible for the due diligence associated with the funds being passed on.

An alternative model has developed in Europe where, despite the rulings by the ECJ, cross-border giving is still not easy. A private initiative, the Transnational Giving Europe ('TGE') network, is a partnership of leading European foundations and associations that facilitates tax-efficient cross-border giving within Europe (Transnational Giving Europe[53]).The TGE network covers 19 countries and enables donors, both corporations and individuals, resident in one of the participating countries, to financially support non-profit organisations in other Member States, while benefiting directly from the tax advantages provided for in the legislation of their country of residence. (Transnational Giving Europe[53])

2.4.3. Arguments in favour of tax incentives for cross-border philanthropy

As the world becomes more interconnected, the argument that countries should treat cross-border philanthropy in much the same way as domestic philanthropy becomes harder to ignore. If governments accept that they should subsidise domestic philanthropy, arguments can also be made as to why they should subsidise cross-border philanthropy. The arguments in favour of tax incentives fall into two categories: arguments that rely on what might be described as the 'moral imperative' to assist others, especially those less well off, and arguments that are based on the 'self-interest' of the country providing the tax relief.

Moral imperative

The global nature of many of the challenges facing the world require global responses. If the relief of poverty, advancement of health and education and preservation of heritage are worthy purposes domestically, they should be seen as 'deserving' globally and so private contributions should be encouraged (Buijze, 2016[54]). Many issues also transcend borders e.g., environmental concerns, or medical research or public health issues such as fighting pandemics, can only be dealt with by countries cooperating. There is already considerable cooperation in the area of development and humanitarian aid, as well as in responding to international disasters. The global public benefit these causes relate to could be a possible reason for some governments to stimulate private contributions to these causes through tax incentives.

Self-interest

The provision of tax incentives for philanthropy directed abroad can also be justified using the subsidy rationale by refocussing on the notion of what constitutes the public benefit. There may be a number of benefits to a country from engaging with global causes by supporting cross-border giving. Just as aid programs enable a country to develop 'soft power' through cultural and economic influence, so does the provision of support for philanthropy (Jenkins, 2007[55]). Certainly, there appears to have been a level of acceptance of this argument by many countries, given the number of domestic philanthropic entities that already have this support. A more focussed notion of self-interest might be present in allowing tax relief in a regional context, where wellbeing of a region, increased sense of solidarity and strengthening of community ties, may generate benefits for the country in which the donors are present.

2.4.4. Arguments against tax incentives for cross-border philanthropy

There are, of course, a number of arguments that can be raised against providing support for cross-border giving. Those arguments tend to focus on the lack of benefit for the 'donor' country and the lack of oversight of the funds once they leave the country. There may also be concerns for the donors or intermediaries about navigating the legal and cultural terrain of the recipient country.

Public benefit

One possible argument is that the granting of tax relief is a cost to the donor country, and there is no matching benefit in terms of spending within the country (Buijze, 2016[54]). This is in effect confining the public in the public benefit requirement to the domestic sphere, although it could be argued that a country derives a benefit from the provision of assistance to less fortunate countries. In some cases, this is recognised as where there is already tax relief for donations to recognised disasters.

Lack of oversight

Lack of oversight of the actual spending of the private contributions is often raised as a concern (Buijze, 2016[54]). This has been exacerbated by the FATF Report in 2012 describing the vulnerability of the non-profit sector. Although the FATF has since moderated its view, the uneasiness remains. There are also issues concerning compliance of domestic entities operating abroad, often in partnership with local entities, to ensure they comply with any codes of conduct as well as the laws of the country in which they are operating e.g., Oxfam in Haiti. Philanthropic activities abroad are also more difficult to administer, which in some cases may raise accountability and transparency issues.

Costs to donors and/or entities operating overseas

Entities that operate across borders may also encounter additional costs of complying with a different legal regime, having to navigate supply arrangements in countries that may have an element of endemic corruption as well as translation and other costs associated with engaging with local populations (Charities Aid Foundation, 2016[51]). All of these costs may mean that less money is actually being spent on the worthy purpose and may discourage countries from supporting philanthropy across borders.

References

Andreoni, J. (1990), “Impure Altruism and Donations to Public Goods: A Theory of Warm-Glow Giving”, *The Economic Journal*, Vol. 100/401, pp. 464-477. [7]

Andreoni, J. and A. Payne (2003), “Do Government Grants to Private Charities Crowd Out Giving or Fund-raising?”, *American Economic Review*, Vol. 93/3, pp. 792-812. [8]

Andrews, W. (1972), “Personal Deductions in an Ideal Income Tax”, *Harvard Law Review*, Vol. 89, pp. 309-385. [33]

Atkinson, A. and N. Stern (1974), “Pigou, Taxation and Public Goods”, *The Review of Economic Studies*, Vol. 41/1, pp. 119-128. [21]

Atkinson, R. (1997), “Theories of the Federal Income Tax Exemption for Charities: Thesis, Antithesis and Synthesis”, *Stetson Law Review*, Vol. 27, pp. 395-431. [23]

Auten, G., C. Clotfelter and R. Schmalbeck (2000), "Taxes and philanthropy among the wealthy", in J. Slemrod (Ed.), *Does atlas shrug: The economics consequences of taxing the rich*, New York: Russell Sage. [56]

Backus, P. and N. Grant (2019), “How sensitive is the average taxpayer to changes in the tax-price of giving?”, *International Tax and Public Finance*, Vol. 26/2, pp. 317-356. [14]

Bekkers, R. and W. Pamala (2011), “A Literature Review of Empirical Studies of Philanthropy: Eight Mechanisms That Drive Charitable Giving”, *Nonprofit and Voluntary Sector Quarterly*, Vol. 40/5, pp. 924–973. [5]

Bittker, B. (1972), “Charitable Contributions: Tax Deductions or Matching Grants?”, *Tax Law Review*, Vol. 28, pp. 37-63. [36]

Bittker, B. and G. Rahdert (1976), “The Exemption of Non-profit Organisations from Federal Income Tax”, *Yale Law Journal*, Vol. 85/3, pp. 299-358. [24]

Boadway, R. and K. Michael (1993), “Public Goods, Self-Selection and Optimal Income Taxation”, *International Economic Review*, Vol. 34/3, pp. 463-478. [22]

Bönke et. al. (2013), “Charitable giving in the German welfare state: fiscal incentives and crowding out”, *Public Choice*, Vol. 154, pp. 39-58. [16]

Bönke, T. and C. Werdt (2015), “Charitable giving and its persistent and transitory reactions to changes in tax incentives: Evidence from the German taxpayer panel”, *School of Business and Economics Discussion Papers, No. 2015/2*, Free University Berlin. [17]

Brody, E. (1999), “Charities in Tax Reform: Threats to Subsidies Overt and Covert”, *Tennessee Law Review*, Vol. 66/3, pp. 687-763. [25]

Brody, E. and J. Cordes (2001), *The Unrelated Business Income Tax: All Bark and No Bite?*, Urban Institue, Washington, D.C. [38]

Buckles, J. (2005), “Community Income Theory of the Charitable Contributions Deduction”, *Indiana Law Journal*, Vol. 80, pp. 947-988. [27]

Buijze, R. (2016), "Approaches towards the Application of Tax Incentives for Cross-Border Philanthropy", *Intertax*, Vol. 44/1, pp. 14-28. [54]

Burton, M. and K. Sadiq (2013), *The Tax Expenditure Concept in Tax Expenditure Management: a Critical Assessment*, Cambridge University Press, Cambridge. [35]

Charities Aid Foundation (2016), *Donation States: An international comparison of the tax treatment of donations,* https://www.cafonline.org/docs/default-source/about-us-publications/fwg4-donation-states. [51]

Charities Aid Foundation (2014), *Why we give*, https://www.cafonline.org/docs/default-source/about-us-publications/caf-why-we-give-jan14.pdf. [6]

Clotfelter, C. (1985), *Federal Tax Policy and Charitable Giving*, University of Chicago Press, Chicago. [9]

Clotfelter, C. and L. Salamon (1982), "The Impact of the 1981 Tax Act", *National Tax Journal*, Vol. 35/2, pp. 171-187. [10]

Diamond, P. and J. Mirrlees (1971), "Optimal Taxation and Public Production I: Production Efficiency, II Tax Rules", *American Economic Review*, Vol. 61/1, pp. 8-27 and 261-78. [19]

Duff, D. (2014), "The Tax Treatment of Charitable Contributions in a Personal Income Tax: Lessons from Theory and the Canadian Experience" in M. Harding, A. O'Connell and M. Stewart (eds.) *Not-for-Profit Law: Theoretical and Comparative Perspectives*, Cambridge University Press, Cambridge. [37]

European Foundation Centre (2017), *Boosting Cross-Border Philanthropy in Europe: Towards a Tax-Effective Environment*, https://www.efc.be/uploads/2019/03/Boosting-Cross-Border-Philanthropy-in-Europe-Towards-a-Tax-Effective-Environment.pdf [47]

Fack, G. and C. Landais (2010), "Are Tax Incentives for Charitable Giving Efficient? Evidence from France", *American Economic Journal: Economic Policy*, Vol. 2/2, pp. 117-141. [15]

FATF (2016), *Outcomes of the Plenary meeting of the FATF*, Paris. [50]

FATF (2012), *International Standards on Combating Money Laundering and the Financing of Terrorism & Proliferation - the FATF Recommendations*, Paris. [49]

Fleischer, M. (2018), *Research Handbook on Not-For-Profit Law: Subsidizing Charity Liberally*, Edward Elgar, Cheltenham. [28]

Hansmann, H. (1987), *Economic theories of non-profit organizations*, Yale University Press, London. [1]

Henry, K. et al. (2009), *Australia's Future Tax System*, https://treasury.gov.au/review/the-australias-future-tax-system-review. [40]

Indiana University Lilly Family School of Philanthropy (2018), *The Global Philanthropy Environment Index*, https://scholarworks.iupui.edu/handle/1805/15958. [52]

Jenkins, G. (2007), "Soft Power, Strategic Security and International Philanthropy", *North Carolina Law Review*, Vol. 85/3, pp. 773-846. [55]

Kahn, H. (1960), *Personal Deductions and the Federal Income Tax*, Princeton University Press, Princeton. [29]

Krever, R. (1991), *Tax Deductions for Charitable Donations: A Tax Expenditure Analysis*, Australian Tax Research Foundation, Sydney. [34]

Lideikyte-Huber, G. (2020), "Tax Incentives for Charitable Giving as a Policy Instrument: Theoretical Discussion and Latest Economic Research", *World Tax Journal*, Vol. 12/3. [43]

Moore, D. and D. Rutzen (2011), "Legal framework for global philanthropy: Barriers and opportunities", *International Journal of Not-for-Profit Law*, Vol. 13/1-2, pp. 5-42. [46]

OECD (2018), *Private Philanthropy for Development*, OECD Publishing, Paris. [48]

Ott, J. and L. Dicke (2016), *The nature of the non-profit sector*, Westview Press, Boulder. [4]

Peloza, J. and P. Steel (2005), "The Price Elasticities of Charitable Contributions: A Meta-Analysis", *Journal of Public Policy and Marketing*, Vol. 24/2, pp. 260-272. [13]

Rabin, E. (1966), "Charitable Trusts and Charitable Deductions", *New York University Law Review*, Vol. 41, pp. 912-925. [30]

Randolph, W. (1995), "Dynamic Income, Progressive Taxes, and the Timing of Charitable Contributions", *Journal of Political Economy*, Vol. 91/1, pp. 371-382. [12]

Reich, R. (2019), *Just Giving: Why Philanthropy is Failing Democracy and How it Can do Better*, Princeton University Press, Princeton. [45]

Rushton, M. (2007), "Why are Non-profits Exempt from the corporate Income tax?", *Non-profit and Voluntary Sector Quarterly*, Vol. 36/4, pp. 662-675. [26]

Saez, E. (2004), "The optimal treatment of tax expenditures", *Journal of Public Economics*, Vol. 88/12, pp. 2657–2684. [18]

Salamon, L. (1987), "Of Market Failure, Voluntary Failure and Third Party Government: Towards the a Theory of Government-Non-profit Relations in the Modern Welfare State", *Non-profit and Voluntary Sector Quarterly*, Vol. 16, pp. 29-49. [3]

Sandmo, A. (1975), "Optimal Taxation in the Presence of Externalities", *The Swedish Journal of Economics*, Vol. 77/1, pp. 86-98. [20]

Sharpe, D. (1996), "Unfair Business Competition and the Tax on Income Destined for Charity: Forty-Six Years Later", *Forida Tax Review,* Vol. 3, p. 367. [39]

Steinberg, R. (1990), "Taxes and Giving: New Findings", *International Journal of Voluntary and Non-profit Organizations*, Vol. 1/2, pp. 61-79. [11]

Steuerle, E. (1998), *The Issue of Unfair Competition*, Center for the Study of Philanthopy and Voluntarism, Institute of Policy Sciences and Public Affairs, Duje University, Durham NC. [41]

Surrey, S. (1970), "Tax Incentives as a Device for implementing Government Policy: A Comparison of Direct Government Expenditures", *Harvard Law Review*, Vol. 83/4, pp. 705-738. [32]

Transnational Giving Europe (n.d.), *How Does it Work?* https://www.transnationalgiving.eu/how-does-it-work. [53]

Treasury Department United States (1968), *Annual Report of the Secretary of the Treasury on the State of Finances for the Fiscal Year Ended June 30,* Washington, D.C. [31]

Weisbrod, B. (1988), *To Profit or Not to Profit: The Commercial Transformation of the Non-Profit Sector*, Oxford University Press. [42]

Weisbrod, B. (1975), *Toward a Theory of the Voluntary Non-Profit Sector in a Three-Sector Economy*, Oxford University Press, Oxford. [2]

Zelinsky, E. (2012), "The Counterproductive Nature of Tax Expenditure Budgets", *Tax Notes*, Vol. 137/12, pp. 1-9. [44]

Notes

[1] The focus of this chapter is on the case for (and against) providing tax concessions for philanthropy. A broader discussion of the benefits to society of philanthropy and the philanthropic sector is beyond the scope of this chapter.

[2] The meaning of the term 'philanthropy' has been discussed in Chapter 1. The term 'philanthropic giving' is used in this report to refer to the act of giving to entities, rather than to individuals, as this is the type of giving that may qualify for tax relief. This report uses the term philanthropic entities to refer to not-for-profit entities with a 'worthy' purpose that typically provide public benefits, and the philanthropic sector to refer to the sector covering such entities.

[3] The price elasticity of philanthropic giving is generally estimated by analysing the effect a change in the price of giving (which, in a country where private contributions are tax deductible, is equal to $(1 - t)$, where t is an individual's marginal tax rate) has on the level of philanthropic giving.

[4] There is also evidence that high income taxpayers are more likely to donate large amounts periodically rather than regular amounts every year (Auten, Clotfelter and Schmalbeck, 2000[56]).

[5] The three assumptions are that there are no income effects on earnings at the individual level, that aggregate earnings are not affected by the level of the contribution good and by the tax rate on contributions, and that the compensated supply of contributions does not depend on the tax rate on earnings.

[6] See for example, Chancellor of the Exchequer in UK, William Gladstone put forward a bill in 1863 to abolish the exempt status of charities on the grounds that it was an undiscriminating public subsidy for a large group of organisations not subject to adequate public scrutiny, including elite schools, but was defeated.

[7] See the discussion relating to 'efficiency'.

3 The tax treatment of philanthropic entities

This chapter provides an overview of the tax treatment of philanthropic entities, starting with the qualification process for entities to become recognised Public Benefit Organisations (PBOs) or funds. This includes a description of countries', worthy purpose, public benefit, and not-for-profit requirements, followed by an overview the administrative application and oversight process. The chapter then analyses the different forms of tax relief that philanthropic entities benefit from, starting with the tax treatment of income of philanthropic entities, followed by Value-Added Tax (VAT) benefits, and an overview of other forms of tax relief that PBOs or funds may be eligible for. Finally, the chapter highlights the potential risk of tax avoidance and evasion schemes involving philanthropic entities and the anti-abuse policies countries have put in place as a result.

3.1. Introduction

Philanthropic entities can be categorised as either funds or Public Benefit Organisations (PBOs). For the purposes of this report, funds are entities such as foundations, associations and trusts that hold assets with which they support PBOs to advance a social objective. The term PBO refers to entities that provide goods and services in pursuit of the public benefit. From a tax perspective, philanthropic entities can benefit from tax incentives in a number of ways. Generally, entities with a philanthropic status may be able to receive tax incentivised gifts from individuals and corporations, or receive tax relief directly in relation to their activities (e.g., exemption from income tax, property tax, VAT[1], etc.). For an entity to receive such a status (fund or PBO status), it must meet a number of requirements that can be separated into three broad categories:

- Not-for-profit requirements.
- Worthy purpose requirements.
- Public benefit requirements.

Additionally a number of administrative requirements must be met to determine that the requirements listed above are met. Countries' approaches to ensuring that the requirements are fulfilled, as well as the stringency of the requirements themselves, vary. Only once the requirements are fulfilled are philanthropic entities eligible to benefit from the tax incentives for philanthropy (such as receiving tax incentivised donations, income tax exemption, capital gains tax exemption, and VAT tax exemption or relief).

By subjecting philanthropic entities to the before mentioned requirements, governments may be able to better keep track of, and have some oversight over, their tax expenditures used to incentivise philanthropy. The not-for-profit requirement ensures that the recipients of tax incentives for philanthropy are entities whose primary objective is the public benefit (and not making profit). The not-for profit requirement does not prohibit a philanthropic entity from making a surplus, instead, it generally includes non-distribution requirements so that the surplus is not distributed as dividends or other benefits beyond the scope of the entity's worthy purpose. The worthy purpose requirement allows the government to direct philanthropic funds, as well as its tax expenditures, towards particular social objectives (and possibly away from others). The public benefit requirement ensures that tax expenditures are used to incentivise activities that benefit a large and inclusive enough section of the public. How large and open the circle of beneficiaries needs to be, depends on the country and is discussed in more detail below. Finally, the administrative requirements may help ensure that the state has (and will continue to have) all the information necessary to evaluate whether an entity meets all the other requirements, particularly if there is an administrative body to monitor approvals and compliance.

3.1.1. Key Findings

The main findings of this chapter are that:

- Countries tend to impose not-for-profit, worthy purpose and public benefit requirements to determine eligibility for tax concessions. Welfare, education, scientific research, and healthcare are deemed worthy purposes most frequently across countries. For the public benefit requirement, countries generally stipulate that the benefit must be open to all, that the benefit can be restricted to groups with specific characteristics, or that the characteristics used to specify who can benefit must relate to the fulfilment of the entities' worthy purpose.
- Almost all countries surveyed in this report require philanthropic entities to undergo a specific application process to become eligible for preferential tax treatment. Countries typically follow three broad approaches: the tax administration is responsible for the accreditation process; the responsibility is shared between the tax administration and a competent authority such as an independent commission; or the responsibility lies with another department and not the tax administration.
- Countries' tax relief for the income of philanthropic entities can be separated into two approaches: (1) to exempt all or specific income, or (2) to consider all forms of income taxable, but allow the entity to reduce its taxable income through current or future reinvestments towards the fulfilment of their worthy purpose. Countries following the first approach generally exclude non-commercial income (received gifts or grants) from the tax base. Approaches to dealing with commercial activities and the income generated from those activities, diverge. A common approach is to exempt commercial income that is related to the worthy purpose and tax unrelated commercial income.

- Finally, countries that offer preferential VAT treatment to philanthropic entities tend to exempt them from having to collect VAT on certain (or all) supplies. Because such an exemption can create an input tax burden, some countries have implemented rules that help philanthropic entities reclaim some of their input tax.

This chapter proceeds as follows. Section 3.2 below summarises the not-for-profit, worthy purpose, public benefit and requirements across countries. Section 3.3 gives an overview of the administrative requirements and application processes that countries have put in place to ensure that the other conditions are being met. Section 3.4 discusses the tax treatment of philanthropic entities' income. Section 3.5 gives an overview of countries' VAT treatment of PBOs. Section 3.6 discusses other taxes and tax benefits that apply to philanthropic entities in some countries. Lastly, section 3.7 analyses the potential risk of tax avoidance and evasion schemes that involve philanthropic entities.

3.2. Qualifying for fund or PBO status and preferential tax treatment

3.2.1. Not-for-profit entities and commercial activity

The first requirement is that entities must be 'not-for-profit'. The term originally used was non-profit but in the last 10 years it has been more commonly referred to as 'not-for-profit' to reflect that the entity may make a surplus, but that its purpose is not to make profits. Thus, the requirement does not in itself limit not-for-profit entities from engaging in commercial activity or even acquiring a surplus (as long as that surplus is not distributed as dividends or as unreasonably high salaries or payments). Nevertheless, countries may choose to limit the degree to which philanthropic entities benefitting from tax incentives are able to engage in commercial activity. Furthermore, in a number of countries philanthropic entities must reinvest their surplus towards activities aimed at fulfilling their worthy purpose. If philanthropic entities engage in too much commercial activity or do not reinvest the surplus into a worthy purpose, countries may choose to tax the commercial activity, as well as the remaining surplus, or strip the entities of their preferential tax status altogether.

When philanthropic entities with a preferential tax treatment engage in commercial activity, it may raise unfair competition concerns if the goods or services supplied by the entity are also supplied by non-philanthropic businesses. To overcome this challenge countries may limit the degree to which a philanthropic entity can engage in commercial activity, tax the commercial activity, limit the commercial activity they can engage in, or only limit the preferential tax treatment of commercial activities that lead to unfair competition with for-profit businesses. More detail on this requirement is provided in the section on the tax treatment of income of philanthropic entities below (Section 3.4).

3.2.2. Worthy purpose requirements

In general, a worthy purpose signifies a cause that is deemed by government to be deserving of the philanthropic gifts of a donor and the resources of a fund or PBO. This characteristic is subjective and can be determined by the donors or philanthropic entities that are choosing what cause to focus their philanthropy on. In this report, however, worthy purposes denote a set of causes that philanthropic entities, which are eligible for tax relief, are able to engage in. That is to say that for a philanthropic entity to receive preferential tax treatment, it must have a purpose that the state (e.g. the legislature or tax administration) accepts as worthy. In a number of countries (e.g. Germany and the United States), PBOs need to focus their resources on the worthy purposes they specified in their application for a PBO status. That is to say that they cannot simply change their objective to any of the accepted purposes without going through an administrative process. In Germany, for example, if a PBO wants to change its worthy purpose, or add a new one, it must report this to the fiscal authorities.

Table 3.1 presents a non-exhaustive list of worthy purpose categories that countries may choose to support by giving tax relief to philanthropic entities with such a purpose. In order to compare worthy purpose requirements across countries, the categories listed are umbrella terms that include any related philanthropic causes. Welfare, for example, includes organisations offering shelter to fight homelessness or foodbanks that distribute food to those in need. Other worthy purposes, such as culture, may include museums or particular movie theatres, but may also apply more generally to heritage organisations or entities supporting the arts through grants. The categories that are deemed worthy most frequently across countries are welfare (37), education (35), scientific research (34), and health care (34).

Welfare qualifies as a worthy purpose in all countries listed except for Bulgaria, which is an anomaly as it only extends preferential tax treatment to the Bulgarian Red Cross. However, Bulgaria does offer tax relief to corporate and individual donors that give to entities other than the Bulgarian Red Cross (for more information see Chapter 4). Of the countries listed, Argentina, Bulgaria and Malta are the only countries that do not include education in their list of eligible causes. All countries listed in Table 3.1, except for Chile, Indonesia, Malta, and Bulgaria, include healthcare in their worthy purposes. South Africa, Malta, and Bulgaria are the only countries listed for which scientific research does not qualify as a worthy purpose. On the other hand, consumer protection (22), civil protection (28), animal protection (28), amateur sports (29), and religion (29) are the least frequently recognised worthy purpose categories across the countries listed.

Table 3.1 also shows that some countries have broad definitions for what constitutes a worthy purpose, while other countries have a more narrow definition. For instance, all of the listed categories could be considered worthy purposes in the Czech Republic, Estonia, Germany, Greece, Ireland, Israel, Lithuania, New Zealand, Norway, Portugal, Romania, the Slovak Republic, Slovenia, and the United States. Argentina, Bulgaria, Chile, Indonesia, Malta, and South Africa, on the other hand, all have a more narrow definition of what constitutes a worthy purpose.

In the majority of countries, funds and PBOs that meet the worthy purpose and public benefit requirements to receive tax incentivised donations also meet the conditions to receive preferential tax treatment and vice versa. However, this is not the case in Australia, Bulgaria, Canada, Germany, New Zealand, Norway, Sweden, South Africa, and the United States.

In countries like Bulgaria, the worthy purpose conditions for incentivising giving are less narrow than those determining whether a fund or PBO can receive direct tax support. In Bulgaria, funds and PBOs with a qualifying worthy purpose can receive tax incentivised donations but only the Bulgarian Red Cross is eligible to receive preferential tax treatment directly.

In Canada, worthy purpose conditions for incentivising giving are not identical to those determining whether a fund or PBO can receive direct tax support. In Canada tax-favoured donations can be made to funds and PBOs that engage in the worthy purpose activities listed in Table 3.1 as well as to: journalism organisations; municipal or public bodies performing a function of government in Canada; universities outside of Canada with Canadians in the student body; registered funds and PBOs outside Canada to which Her Majesty has made a gift; and the United Nations and its agencies. In general, however, it is more onerous for an organisation in Canada to become a registered charity organisation benefiting from tax-favoured donations than it is to be considered a non-profit.

Conversely, in Norway, Sweden and South Africa, the conditions for receiving tax incentivised donations are more restrictive than those for receiving tax support directly. In Norway, for example, only a specific subset of the philanthropic entities eligible for tax exemption qualify to receive donations from which the donating party can claim a tax deduction. In order to qualify, the receiving entity's worthy purpose must fall within the following categories: healthcare; activities directed at children and young people engaged in culture or amateur sports; religion; human rights; development aid; disaster relief; and environmental and cultural preservation. In South Africa, funds and PBOs are only eligible to receive tax incentivised donations if their worthy purpose falls within healthcare, welfare and education.

Table 3.1. Worthy purposes by country

	Welfare	Education	Science	Health-care	Cultural	Environmental	Disaster relief	Civil society	Community service	Human rights	Development finance	Child-care	Humanitarian aid (abroad)	Religious	Amateur sport	Animal protection	Civil-protection	Consumer protection	Other
Argentina	X		X	X					X			X		X					X[1]
Australia	X	X	X	X	X	X	X	X	X	X	X		X	X	X	X	X		X[2]
Austria	X	X	X	X	X	X	X	X		X	X	X	X	X	X	X	X		
Belgium	X	X	X	X	X	X	X	X	X	X	X	X	X			X	X		
Bulgaria	X	X		X	X	X	X	X	X			X	X	X					X[3]
Canada	X	X	X	X	X	X	X	X	X	X	X	X	X	X	X	X	X		
Chile	X	X	X		X		X		X		X	X			x		X		
Colombia	X	X	X	X	X	X	X	X	X	X	X	X		X	X		X		
Czech Republic	X	X	X	X	X	X	X	X	X	X	X	X	X	X	X	X	X	X	
Estonia	X	X	X	X	X	X	X	X	X	X	X	X	X	X	X	X	X	X	
Finland	X	X	X	X	X	X		X	X			X			X			X	X[4]
France	X	X	X	X	X	X	X	X	X	X	X	X	X	X		X	X	X	
Germany	X	X	X	X	X	X	X	X	X	X	X	X	X	X	X	X	X	X	
Greece	X	X	X	X	X	X	X	X	X	X	X	X	X	X	X	X	X	X	
India	X	X	X	X	X	X	X	X	X	X	X	X	X	X	X	X	X	X	X[5]
Indonesia	X	X	X				X							X	X				X[6]
Ireland	X	X	X	X	X	X	X	X	X	X	X	X	X	X	X	X	X	X	
Israel	X	X	X	X	X	X	X	X	X	X	X	X	X	X	X	X	X	X	
Italy	X	X	X	X	X	X	X	X	X	X	X	X	X		X	X		X	
Japan	X	X	X	X	X	X	X	X	X	X	X	X	X	X	X	X	X	X	
Latvia	X	X	X	X	X	X	X	X		X		X	X		X	X	X		
Lithuania	X	X	X	X	X	X	X	X	X	X	X	X	X	X	X	X	X	X	
Luxembourg	X	X	X	X	X	X	X	X	X	X		X	X	X	X	X	X		
Malta	X									X			X						
Mexico	X	X	X	X	X	X	X	X	X	X	X	X				X	X	X	X[7]
Netherlands	X	X	X	X	X	X	X	X	X	X	X	X	X	X		X	X		
New Zealand	X	X	X	X	X	X	X	X	X	X	X	X	X	X	X	X	X	X	
Norway	X	X	X	X	X	X	X	X	X	X	X	X	X	X	X	X	X	X	X[8]
Portugal	X	X	X	X	X	X	X	X	X	X	X	X	X	X	X	X	X	X	
Romania	X	X	X	X	X	X	X	X	X	X	X	X	X	X	X	X	X	X	
Singapore																			X[9]
Slovak Republic	X	X	X	X	X	X	X	X	X	X	X	X	X	X	X	X	X	X	
Slovenia	X	X	X	X	X	X	X	X	X	X	X	X	X	X	X	X	X	X	X[10]
South Africa	X	X		X		X					X			X	X				
Sweden	X	X	X	X	X	X	X	X		X	X		X	X	X				
Switzerland	X	X	X	X	X	X	X	X	X	X	X		X			X		X	
United Kingdom	X	X	X	X	X	X	X	X	X	X	X	X	X	X	X	X	X	X	
United States	X	X	X	X	X	X	X	X	X	X	X	X	X	X	X	X	X	X	X[11]
Frequency	**37**	**35**	**34**	**34**	**33**	**33**	**33**	**32**	**31**	**31**	**30**	**30**	**30**	**29**	**29**	**28**	**28**	**22**	

Notes:

1. Charity, Art and Literature, Unions
2. Sporting clubs in general, employer and employee associations, trade unions, associations promoting primary and secondary resources and tourism.
3. The activities of the Bulgarian Red Cross.
4. Finland does not have an exhaustive list of worthy purposes and categories identified in this table are from a list of non-exhaustive examples in the income tax act.
5. Yoga and the advancement of any other object of general public utility.
6. Scholarship awarding; environmental preservation.

7. The worthy purposes for Mexico in this table, are limited to those that receive deductible donations. Other worthy purposes, such as amateur sports, religious or some mutual societies can only benefit from preferential income tax treatment.
8. The tax act does not contain a specification of what constitutes an entity with worthy purposes or activity of public benefit.
9. Recognises charitable purposes as defined in common: (i) relief of poverty; (ii) advancement of education; (iii) advancement of religion; and (iv) other purposes beneficial to the community, such as health-promotion, advancement of arts and heritage, and environmental protection.
10. Must be considered "generally useful" (*splošnokoristen*).
11. Amateur athletics (added for 1976 Olympics).
Source: OECD Taxation and Philanthropy Questionnaire

3.2.3. Public benefit requirements

For an entity to be philanthropic, its worthy purpose must be for the public benefit. Generally speaking this means that the worthy purpose of a fund or PBO has to benefit the public as a whole or a sufficient section of the public (sometimes referred to as a charitable or public class). If the circle of beneficiaries does not constitute a sufficient section of the public, the entity's purpose would only be for the private benefit of a few individuals and therefore not meet the necessary requirements to qualify as a philanthropic entity worthy of receiving preferential tax treatment.

Typically, some worthy purposes are considered to benefit the public as a whole, meaning that the benefit is not limited to people who satisfy a particular criteria. Such worthy purposes may include, for example, protecting the environment, scientific discovery, or animal protection. Other worthy purposes, however, tend to benefit a circle of beneficiaries and countries typically regulate the size and/or the criteria used to specify who can benefit. An example of a worthy purpose that specifies who can benefit, is a disability support group. Generally, countries consider a circle of beneficiaries that is defined by need to be a sufficient section of the public.

Some entities, however, define their circle of beneficiaries using characteristics such as age, disability, gender, sexual orientation, race, nationality, pregnancy, or religion. Public benefit rules addressing this issue can be categorised into three approaches: countries may restrict philanthropic entities from using individual characteristics to define who can benefit altogether; countries may approve a list of characteristics (sometimes referred to as protected characteristics) that philanthropic entities are permitted to use in order to specify who can benefit; or countries may only allow limiting benefits to people with these characteristics if the criteria can be justified in relation to the worthy purpose (e.g., under this approach, a PBO committed to the health and well-being of pregnant women can use pregnancy as a characteristic to limit the circle of beneficiaries but cannot specify that only individuals of a particular religion may benefit from its services).

The benefit must be open to all and cannot be restricted

Some countries (e.g. Austria, France, and Slovenia) stipulate that the circle of beneficiaries needs to be open to the public and cannot be restricted by specific characteristics of individuals such as gender, sex, religion, or origin. In Austria, the circle of beneficiaries has to be the general public in the sense that the activity is in line with public interest in regard to intellectual, cultural or material subjects. Furthermore, the circle of beneficiaries of public benefit activities cannot be restricted by specific characteristics, including sex and gender. In Slovenia, there is no minimum number of people that need to be in the circle of beneficiaries and the benefit cannot be limited by individual characteristics including skill, gender, religion, nationality, or origin.

In France, PBOs are referred to as general interest organisations (*association d'intérêt general*) and can issue tax receipts to their donors so that they can benefit from the tax incentive for giving. To be eligible for such a status, an entity must meet the public benefit requirement of not working for the benefit of a small circle of people. Furthermore, the interests and activities of a general interest organisation must be able to benefit everyone, without being limited to any criteria (e.g., race, sex, profession, or religion). Additionally, a general interest organisation can become an association of public utility (*association d'utilité publique*). An association of public utility can receive, in addition to gifts which any PBO can benefit from, donations and bequests. To become an association of public utility, a PBO must fulfil additional public benefit requirements, such as having an influence and outreach beyond the local context and a minimum of 200 members.

The benefit can be restricted by specified characteristics

A number of countries allow philanthropic entities to restrict who can benefit using certain characteristics (e.g., Chile, Colombia, Greece, Israel, Lithuania, Malta, Mexico, Norway, Romania, Singapore, the Slovak Republic, South Africa, and Switzerland). In Colombia and Switzerland, for example, entities are allowed to benefit only one gender but may not use any other characteristics to further restrict who can benefit. In Mexico, no restrictions are allowed regarding origin, religion, or nationality. However, restrictions based on gender and potentially other characteristics are possible. For instance, philanthropic entities can concentrate their support on single mothers. The rule is that they must fulfil their specific purpose.

In Israel philanthropic entities can target only one gender and can specify origin, or nationality. In Latvia a worthy purpose can benefit target groups such as children, young people, people in poverty, and disabled people but the philanthropic activity must reach people regardless of their skill, origin, religion or nationality.

In Lithuania there are no rules that prohibit entities selecting their beneficiaries based on gender or skill as long as the activity is in line with the Law on Equal Opportunities for Women and Men. The philanthropic activities of the entities must also reach people regardless of their origin, religion, or nationality. In Romania, on the other hand, entities cannot benefit only one gender but may specify their circle of beneficiaries using other individual characteristics such as skill, religion, or nationality. Singapore permits entities to target only one gender if their activities also benefit the public as a whole. For example, PBOs such as the Boys Brigade and Girls Brigade engage in activities that benefit the wider community. Chile, Greece, Malta and the Slovak Republic have no rules regarding whether or not entities can limit their philanthropic activity to individuals with particular characteristics.

The characteristics used to specify who can benefit must relate to the worthy purpose

Lastly, a number of countries (Australia, Belgium, Canada, Estonia, Germany, India, Japan, the Netherlands, New Zealand, Portugal, South Africa, Sweden, and the United States) only permit philanthropic entities to limit the circle of beneficiaries to people with particular characteristics if it can be justified with their worthy purpose.

In Australia, philanthropic entities must have a purpose that provides a benefit to the general public or a sufficient section of the general public. Whether a purpose benefits a sufficient section of the general public is to be assessed on registration. Certain PBOs are presumed to be for the public benefit, such as those involved in the relief of poverty. PBOs can limit their beneficiaries to a gender if such a restriction relates to the worthy purpose. For example, a charity providing support to victims of domestic violence may be permitted to provide services only to women, and a charity with a purpose of advancing health may provide services only to men with mental health concerns. Similarly, a tax-exempt PBO may promote a specific religion or provide services to people who have migrated to Australia from a specific country.

Belgian law prohibits discrimination on grounds of age, sexual orientation, marital status, birth, property, religious or philosophical belief, political conviction, language, present or future state of health, disability, physical or genetic characteristic or social origin. However, if the PBO receives its accreditation for the purpose of benefiting a defined category of people (e.g. disabled persons), it may limit its action to this specific section of the public. Such PBOs include associations that specifically defend women's rights with a view to achieving greater gender equality. Regarding the geographic reach of an entity's activities, specific criteria are defined by both the Ministry of Finance and the competent authority:

- Scientific research: Entities must be active throughout the national or regional territory and not only at the local level.
- Culture: Entities must be active throughout the national territory and not only at the local level, and may not be related to teaching activities which fall within the responsibility of the Ministry of Education.
- Protection of nature and the environment: Entities must demonstrate that their activities are of a continuous and sustainable nature, have an area of influence that extends to more than one municipality.
- Assistance to war victims, to the disabled, the elderly, minors of protected age and people living in poverty: Entities must be active throughout the national territory and not only at the local level.
- Aid to victims of natural disasters recognised in Belgium, aid to developing countries, assistance to victims of major industrial accidents and sustainable development: Entities must be active throughout the national or regional territory and not only at the local level.
- Donations to associations that assist the disabled may only benefit the disabled and not their families.
- For cultural associations, activities must be organised in three different provinces. Local associations are excluded. A calendar of activities and an activity report for the past year must be provided.

In Canada an entity that benefits only one gender may be eligible to be a registered PBO and receive preferential tax treatment if it can show that there is a need to do so. All types of limitations to access have the potential to prevent an entity from being registered as a PBO, although to differing degrees. Entities that want an outright restriction of benefit or exclusion of services have a far greater burden of establishing public benefit than those entities that want only to focus attention on a specific group, but extend service delivery to the general public. Most importantly, when a PBO proposes to restrict the beneficiaries of an activity in any way, the nature of the restriction must be clearly linked to the proposed benefit. For example, a religious charity may well be limited to those who are adherents of that particular religious faith, whereas that same limitation would not suffice for an organisation established to assist persons with a disability. Overall, an entity with an unreasonably limiting service or programme, will not meet the public benefit requirements, unless the restrictions are shown to be relevant to achieving the charitable purpose.

Within the public benefit requirements, there are several sub-requirements. For instance, the benefit should generally be tangible; the beneficiaries must be the public-at-large or come from a sufficient segment of the public as determined by the charitable purpose being considered; the entity may not otherwise benefit private individuals except under certain limited conditions; subject to some exceptions, the entity cannot exist for the benefit of its members; the entity cannot charge fees for its services where the effect of the charge would unduly exclude members of the public.

In Estonia, the benefits of the philanthropic activity must be identifiable and justifiable, but not quantifiable. Philanthropic activities cannot only be aimed at individuals with specific characteristics and need to benefit a sufficient section of the public. If targeting only one gender can be justified with the entity's worthy purpose, that would be considered a sufficient section of the public. The worthy purpose must not benefit a fixed number of people. If the not-for-profit entity has members, it must have two or more.

In Germany, the worthy purpose must be dedicated to the altruistic advancement of the general public. In 2017 the federal fiscal court in Germany decided that a PBO cannot be for the common-benefit if it excludes women from its membership without a relevant justification. The ruling has led to public debate. Member based entities are eligible for preferential tax treatment. There is a minimum number of seven members in order to establish a registered association. Non-registered associations may also be eligible for the preferential tax treatment.

In India a philanthropic entity cannot be for a private religious purpose or be a trust "for the benefit of any particular religious community or caste". Activities may cater to women, children and vulnerable sections of society. Similarly in Japan, the beneficiaries can be specified by characteristics such as gender, religion, or ability as long as the there is a relevant connection with the worthy purpose. For example, a women's rights organisation can target people based on gender, a religious organisation can target people based on religion, or an educational facility can target people based on skill or ability.

In Italy, most philanthropic entities are open to all, without restrictions to beneficiaries. However, some kinds of entities can restrict the benefits from their activities to some groups with characteristics related to the PBO's worthy purpose (for example, philanthropic organisations that help disadvantaged people to find employment).

In the Netherlands, there is no specific definition of 'public benefit'. In the legislation as well as in case law, this term is neutrally described, so that there may be different opinions as to whether the organisation benefits the public. The circle of beneficiaries can be restricted by the entity if, for example, its worthy purpose is promoting equal treatment of men and women and therefore focusses only on women. Importantly, however, the purpose and activities of a philanthropic entity may not violate the constitution or international treaties, which forbid discrimination based on (amongst other characteristics) gender, race and religion.

In New Zealand, philanthropic activity needs to benefit a sufficient section of the public. Imposing fees for access to a benefit can be acceptable if done reasonably. For example, by providing a benefit that can only be accessed by members of a certain group (e.g. a scholarship for Māori students). Limits on public access must be reasonable and appropriate. When members of an organisation can also benefit, any limitations on membership must also be reasonable in the context of the benefit to the public. For example, a society of doctors set up to improve medical practice may reasonably limit its membership to qualified doctors, because the real benefit is to the wider public from the improvement of public health.

In Sweden, member based entities are eligible if they are open to the public. Nevertheless, they are allowed to make certain restrictions (e.g., age limit for a shooting club, the ability to play an instrument for an orchestra etc.). Similarly, their activities can target only one gender only if this target is naturally associated with the objective of the member based entity.

In the United States, entities need to support a charitable "class", and not provide a more than insubstantial private benefit. There is not a specific number that constitutes a charitable class, however it must either be large enough that potential beneficiaries cannot be individually identified, or sufficiently indefinite that the community as a whole, rather than a pre-selected group of people receive benefits. Clubs and associations that are not charities are eligible for limited preferential tax treatment and there is not a specific minimum number of members needed.

3.3. Tax Administration and application processes

3.3.1. Application process

To ensure that the entities receiving preferential tax treatment meet the public benefit, worthy purpose, and not-for-profit conditions, almost all countries surveyed in this report require philanthropic entities to undergo a specific application process to become eligible for preferential tax treatment. The assessing body must therefore approve entities before they are able to receive the preferential tax treatment. In a number of countries (e.g., Canada, France, Ireland, New Zealand, Colombia, and Germany), entities are able to apply before starting to operate. An advantage of this approach may be that entities can address issues from the start and thereby reduce the chance that they do not receive preferential tax status after they have already started operating. On the other hand, the shortcoming of such an approach may be that countries grant entities preferential tax status without being able to evaluate their performance or operations. Following up with the entity after it receives its initial tax privileges is a potential way in which countries could address this issue. For example, within three years after the approval of the status, the German tax administration monitors whether the requirements of the preferential tax treatment are still met. In France, the tax administration has six months to respond from the date of receipt of the application. After six months without notification of an administration agreement, a general interest association can receive preferential tax treatment. When it is negative, the tax administration must justify its decision. If the general interest organisation does not agree with the tax administration, it can send a second application within two months.

On the other hand, some countries (e.g., Belgium, Romania, and Argentina), require entities to have already been operating for a minimum period of time before they can apply. In Belgium, for example, PBOs must provide an activity report for the past year as well as a detailed statement of the current year's projects. In Argentina, entities that apply to receive PBO status with preferential tax treatment must demonstrate an initial (and largely symbolic, given recent inflation rates) social capital of ARS 1 000 in the general case, and ARS 200 for entities with a worthy purpose to promote economic, social and cultural rights of vulnerable groups and/or ethnic communities with a poverty or vulnerability status. In the case of foundations, the minimum initial social capital required is ARS 80 000. In Romania, entities must have been operating for at least three years and have achieved part of their philanthropic objectives before they can apply for tax relief.

In some countries (e.g., Norway and Lithuania), there is no application process for philanthropic entities to receive some of the preferential tax treatments. The benefits of not having an application process for preferential tax treatment may be to reduce the administrative burden on the entities as well as on the assessing body but this may raise issues of accountability. In Norway, for instance, there is no application process for qualifying philanthropic entities to benefit from direct preferential tax treatment. For funds and PBOs to be able to receive tax-incentivised donations, however, the entity must apply to the tax administration and fulfil the accounting and auditing requirements. Similarly, in Lithuania, there is also no registration process for philanthropic entities to receive most forms of preferential tax treatment, but if a PBO would like to receive sponsorship, it must apply to become an eligible sponsorship recipient.

3.3.2. Assessing body

To ensure that philanthropic entities meet the necessary conditions to benefit from preferential tax treatment, countries task their tax administration, other ministries or independent commissions with accreditation and oversight responsibilities. Table 3.2 shows that the majority of countries (16) have specific departments or units within their tax administration and/or Ministry of Finance that are dedicated to the philanthropic sector. Such countries may or may not have another department or independent body that oversees the funds and PBOs. To ensure that tax relief is targeted efficiently, the oversight body has to be able to determine whether the entity is productively fulfilling its worthy purpose. For PBOs with a cultural purpose, for example, such a determination may require a very different set of expertise as for PBOs with a welfare or environmental objective.

Table 3.2. Departments devoted to the tax treatment of philanthropic entities

Countries <u>with</u> a specific department/unit in the Ministry of Finance and/or tax administration that is dedicated to philanthropy:	*Argentina; Australia; Belgium; Canada; Estonia; Germany; India; Ireland; Israel; Italy; Malta; Mexico; the Netherlands; New Zealand; Singapore; South Africa; Sweden; Switzerland; and the United Kingdom and the United States[1];*
Countries <u>without</u> a specific department/unit in the Ministry of Finance and/or tax administration that is dedicated to philanthropy:	*Austria; Bulgaria; Chile; Colombia; Czech Republic; France; Indonesia; Lithuania; Latvia; Norway; Portugal; Romania; the Slovak Republic; and Slovenia*

Note:
1. In the United States, the IRS has an office devoted to Exempt Organizations (including philanthropic entities).
Source: OECD Taxation and Philanthropy Questionnaire

Table 3.3 indicates where within the government the administrative process of accrediting and overseeing philanthropic entities takes place. Countries typically follow one of three broad approaches: the tax administration is responsible for the accreditation process; the responsibility is shared between the tax administration and a competent authority; or the responsibility lies with another department and not the tax administration.

Table 3.3. Administering body by country

	Tax administration	Ministry of Finance	Another ministry	Independent commissions	A combination	Other
Argentina	X					
Australia	X			X[1]	X[2]	
Austria	X					
Belgium	X	X			X[3]	
Bulgaria			X[4]			
Canada	X	X				
Chile	X				X[5]	
Colombia	X					
Estonia	X					
Finland	X					
France	X		X[6]			
Germany	X	X				
Greece	X				X[5]	
India	X					
Indonesia	X		X[7]			
Ireland	X			X[8]		
Israel	X					
Italy	X		X[9]			
Japan	X		X[3]			
Latvia	X					X[10]
Lithuania						X[11]
Luxembourg	X				X[12]	
Malta	X	X				
Mexico	X					
Netherlands	X					
New Zealand	X		X[13]			
Norway		X[14]				
Portugal	X				X[5]	
Romania			X[15]			
Singapore			X			
Slovak Republic	X					
Slovenia	X		X[3]			X[16]
South Africa	X					
Sweden	X					
Switzerland	X					
United Kingdom	X					
United States	X					X[17]

Notes:

1. The Charities Registration Board is responsible for all decisions regarding the registration and removal of organisations from the charities register; Australian Charities and Not-for-profits Commission.
2. Eligibility for some concessions requires endorsement by both the ATO and the ACNC.
3. PBOs must be accredited by the Ministry of Finance/ tax administration as well as the competent authority (e.g. Ministry for Development Cooperation for humanitarian NGO's).

4. Registry Agency to the Ministry of Justice.
5. Tax administration and other competent entities, depending on the activity (e.g., social security, ministry of education, etc.).
6. Ministry of Interior ("Ministère de l'Intérieur").
7. Ministry of Law and Human Rights (for the record of establishment and financial report.
8. The Charities Regulatory Authority.
9. With the implementation of the reform, the Ministry of Labour and Social Policies will be in charge of administering the new National Register of PBOs together with the Tax Administration.
10. The Commission is a collegial consultative body which includes, in equal number, authorized officials as well as representatives of associations and foundations.
11. Centre of Registers under the supervision of Ministry of the Economy and Innovation of the Republic of Lithuania.
12. The Ministry of Justice as well as the Direct Tax Administration play a role in the administration of PBOs and funds.
13. Charities Services (Department of Internal Affairs).
14. There is no accreditation process. However, organisations can request either a binding or advisory advance ruling from the tax administration with respect to whether it would qualify for tax exempt status.
15. General Secretariat of the Government.
16. Administrative office (as part of state).
17. Organizations are generally registered as non-profits by the states before they apply to the IRS to receive preferential tax treatment.
Source: OECD Taxation and Philanthropy Questionnaire

Tax administration

In the majority of countries, the responsibility over the accreditation process lies within the tax administration (see Table 3.3). This is the case in, for example, Argentina, Austria, Colombia, Estonia, Finland, India, Israel, Mexico, the Netherlands, Norway, the Slovak Republic, South Africa, Sweden, and Switzerland. In all of these countries, entities applying for preferential tax treatment need to apply directly to the tax administration, which is then tasked with reviewing the provided materials and determine eligibility. The majority of the countries following this approach (Argentina, Australia, Estonia, India, Israel, Mexico, the Netherlands, the Slovak Republic, South Africa, and Sweden) have a department or unit in their tax administration that is dedicated to philanthropy (see Table 3.2). For those countries in particular, a benefit of this approach may be to centralise the oversight process. On the other hand, this approach may require the tax administration to devote a significant amount of resources to entities that pay little to no taxes. Depending on the political environment, there could be competing pressures to prioritise revenue-raising activities over administering tax incentives for funds and PBOs. In such cases, there may be advantages in involving other parts of the government.

The Colombian approach is unique because it allows the public to be involved in the accreditation process. As Figure 3.1 below shows, once the submission of the request and the fulfilment of the online registry are correctly completed, the information of the entity will be published online, allowing the public to comment on it for five business days. After this, the Colombian tax administration will have four months to decide if it approves or denies the request of the entity to be classified as a philanthropic entity benefiting from the special tax regime (see the Figure 3.1 for more details on the timeline).

Figure 3.1. Colombian special tax regime application process

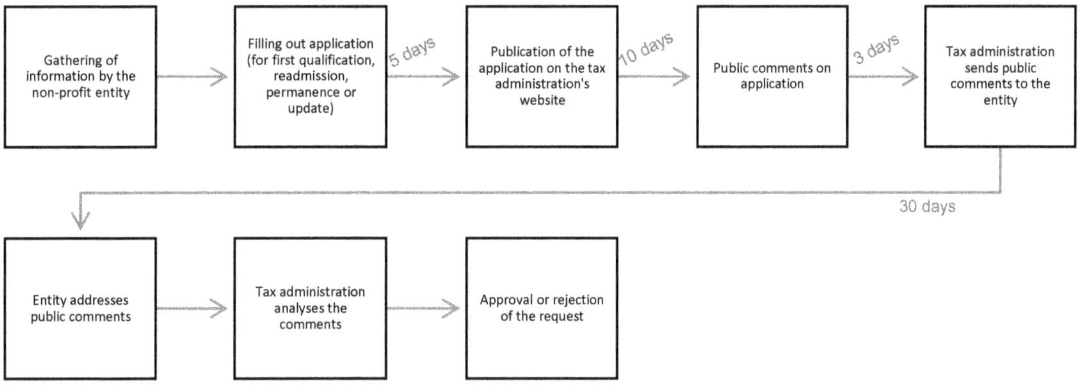

Note: The days in the infographic correspond to business days
Source: OECD Taxation and Philanthropy Questionnaire

Tax administration as well as other competent authority

In a number of countries (e.g., Australia, Belgium, Canada, Chile, France, Germany, Greece, Indonesia, Ireland, Japan, Latvia, Malta, Portugal, Slovenia, the Unites States) the administrative responsibilities are shared between the tax administration and other competent authorities. The range of activities that philanthropic entities may engage in is typically very broad and thus it could be challenging to properly assess and oversee entities that engage in fields that are not within the expertise of the tax administration or ministry of finance. Especially for countries that do not have a specific department or unit devoted to administering philanthropic entities (see Table 3.2), the additional resources and expertise of another competent authority may be an advantage. Some countries (e.g., Belgium, France, Slovenia, Portugal, and Chile) have addressed this challenge by assigning a competent authority in addition to the tax administration to oversee philanthropic entities. For example, the tax administration as well as the ministry of culture may process a cultural heritage organisation's application for PBO status. In France, general interest organisations must register with the tax administration, while those seeking to be additionally recognised as being of public utility, must send their application to the Ministry of the Interior.

Another approach is to make an independent commission of experts responsible for the accreditation and oversight process (e.g., Australia, Ireland, Latvia and New Zealand). Having a dedicated commission of experts as an oversight body may have the advantage of overcoming institutional constraints of tax administrations. The primary purpose of a tax administration is the collection of tax revenue on behalf of citizens to fund the work of the government (OECD, 2019[1]). Managing a largely untaxed philanthropic sector, may therefore compete with limited resources needed for revenue raising activities. Dedicated commissions are typically able to collect and analyse data, develop expertise in the field of philanthropic entities, publish reports, and offer a clear point of contact for funds and PBOs.

Nevertheless, tax administrations have a crucial proficiency of the applicable tax rules and the way in which they interact with the country's overall tax system. As a result, countries with commissions typically follow two approaches to incorporate the tax administration in the oversight process. The first approach, followed by Latvia, is to include tax administration officials in their commissions. The second approach, followed by Australia, Ireland and New Zealand, is to make use of a two-step process where entities must apply for approval to both a commission dedicated to philanthropic entities and the tax administration.

For example, in Latvia, entities are evaluated by a commission that is a collegial consultative body which includes (in equal number) authorized officials from the Ministry of Finance, the Ministry of Education and Science, the Ministry of Culture, the Ministry of Welfare, the Ministry of Justice and the Ministry of the

Environment and Regional Development, as well as representatives of funds and PBOs who are competent and have experience in one of the worthy purpose fields.

In Ireland, philanthropic entities must firstly apply to an independent charity commission in order to be granted philanthropic status. Following that, philanthropic entities can apply to the tax administration for tax exemption. To be eligible for tax concessions in New Zealand, charities must first register with the Charities Services (a group within the Department of Internal Affairs with an independent charities registration board of three people). As part of the registration process, entities must disclose to Charities Services if they operate, or intend to operate, overseas. This information is passed on to the tax administration to further consider the charity's eligibility for income tax concessions and for receiving tax-incentivised donations. Other PBO's that may be fully income tax exempt, but are not considered charities in New Zealand (e.g., amateur sports bodies, or 'friendly societies') must apply to the tax administration directly and provide a copy of their company rules to ensure their funds can only be applied to their worthy purposes before the tax exemption is approved. Other clubs and associations, which are not eligible for full income tax exemptions, are also required to supply the tax administration with copies of their rules as they may be entitled to a limited NZD 1 000 tax deduction but unlike registered charities, are expected to file a tax return.

In Australia, the assessing body responsible for all decisions, regarding the registration and removal of organisations from the charities register is the Australian Charities and Not-for-profits Commission (ACNC). A charity must be registered with the ACNC to be exempt from income tax and obtain other tax concessions. Furthermore, a charity must be endorsed by the tax administration to be exempt from income tax. An entity wishing to be a deductible gift recipient must be endorsed by the tax administration or specifically named in tax legislation. The tax administration's endorsement process typically takes less than 28 days.

Other department

Not all countries follow the above approaches of involving the tax administration in oversight responsibilities. In Lithuania, for example, the assessing body in charge of the application process to becoming a sponsorship recipient is the Centre of Registers under the supervision of the Ministry of the Economy and Innovation of the Republic of Lithuania. In Luxembourg, a PBO (like any other corporation) has to file annual accounts with the Company and Trade Register, which have to be supervised and approved by an independent auditor. PBOs may only own property or buildings necessary to carry out its mission. In Romania, the assessing body is the General Secretariat of the Government. In Bulgaria, the Registry Agency to the Minister of Justice is the body responsible for accrediting philanthropic entities, which enables them to receive tax-incentivised donations.

3.3.3. Additional reporting requirements

Regardless of what authority is tasked with approving philanthropic entities for tax privileges, the assessing body typically requires funds and PBOs to provide them with the information they need to evaluate whether or not the entities are, and continue to be, eligible to receive the philanthropic status as well as the associated preferential tax treatment. The requirements differ across countries and there is a trade-off between requiring entities to provide a lot of detailed information at the cost of a high administrative burden and minimal information at the cost of less oversight and perhaps more misconduct. The information requirements that countries implement can be categorised into record keeping requirements (so that entities can be audited effectively); annual reporting requirements (to help the administrative body oversee whether the entities continue to meet the worthy purpose, public benefit and not-for-profit conditions); constitutional requirements (to align the company rules with the tax rules); and an activities plan requirement (to help the assessing body evaluate the entity's future plans).

Application and record keeping requirements

Record keeping requirements are necessary for effective auditing. For example, the Canadian tax administration conducts selective audits of registered philanthropic entities each year to evaluate whether they continue to qualify for registration and ensure they follow the rules (the tax administration maintains an audit coverage of approximately 1%). Funds and PBOs are required to provide books and records to demonstrate that their resources were used for worthy purposes and to ensure that official donation receipts were issued. So that entities have all the necessary information available during an audit, registered funds and PBOs in Canada are obliged to:

- maintain direction and control of the use of all their resources;
- meet their annual spending requirement (disbursement quota);
- keep reliable and complete books and records;
- issue complete and accurate official donation receipts (see Chapter 4 for more details on requirements relating to donation receipts).

In Belgium, PBOs must provide a budget for the current fiscal year; and the accounts of the last two accounting years. Furthermore, they must formally commit to limit management fees to less than 20%, limit advertising costs to less than 30%, and make no profits. The minimum duration of the process of accreditation is three months. Similarly, in Ireland the application for tax-exempt status must include a full set of recent financial accounts; a constitution; a plan for activities for the year ahead; and proof of registration of PBO or fund status with an independent charity commission.

Philanthropic entities in the Netherlands must keep accounting records from which the following can be inferred:

- the nature and scope of the expense allowances and/or attendance fees granted to the separate members of the board;
- the nature and scope of the management activities, and the other costs incurred by the entity; and
- the nature and scope of the income and the assets held by the entity.

In Lithuania, philanthropic entities entitled to receive sponsorship must keep separate accounts for sponsorship received as well as for donations and/or services provided. Additionally, they must submit their monthly or annual reports to the tax administration. If the amount of the sponsorship received since the beginning of a calendar year from a single provider of sponsorship exceeds EUR 15 000, the entity must submit a monthly report.

In Colombia, the application process requires the following information:

- a description of the entity's worthy purpose;
- the amount and destination of the reinvestment of the net benefits or surpluses, when applicable;
- the amount and destination of permanent assignments that have been made in the taxable year;;
- names of the persons that manage, direct or control the entity;
- the salary of the members of the governing body of the entity;
- names of the founders;
- the amount of equity as of December 31st of the previous year;
- the identification of the donors and the amount of the donations, as well as the destination of such donation and the projected term for expenditure or investment (if applicable);
- an annual report of the results that establishes the information about ongoing projects and concluded ones, income, agreements entered into, subsidies and contributions received, as well as goals achieved for the public benefit;

- financial statements of the entity;
- a certificate of the legal representative or controller, as well as the income tax return that establishes that the entity has complied with all requirements for the taxable year;

In France, PBOs benefiting from a preferential tax treatment are subject to audit by the Court of Auditors. Organizations receiving more than EUR 153 000 in grants or more than EUR 153 000 in philanthropic gifts, must have their account records certified by an external auditor each year.

In Luxembourg, PBOs must determine who their beneficial owners are and have to declare them in the register of beneficial owners. A form must be completed with the information required by law in order to complete this declaration (in most cases, it will be the members of the board of directors).

Annual reporting requirements

A number of countries have annual reporting requirements (e.g., Australia, Colombia, Estonia, Lithuania, and Singapore). Typically, annual reporting helps the assessing body monitor an entity's activities and assess whether they are still meeting all the necessary requirements. In Australia, for example, a registered entity must provide annual reports – an Annual Information Statement and for medium and large entities, a financial statement - to the ACNC. If a philanthropic entity is income tax exempt, it does not need to submit an income tax return, although there is a requirement to do so if requested by the tax administration. However, if applicable, such an entity may need to submit statements in relation to the VAT. Similarly, in order for philanthropic entities to maintain their status in Colombia, funds and PBOs of the special tax regime must annually submit their financial and legal information to the Colombian tax administration. Furthermore, all entities belonging to the special tax regime must file an annual income tax return.

Some countries require funds and PBOs to make their information publicly available. This is the case in the Netherlands, where philanthropic entities must publish information about the organisation on their own website or on a communal website of a trade organisation for example. An advantage of this approach may be in fostering the public's trust in the philanthropic sector.

A number of countries require philanthropic entities to submit tax returns regardless of whether or not they are liable to pay taxes. In Germany, for example, funds and PBOs that receive preferential tax treatment can self-assess but are required to submit tax returns even if no tax is payable. Similarly, funds and PBOs in Slovenia can self-assess but are required to submit tax returns. On the other hand, for an entity to receive preferential tax treatment in the Slovak Republic, the only condition is to establish a business with a worthy purpose. The philanthropic entity is then required to submit tax returns but only if their income includes non-exempt income.

In the United States, philanthropic entities (other than churches) must apply for tax exemption from the tax administration and receive a tax-exempt status. After the tax-exempt status is granted, the entities (other than churches) must file annual information tax returns, which are available to the public. Additionally, if they engage in any unrelated trade or business activity, the philanthropic entities (including churches) must file a separate tax return, which is also available to the public.

Company rules and related requirements

Some countries (e.g., Ireland, New Zealand, Estonia, Mexico, and the Netherlands) require entities to report their company rules, constitution or bylaws with the administration, so that they can ensure that they are in line with the requirements necessary to receive preferential tax treatment. For example, to be qualified as a fund or PBO in the Netherlands, the articles of association of the philanthropic entity must stipulate that, in the event of liquidation, the assets remaining are to be passed on to a philanthropic entity with a similar purpose or on a foreign philanthropic entity that is (entirely or almost) exclusively committed to the public good and has a similar worthy purpose. In New Zealand, clubs and associations which are not eligible for full income tax exemptions are required to supply the tax administration with copies of their rules as they may be entitled to a limited NZD 1 000 tax deduction, but are also expected to file a tax return. Funds and PBOs in Mexico must include the current company bylaws in their application along with a proof of the nature of their activities.

Activities plan requirement

In a few countries (e.g., Belgium, Ireland, Colombia, Estonia, and Romania), entities have to provide the administration body with an activities plan. A benefit of this approach may be that countries can evaluate whether the entities have successfully made progress on their objectives but also allows them to flag any issues of eligibility ahead of time. For example, Belgium requires entities to provide a calendar of activities and an activity report for the past year as well as a detailed statement of the current year's projects.

In order to receive preferential tax treatment in Estonia, a philanthropic entity must submit an application complying with the requirements of the tax administration. The application should describe the activities of the association in the current year (including planned activities), explain the philanthropic activities carried out for the public benefit, describe the future visions of the entity and provide the necessary information on its founders. In addition to the application, the objectives set out in the articles of the entity and in the annual report are reviewed by the tax administration.

Philanthropic entities in Romania must present an activity report accompanied by annual financial statements as well as revenue statements and expenditure budgets for the three years prior to the application. The entity must also show proof of collaboration and partnership contracts with public institutions, associations or foundations in the country or abroad. Lastly, the entity should be able to show significant results in the fulfilment of its worthy purpose or present recommendation letters from competent authorities.

In Singapore, entities that wish to be a registered charity have to apply to the Commissioner of Charities, who assesses the application. Once registered, the philanthropic entity is required to make an annual submission to the Commissioner of Charities, which includes an annual report (including financial statements and a governance evaluation checklist).

3.4. Tax treatment of income of philanthropic entities

3.4.1. Sources of income

Philanthropic entities may have commercial and/or non-commercial income, but the distinction is not always clear or the same across countries. Generally, non-commercial income refers to income from philanthropic gifts (discussed in Chapter 4) and government grants, or (in the case of PBOs) grants from supporting funds. Income from philanthropic gifts includes donations from individuals and corporations and testamentary transfers from individuals. In relation to these transfers, in countries that levy an inheritance tax instead of an estate tax, the tax liability is with the beneficiary and therefore an inheritance tax incentive for giving would benefit the philanthropic entity receiving the inheritance.

Broadly, commercial income is income derived from the supply of goods or services in return for some form of payment. When a corporation makes a payment as sponsorship (i.e. in return for publicity) to a philanthropic entity, it may, in some countries, be considered commercial income. That is to say that to the extent that the publicity resulting from sponsoring a philanthropic entity is a service, such income could be considered commercial.

Countries' tax relief for the income of philanthropic entities can be separated into two approaches: (1) to exempt all or specific income (e.g. income from philanthropic gifts), or (2) to consider all forms of income taxable, but allow the entity to reduce its taxable income through current or future reinvestments towards the fulfilment of their worthy purpose. Table 3.4 shows that most countries tend to follow the first approach.

Colombia, Indonesia, Lithuania, and Ireland follow the second approach, where all income (including philanthropic gifts) is considered taxable unless it is reinvested towards the fulfilment or the worthy purpose (see Table 3.5 for a detailed explanation of how the income tax liability of philanthropic entities is determined in Colombia).

Table 3.4. Approaches to providing tax relief for the income of philanthropic entities

Countries following the exempt all or specific sources of income approach:	*Australia; Austria; Belgium; Bulgaria; Canada; Chile; Finland; Germany; Greece; Ireland; Israel; Italy; Latvia; Malta; Mexico; the Netherlands; New Zealand; Norway; Portugal; Romania; Singapore; the Slovak Republic; Slovenia; South Africa; Sweden; Switzerland; the United Kingdom, and the United States.*
Countries following the exempt income if reinvested towards worthy purpose approach:	*Colombia, Indonesia; Lithuania; and Ireland*

Source: OECD Taxation and Philanthropy Questionnaire

3.4.2. Exempting all or specific sources of income approach

Countries generally exclude non-commercial income (such as income from philanthropic gifts or government grants) from the tax base and do not consider it as taxable income. Countries with inheritance taxes tend to exempt philanthropic entities from paying such taxes on the testamentary transfers they receive (Belgium and France apply a reduced inheritance tax rate on income from bequests).

Approaches to the tax treatment of income from commercial activities diverge. The first subsection below, discusses a small number of countries that exempt all commercial income of philanthropic entities. The second subsection provides an overview of countries whose philanthropic entities are fully income tax exempt and restrict these entities from engaging in certain kinds of activities. The third subsection discusses the countries that want philanthropic entities to pay taxes on some of their income, and thus generally differentiate between income that is related to their worthy purpose and income that is unrelated (also referred to as related and unrelated business income). The fourth subsection covers countries that tax commercial income above a threshold. Finally, there are also countries that simply tax commercial income and are thus not included in the following subsections (this is the case in Greece, Luxembourg, and Slovenia, where income derived from commercial activities is taxed).

Exempting all income from commercial activity

In Australia, philanthropic entities are fully exempt from paying income tax on both commercial and non-commercial income. Notably, a 2008-2010 review of the Australian tax system considered the issue of taxing the unrelated business income of philanthropic entities. The review found that the tax exempt entities are not incentivised to undercut the prices of their for-profit counterparts and thus the income tax concessions do not violate the principle of competitive neutrality and should be retained (Henry et al., 2009[2]). Entities may also receive a refund for franking credits (see Box 3.1 for more information).

New Zealand follows a similar approach: philanthropic entities are exempt from paying corporate income tax on non-commercial income and are also exempt from income tax on commercial income if the philanthropic entity meets the not-for-profit requirement and has no activities overseas. The issue of competitive neutrality concerns arising from exempting the commercial income of philanthropic entities was considered in the recent New Zealand Tax Working Group report. The report concluded that the underlying issue was the extent to which the philanthropic entity directs its surplus to their worthy purpose activities for the public benefit. As a result, the Working Group recommended that the Government regularly review the philanthropic sector's use of tax expenditures to ensure that the intended social outcomes are being achieved (Tax Working Group, 2019[3]). In Malta too, philanthropic entities benefit from a tax exemption on all their income.

Restricting the commercial activities an entity can engage in

In Canada, qualifying philanthropic entities are exempt from paying income tax. PBOs are not permitted to undertake commercial activities unless they are related to the charitable purpose the entity is undertaking or the entity is run almost entirely with volunteer labour. Philanthropic entities are prohibited from carrying out unrelated commercial activities themselves and may have their registration revoked or be subject to financial penalties if they do so. A philanthropic entity may, however, carry out commercial activities through separate business corporations or trusts, provided the proper separations between the philanthropic entity and the business are in place. There are also expenditure requirements: if the average value of an entity's property not used directly in philanthropic activities (during the 24 months before the beginning of the fiscal year) exceeds CAD 100 000, the philanthropic entity's disbursement quota is 3.5% of the average value of that property.

In Belgium, philanthropic entities are subject to the legal entities income tax (LEIT). The LEIT is not specific to philanthropic entities and is applied to all legal entities that are not subject to the corporate income tax. A philanthropic entity can engage in economic activity if it does not constitute a principal activity, and is a secondary activity whose profits are reinvested in the entity's worthy purpose. Philanthropic entities liable to the LEIT are not taxed on their total annual net income, but only on:

- their real estate income,
- their income from capital and movable property, inclusive the first EUR 1 880 euro bracket of income from savings deposits and the first EUR 190 bracket of dividends from recognised cooperative companies and to companies with a social purpose.
- certain miscellaneous forms of income.

Thus, income from donations is exempt from the LEIT, but regional inheritance taxes may still apply to bequests.[2]

The LEIT is collected as a withholding tax. Where philanthropic entities receive income from movable property or miscellaneous income of movable origin without the withholding tax being deducted at source, the withholding tax is due by the recipient of the income. In the following cases specific assets are put on the Belgian tax roll:

- Certain types of real estate income, notably net income from land and buildings situated in Belgium and leased, are subject to a 20% tax.
- Capital gains made through the transfer of developed or undeveloped real estate are taxable at 16.5% or 33%.
- The transfer of important participations is taxable, at the 16.5% rate, according to the same arrangements as for personal income tax.
- Unjustified expenses, in-kind benefits or financial advantages, are taxable according to the same arrangements as for the corporate income tax (contribution of 100% on secret commissions and 50% if it can be established that the beneficiary for those expenses, in-kind benefits, and financial advantages is a legal person).
- Pension contributions and pensions considered as disallowed expenses under the corporate income tax, financial advantages or in-kind benefits, as well as the amount equal to 17% of the benefit in kind resulting from the private use of a company car, are liable to a 33% tax.
- Inter-municipal associations operating a hospital or an institution assisting war victims, disabled persons, etc., are taxable on dividends attributed to other legal entities except public administrations. The rate of this tax is 25% and the increase for lack or insufficiency of advance payments is applicable according to the same arrangements as for corporate income tax.

In Latvia, philanthropic entities are not subject to corporate income tax if the purpose of the establishment is not to make profit or achieve an increase in capital for their members, religious organisations, trade unions, and political parties. Furthermore, monetary assistance received from a public benefit organisation for covering expenditure for medical treatment (including in order to ensure transport of a patient and accompanying person to a medical treatment institution) is not included in the annual taxable income and is thus exempt from personal income tax.

Box 3.1. Imputation credits

Overview

The rationale behind imputation credits (also termed refundable franking credits') is to reduce the double taxation of dividends by imputing the corporate tax to the shareholder. Dividends paid from taxed profits are 'franked' (i.e. receive an imputation credit) if the company that distributes its dividends has paid tax on its profits. Therefore, individuals or corporations receiving the franked dividends may receive an imputation credit under certain conditions.

Imputation Credits in Australia and New Zealand

In Australia, some tax-exempt entities (i.e. charities and deductible gift recipients) that receive franked dividends are eligible to benefit from a refund of franking credit. Since these tax-exempt entities do not pay tax on the income received from dividends, the refundable credit is essentially additional income for the entity to use for its worthy purpose. In New Zealand, on the other hand, tax-exempt entities that receive franked dividends will not be taxed on those dividends but will not be able to use the imputation credits attached to the dividends. The effect is that they are effectively subject to tax at the company rate, 28%, on the income that is taxed within any companies they invest in.

Source: Australian Taxation Office website.

In Japan, the income of PBOs (that fulfil the not-for-profit requirement) is tax exempt. The commercial activities that exempt PBOs are permitted to engage in without losing their tax exempt status, are stipulated by the most applicable ministry (i.e. the ministry that has the most expertise regarding the particular worthy purpose). Furthermore, if half or more of the employees of a commercial activity are persons with disabilities and the PBO contributes to the protection of the lives of these persons, than the activity is not considered a profitable business, which would otherwise be taxable.

In Singapore, the income of all philanthropic entities registered under the Charities Act, is exempt from income tax. PBOs may engage in commercial activities to generate additional income, or to provide goods or services for their members or clients to further their worthy purposes. However, these commercial activities, may not undermine the philanthropic entity's focus and distract the charity from its exclusively worthy purpose. Charity boards should also be prudent and must not expose their charitable assets to significant risk. Where business activities may expose charitable assets to significant risk, they must be carried out by a business subsidiary. Business subsidiaries that are set up by charities are treated in the same manner as any other company. The income of these business subsidiaries is subject to income tax.

In Argentina, philanthropic entities are exempt from corporate income taxes. In Switzerland, PBO's are exempt from income and wealth taxes. In Israel, donations, inheritances, government grants and passive income are tax exempt. In Chile, some PBOs may be exempt from the corporate income tax when the exemption is granted by the President of the Republic. This benefit can only be requested by PBOs where their main and effective purpose is to provide aid directly to people with limited economic resources who are unable to meet their basic needs.

Exempting commercial income if related to worthy purpose activities

Austria distinguishes between three types of commercial activities: necessary, related, and unrelated. A commercial activity is considered necessary if the worthy purpose of the philanthropic entity cannot be achieved without it and the exempt entity does not significantly compete with other taxed entities that engage in a similar commercial activity. The income generated through necessary commercial activities (e.g., selling entry tickets as a museum) is fully tax exempt. A commercial activity is considered related if it is a means to achieving the worthy purpose, although not a necessary one. Income generated from related commercial activities is liable for the corporate income tax but a EUR 10 000 exemption remains. Philanthropic entities that engage in unrelated commercial activities risk losing their tax-exempt status all together. If, however, the commercial activities that a philanthropic entity engages in, generates under a threshold of EUR 40 000 in the tax year, the entity may keep its tax-exempt status. Furthermore, some capital gains of PBOs are tax-exempt. For example, the capital gain from shares (and interest from capital assets) that is verifiably used for worthy purposes is tax-free if the business is related to the PBO.

In Finland, philanthropic entities are liable to a tax on income derived from business activity, as well as a 6.26% tax on income derived from real property that is used for a purpose other than the eligible worthy purposes. For philanthropic entities in Finland, the income from the following activities is not considered to be income derived from business activity and is therefore tax exempt:

- income derived from organising lotteries, fairs, athletic competitions, dances, bingo and other entertainment events, as well as the income derived from buffets, sales and other similar activities;
- income derived from member magazines and other publications directly serving the purpose of the entity;
- income derived from collecting funds through selling remembrance cards, badges, cards, vanes or other such products;
- income derived from selling goods or services, which are manufactured or produced for the purposes of therapy, or teaching in hospitals, mental hospitals, penal institutions, workhouses, old people's or disabled people's homes or other similar care-taking institutions.

Income subject to tax can be deemed to be wholly or partly income tax exempt by the tax administration. A tax exemption can be granted only when the exemption can be regarded as justified with respect to the benefit that the entity produces for society. When an exemption is considered, attention is paid to what degree the entity's assets and income are used worthy purpose activity that is important for society. Attention must also be paid to whether the exemption for an entity's business leads to unfair competition.

In Germany, the income generated from activities related to the worthy purpose is exempt from corporate income and trade tax. Income attributable to economic activities which are not related to the designated worthy purpose are not subject to corporate income tax or trade tax if the total annual income including VAT from these commercial activities does not exceed EUR 35 000. Furthermore, the income of capital assets of philanthropic entities is exempt from the withholding tax on capital investments.

Philanthropic entities in Bulgaria are not taxed on their non-commercial income (such as income from grants or donations), i.e. the income that supports their main purpose, but income from commercial activities is subject to the corporate income tax for all philanthropic entities except for the Bulgarian Red Cross.

Similarly in Greece, any income acquired by philanthropic entities through the pursuit of the fulfilment of their worthy purpose (such as membership fees, public or private grants, donations, etc.) is not subject to income tax. On the other hand, any income generated from commercial/business activities is taxable, regardless of whether it is used to fulfil the worthy purpose of the not-for-profit entity (e.g., interest on deposits, public events etc.).

In Portugal, the income of philanthropic entities that is derived from donations is untaxed. Income derived from worthy purpose activities is generally also untaxed. Other sources of income, such as unrelated commercial activity or financial assets and investments are considered taxable income.

In Sweden, as in most other countries, PBOs are exempt from paying income taxes on income received or derived from donations, grants, investments, and worthy purpose activities. Furthermore, income earned by carrying out philanthropic activities, including under contracts with government, is also tax-exempt. This suggests that income from unrelated activities will be taxable income.

In the United States, PBO's are generally exempt from corporate income taxes. However, income from unrelated business activities (i.e. activities that are not substantially related to the exempt purpose), is taxable at the corporate tax rate. More specifically, such income is taxed at the top corporate tax rate with an exclusion of USD 1 000. Income related to the exempt purpose of the non-profit organisation is generally income tax exempt. The rules on income from outsourcing work depend on the way in which it is outsourced. If, for example, an entity pays a management company to run a business and transfer all of the income over to the entity itself, then the income would be taxable as unrelated business income. Similarly, if the philanthropic entity is a partner in a partnership and the partnership is running the business, then the income would be taxable also. If, on the other hand, the income is from a business that just pays the PBO rent, then the income would usually not be taxable. If the income is passive income, for example royalty or dividend income, it would also not be taxable.

Using a threshold to exempt commercial income

As noted in the section above, Austria, Germany and the United States apply thresholds as well as distinguish between related and unrelated commercial income. In Austria, philanthropic entities that generate related or unrelated commercial income above the respective thresholds, risk losing their tax-exempt status. In Germany and the United States, on the other hand, unrelated commercial income above the threshold is taxed. In addition, several other countries (France, Hungary, Mexico, the Netherlands, Norway, the Slovak Republic, and South Africa) use thresholds to determine how to tax the income of philanthropic entities.

In France, PBOs which carry out commercial activity on a regular or occasional basis, may be exempt from corporate taxes (value added tax, corporate income tax, corporate property tax) if the activity does not compete with the business sector and if the revenues collected during the calendar year for this activity do not exceed EUR 72 000. PBOs that benefit from the corporate tax exemption remain liable for corporate income tax at reduced rates for income from asset management such as:

- income from the rental of built and undeveloped buildings owned by the association (CIT rate at 24%);
- profits from the exploitation of agricultural or forestry properties (CIT rate at 24%);
- dividends (CIT rate at 15%);
- other securities (CIT rate at 10 % or 24%).

In Hungary, PBOs are exempt from corporate tax if their income derived from commercial activities (including managing real estate) does not exceed 15% of the total income. In India, philanthropic entities that are not engaged in certain specified charitable activities and are classified as being engaged in the advancement of any other object of general public utility can derive up to 20% of their income from trade, commerce or business, provided it is earned in the course of advancing the charitable purpose of the entity.

In Mexico, philanthropic entities are exempt from income tax on income from donations; government grants; the sale of fixed or intangible asset; membership fees; recovery fees; interest; economic rights derived from intellectual property; temporary use or enjoyment of real estate, or from yields obtained from shares or other credit instruments, provided they are used for the purposes for which they were authorised.

Additionally, they may obtain income from activities other than the purposes for which they were authorised, provided it does not exceed 10% of their total income.

In the Netherlands, philanthropic entities are only liable to the corporate income tax if (1) they participate in the market economy with labour and capital and thereby make a profit, or (2) if their activities compete with commercial businesses, or (3) if no exemption applies. The exemption applies if the entity's surplus is below EUR 15 000 a year or less than EUR 75 000 combined for the prior four years.

In Norway, a philanthropic entity is exempt from paying income taxes on received donations, inheritances and grants. The entity is exempt from income taxes on income generated from any commercial activity it undertakes that does not contribute towards the realisation of the institution's worthy purpose, provided that the annual revenue from the commercial activity does not exceed a threshold of NOK 140 000. This includes any capital gain as a result of economic activity. On the other hand, capital gains resulting from the tax-exempt worthy purpose activities are tax-exempt.

In the Slovak Republic, the income received by philanthropic entities is generally tax-exempt, except for commercial income, including income derived from property (rent), the sale of assets, membership fees and advertising income above EUR 20 000 per year.

In South Africa, only welfare, education, healthcare and conservation activities qualify for an income tax deduction. The other worthy purposes (shown in Table 3.1 are only exempt from gift tax. Furthermore, 15% of all commercial income of philanthropic entities is tax exempt, amounts above that are taxable at the corporate income tax rate.

3.4.3. Exempting income if reinvested towards the worthy purpose

For countries following the second approach (exempting income if reinvested towards the worthy purpose), the source of the income is generally secondary to its destination. That is to say that as long as the surplus of a philanthropic entity is reinvested towards the worthy purpose within a given time period, the income of the entity is exempt. If, on the other hand, the entity decides to defer reinvestment, stockpile its surplus or invest it towards something other than its worthy purpose, the surplus may become taxable.

In Colombia the income tax treatment of philanthropic entities is determined based on whether, and how, the net benefit or surplus is reinvested. Other countries discussed in this report tend to exempt non-commercial income automatically (i.e. not consider it taxable income). In Colombia, however, all forms of income are considered taxable and the tax relief instead allows the entity to reinvest the net benefit or surplus (resulting from the income) towards the fulfilment of its social objective.

In Indonesia, donations and grants to philanthropic entities are tax exempt income. If an entity engaged in education or research and development has a surplus, it is only tax exempt if the surplus is reinvested in its worthy purpose (education or research and development) within a four year period after the income was received. Similarly, in the Czech Republic, the corporate income tax exemption only applies to the income of a PBO if such income is or will be used for specified worthy purposes.

In Ireland, philanthropic entities do not enjoy automatic income tax exemption simply by virtue of registering with charities commission. As discussed at the beginning of the chapter, entities must apply to the revenue for the tax exemption separately. Once the tax-exempt status is approved, entities are also exempt from capital gains tax and tax on commercial income, provided that the income is applied towards the fulfilment of the entities' worthy purposes. Philanthropic entities also benefit from a matching scheme for donations which is described in more detail in Chapter 4.

Table 3.5. Tax liability formula for philanthropic entities in Colombia

+	Ordinary or extraordinary income of the taxable year
-	Expenses of the taxable year, including those not related to the worthy purpose
-	Investments made to strengthen the equity (for more than one year), which are not susceptible to amortisation or depreciation and generate returns for the worthy purpose.
=	Net Benefit or Surplus
-	The assets of the Net Benefit or Surplus reinvested during the following taxable year towards the worthy purpose of the philanthropic entity.
-	The assets of the Net Benefit or Surplus reinvested into long-term projects (between 2 to 5 years) towards the "worthy purpose" of the entity. These long-term reinvestment projects will be recognized as "Permanent Assignments". In case the long-term reinvestment project surpasses five (5) years, the entity must submit a request to the Colombian Tax Administration to extend the reinvestment term.
=	Taxable Net Benefit or Surplus
×	Income tax rate of 20%
=	**Total income tax liability**

Source: OECD Taxation and Philanthropy Questionnaire

In Lithuania, philanthropic entities are subject to the corporate income tax. The rules for calculating taxable profits of such organisations do not differ from the rules applicable for commercial entities. Nevertheless, the preferential tax treatment allows philanthropic entities to reduce the taxable surplus calculated in accordance with the general corporate income tax rules by deducting the funds directly allocated to a worthy purpose in the current or subsequent two tax periods. Where the amount of funds directly allocated to the financing of activities with a worthy purpose in the current tax period exceed the amount of taxable surplus calculated for that tax period, the funds exceeding this amount may be carried forward to reduce the amounts of taxable surplus calculated for the two subsequent tax periods. Donations in cash from a single donor which exceed EUR 9 750 during a tax period, and other donations not used for public benefit purposes are taxed at a general 15% corporate income tax rate.

3.5. Value-added taxes

Preferential VAT treatment may apply to a philanthropic entity's inputs (purchases) as well as its outputs (supplies - sales or disposals). Regarding its inputs, philanthropic entities pay VAT on their purchases (as long as those purchases are not exempt goods or services). If they are not registered for VAT purposes, the entity is likely treated as a final consumer and cannot recover the VAT paid on its inputs without specific tax relief. Similarly, if the entity is registered for VAT purposes but does not make any taxable sales, it will also not be able to recover the VAT paid on its inputs. A philanthropic entity may not make any taxable sales because its supplies (outputs) are exempt, or because they are out of the scope of the VAT. On the other hand, philanthropic entities that do charge VAT on their sales (including zero rated goods and services) are able to recover the VAT paid on their inputs.

Consequentially, countries may choose to allow philanthropic entities to not charge VAT on their supplies (or the entities may be under the revenue threshold), which could in return create an input tax burden for those entities. As a result, some countries offer tax relief to philanthropic entities that are not able to recover VAT paid on their inputs (or are only able to recover a share of it).

VAT exemptions, reduced rates, and zero rates can create unfair competition, especially if the VAT exempt goods or services supplied by a philanthropic entity are also provided by businesses that charge VAT on their sales. Thus some countries do not exempt from VAT certain goods and services provided by philanthropic entities in order to avoid unfair competition (e.g. Canada and Ireland). Belgium, Chile, Colombia, Estonia, Indonesia, Italy, and the Slovak Republic, do not have preferential VAT treatment for philanthropic entities and apply the standard VAT rules. Although Italy does not allow a preferential VAT regime for philanthropic entities, PBOs are exempt from the requirement to provide evidence of their sales through invoices and sales receipts.

3.5.1. VAT exempt

Entities (or the activities of entities) can be exempt from VAT due to their philanthropic nature (e.g., France), because their activities do not fall within the coverage of the VAT, or because they operate below a VAT registration threshold.

In Argentina, the services of philanthropic entities that are directly related to the PBO's main purpose are exempt from VAT. That means that donations by third parties, membership dues, and fees charged to members for specific statutory activities, are all VAT exempt services for PBOs. Other transactions of PBOs are subject to the standard VAT rules.

In Australia, philanthropic entities have a higher revenue threshold for registering for VAT. Eligible entities do not need to register for VAT until their turnover is AUD 150 000 or more (normally registration is required at AUD 75 000). In some cases, PBO may choose how activities are treated. If, for instance, a PBO (e.g., a parents association) operates a school canteen on the grounds of a primary or secondary school, the PBO can choose to be VAT exempt, meaning it does not need to remit VAT on its sales of food. However, the school canteen cannot claim VAT credits for its purchases. Once the PBO chooses to be VAT exempt (i.e. pay input tax) it cannot revoke that choice for 12 months. Similarly, all philanthropic entities can choose to exempt their fundraising events from VAT, which in turn means they will have to pay input tax on their purchases since they will not be able to claim the VAT credits. This is aimed at reducing the administrative burden.

In Austria, not all philanthropic entities are exempt from the VAT. Instead, only PBOs with a "cultural" or "sports promoting" worthy purpose, as well as those running care facilities or health institutions, or providing accommodation and food to trainees below the age of 27, are VAT-exempt. Other philanthropic entities are subject to the standard VAT rules.

In Greece, philanthropic entities are exempt from charging VAT on several goods and services, subject to certain conditions. Examples of exempted activities are: The provision of services closely related to sport to persons engaged in sports or physical education by philanthropic entities. The provision of services to their members by philanthropic entities and organizations pursuing religious, philosophical, charitable purposes. The provision of cultural or educational services by philanthropic entities operating for cultural or educational purposes (in particular those services provided to visitors of museums, monuments, archaeological or other similar sites, as well as the organisation of art events, exhibitions and lectures). And finally, services provided by the above-mentioned entities in the context of events organised by them for their financial support.

In Israel, PBOs pay VAT on the goods and services they purchase and use as part of the philanthropic activity. The VAT paid by the PBOs cannot be deducted as an input tax, as there is no VAT on goods or services supplied by the PBO as part of its philanthropic activity. Commercial activity by the PBO is subject to VAT and therefore the VAT paid on inputs for the commercial activity can be deducted against VAT collected from the commercial activity.

In Latvia, the non-commercial activities of PBOs are generally considered to be outside the scope of the VAT. On the other hand, the commercial activities of PBOs are subject to the standard VAT rules. However, the VAT treatment is evaluated on a case-by-case basis. For example, VAT paid on inputs that are used as part of the philanthropic activity are not deductible. VAT paid on inputs for the commercial activity on the other hand, are deductible. However, if a PBO 'sells' the goods and services as part of its philanthropic activity, this activity would be regarded as a taxable transaction. The taxable amount of this transaction shall be the purchase price of the goods or full cost to the PBO of providing these services.

In Mexico, philanthropic entities are exempt from VAT for the sale of goods, the provision of services and the temporary use or enjoyment of goods as part of their activities. However, the entities have the obligation to pay and withhold the VAT when they receive independent personal services or goods provided or granted by individuals.

In Portugal, philanthropic entities are exempt from charging VAT on goods and services related to:

- health, social security and social assistance (provided that they do not receive any compensation);
- education – including day-care centres, kindergartens, leisure centres, establishments for children and young people with no normal family environment, establishments for disabled children and young people, rehabilitation centres for the disabled;
- sport, art, and culture – including artistic, sporting, recreational, physical education and cultural activities (e.g., visiting museums, art galleries, and castles);
- civic activities (e.g., political, union);
- religious activities;
- and humanitarian activities.

Fundraising activities (such as access tickets, registration fees, buffet, bar, stand rental, advertising revenue, etc.) are also exempt from VAT, as long as the fundraising is on an occasional basis and for the exclusive benefit of these entities (and provided they do not distort competition) and is limited to a maximum of eight fundraising events.

In Romania, some activities for the public benefit are exempt from VAT. These activities include the supplies of services closely related to sports or physical training, performed by PBOs for persons who practice sports, as well as the supplies of cultural services by cultural PBOs, recognised by the Ministry of Culture.

In South Africa, PBOs need to apply separately to be exempt from VAT. However, in general a PBO will not have to register for VAT as a vendor since it cannot be a predominantly commercial enterprise. In Switzerland, the VAT threshold for PBOs is supplies of CHF 150,000. In Finland, philanthropic entities are only liable for VAT on their commercial activities.

In the Netherlands, VAT is not applicable to non-commercial activities and therefore the VAT paid on inputs is not deductible. Within commercial activities there is a distinction between activities that are exempt and not exempt from VAT. Where activities are exempt from VAT, the VAT paid on the inputs is not deductible either. If a PBO is located in the Netherlands and has sales of no more than EUR 20 000 a year, the PBO can choose to be exempt from charging VAT, like any other small business, but will not be able to deduct or claim VAT on inputs.

In Singapore, PBOs are subject to standard VAT rules. PBOs may be regarded as carrying on both business and non-business activities for VAT purposes. Non-business activities include the provision of free services that are funded by grants, donations or sponsorships. PBOs are liable for VAT registration in Singapore if the annual value of taxable supplies arising from business activities exceeds the registration threshold of SGD 1 000 000. Once VAT-registered, PBOs are required to charge and account for VAT on their taxable supplies made. These include supplies made in the course of commercial activities (e.g. school or course fees, and day-care facility fees), as well as subsidised services as part of their philanthropic or religious purposes (e.g. dialysis fees, medical consultation fees). Like other businesses under standard VAT rules, PBOs are allowed input VAT claims on business purchases if these inputs are incurred for the making of taxable supplies in the course or furtherance of their business. Input VAT incurred for carrying out wholly non-business activities or exempt supplies is not claimable, while input VAT incurred for carrying out subsidised activities (partly business and partly non-business) is to be apportioned such that only the portion relating to the business of making taxable supplies is claimable.

3.5.2. VAT exempt with possibility of reclaiming input tax

Exempting entities or activities from VAT can lead to entities having to pay VAT on their inputs and some countries have put in place policies that enable philanthropic entities to reclaim some of the VAT they paid on inputs.

In Canada, most supplies of services and some supplies of goods made by registered charities and other PBOs are exempt from VAT (e.g. supplies of food and lodging made for the relief of poverty or distress; meals on wheels; recreational programs established for children, individuals with a disability and disadvantaged individuals; memberships in organizations providing no significant benefit to individual members; and trade union and mandatory professional dues). However, the VAT generally applies to certain supplies of goods and services made by charities that are similar to goods and services supplied by non-charitable businesses. For example, VAT typically applies to admissions to a place of amusement (e.g., a theatre), even when supplied by a philanthropic entity. If all or substantially all (90%) of a philanthropic entity's supplies (outputs) are taxable, the entity would typically be entitled to full input tax credits for VAT paid on its purchases of inputs to those taxable supplies. For VAT paid on purchases that do not qualify for input tax credits, philanthropic entities are eligible for partial rebates. The typical rebate rate for PBOs is 50%, however, higher rebate rates are available if the PBO is also a public hospital or a non-profit school, college or university. Registered charities that produce or offer a mix of taxable and exempt supplies (outputs) use a special streamlined method for calculating their VAT obligations: registered charities generally retain 40% of the VAT they collect on their taxable supplies (outputs) and receive a rebate on the VAT paid on most of their inputs, but are not entitled to input tax credits on these inputs.

In Ireland, a PBO may have activities which are taxable from a VAT perspective, outside-the-scope of VAT or even exempt from VAT. If their activity is an outside-the-scope or exempt activity, they are neither obliged nor entitled to register and account for VAT on the income generated from those income activities. In certain circumstances, the activities of a PBO may be considered to be in competition with commercial traders and the charity may then be required to register and account for VAT on these activities. Additionally, where a PBO acquires, or is likely to acquire more than EUR 41 000 worth of goods from other EU Member States in any period of twelve months, there is an obligation to register and account for VAT in respect of those intra-Community acquisitions. Overall, the VAT status of the PBO's activities is important in determining the VAT treatment of any income generated and the resultant entitlement to deduct VAT on costs associated with that income. In other words, the activities of a PBO must be considered on a case by case basis to decide their VAT status.

Under Irish legislation, a PBO can only recover VAT on its costs if it makes taxable sales, that is, if it is registered for VAT and charges VAT (including sales subject to the zero rate) on its sales. If the PBO has taxable supplies, it can reclaim its VAT on inputs. If the supplies are exempt or out-of-the-scope of VAT, no VAT recovery is possible. If the PBO has a mix of both exempt income and income which is subject to VAT, and income which is outside the scope of VAT, it can reclaim VAT incurred on the direct costs of making its taxable sales as well as a proportion of the VAT incurred on its general costs using an apportionment method. Furthermore, Ireland has a unique VAT compensation scheme for PBOs, which is described in more detail in Box 3.2. Other reliefs from VAT are available for the following PBOs, goods and services:

- PBOs involved in the transport of severely and permanently physically disabled persons: a refund of the amount of VAT paid may be claimed in relation to the purchase and adaptation of vehicles for use by qualifying bodies for the transport of severely and permanently disabled persons.
- Radios for the blind: a refund of the amount of VAT paid may be claimed in respect of radios where the PBO has a primary objective of improving the circumstances of blind persons and where the radios are intended for the use of blind persons.

- Appliances for use by disabled persons: a refund of the amount of VAT paid may be claimed on certain aids and appliances purchased by or on behalf of a disabled person to assist that disabled person in the performance of essential daily functions or in the exercise of a vocation.
- Rescue craft and equipment: a refund of the amount of VAT paid may be claimed on certain small rescue craft, ancillary equipment and special boat buildings and also on the hire, repair and maintenance of these craft to PBO's who provide a sufficient standard of rescue and assistance services at sea and on inland waterways.
- Humanitarian Goods for Export: a refund for VAT can be granted for goods purchased for exportation by philanthropic organisations for humanitarian, charitable or teaching activities abroad e.g. Apostolic Societies, Chernobyl Children Projects etc.
- Donated medical equipment: a refund of the amount of VAT paid may be claimed by a hospital or a donor on the purchase of certain new medical instruments and appliances which are funded by voluntary donations. The VAT refund may be claimed by whoever suffers the tax i.e. the hospital or the donor, as appropriate, but not, of course, both.
- Donated Research Equipment: a refund of the amount of VAT incurred in the purchase or importation of any new instrument or appliance (excluding means of transport) through voluntary donations, to a research institution or a university, school or similar educational body engaged in medical research in a laboratory.

In New Zealand, PBOs that make taxable supplies of more than NZD 60 000 per annum are required to register for the VAT. PBOs that do not reach this registration threshold may voluntarily register so long as they do make taxable supplies of goods or services. The rules do not distinguish between different types of activities. PBOs can, as long as they make some taxable supplies, claim back the VAT on any inputs they have other than inputs used for making exempt supplies (i.e. rental accommodation or financial services). As such, they can claim back the VAT on inputs that are not actually used for making a supply of goods or services. This is more generous than the input tax deduction rules for other registered-persons who can normally only claim an input tax deduction if the input is applied towards making a taxable supply of goods or services. All goods and services sold by PBOs, other than exempt supplies, are subject to VAT. Whether the goods and services are sold as part of a commercial activity or a philanthropic activity is irrelevant for VAT purposes.

The United States does not have a VAT although the States and local authorities imposes retail sales taxes. In the United States, the specific rules about exemption from State and local retail sales taxes are made by the States and can vary. Philanthropic entities are generally exempt from paying sales tax on their purchases and from collecting sales taxes from related business activities provided they meet state requirements, which may include a certificate or application for eligibility.

Germany is an outlier, because it offers a reduced VAT rate for some supplies by philanthropic entities, while others are VAT-free (e.g. some medical services). Entities can reclaim the VAT paid on their inputs for supplies subject to a reduced VAT rate. If the activities of PBOs are not part of a commercial activity and meet the worthy purpose and public benefit requirements, philanthropic entities in Germany are subject to the reduced VAT rate of 7%.

Box 3.2. Irish VAT compensation scheme for charities

To mitigate the VAT cost for registered charities that cannot recover VAT on their costs, a VAT Compensation Scheme for PBOs was introduced in Ireland in 2019. This scheme aims to reduce the VAT burden on qualifying charities to partially compensate them for irrecoverable VAT which they have suffered in the previous calendar year. They are entitled to claim a refund of a proportion of their VAT costs based on the level of non-public funding they receive.

The scheme is capped at EUR 5 000 000 per year and, where the total amount of all eligible claims in each year exceeds the capped amount, claims are paid on a proportional basis. VAT may only be reclaimed on goods and services which were applied only to the PBOs charitable purpose. The charity must also provide proof that the charity was not entitled to a deduction or refund of the tax being claimed under any other legislation administered by the tax authority.

3.6. Other taxes

3.6.1. Recurrent taxes on immovable property

Philanthropic entities may own real-estate that they use to fulfil their social objectives, or they may own it as a source of income. If entities use their real-estate for their worthy purpose such as the location of offices or philanthropic activities such as treatment centres, athletic infrastructures, events, or distribution centres, some countries may exempt them from property taxes. Philanthropic entities that own immovable property as a source of income are generally liable for property taxes on those properties if such a tax is levied in their jurisdiction.

In certain cases philanthropic entities in Canada may be exempt from property taxes. However, property tax is predominantly levied at the municipal level and exemptions, rebates and credits vary provincially and by municipality. In Germany, real estate used by PBOs for charitable purposes is exempt from local property tax. In Ireland, residential properties that are owned by a PBO and used for the sole purpose of providing residential accommodation in connection with the facilitation of recreational activities are exempt from property taxes. This exemption is intended to benefit philanthropic entities who own residential properties that are used by its members when taking part in recreational activities. In Italy, local authorities (municipalities and regions) can exempt philanthropic entities from local taxes (such as real estate taxes). In Romania, there is an exemption from the tax on buildings for structures owned by the entities established either by will or set up according to the law, in order to maintain, develop and help national cultural institutions, as well as to support humanitarian, social and cultural actions. Local councils may decide to grant exemption or reduction of tax on buildings used for the supply of social services by philanthropic entities. In Singapore, PBOs benefit from a property tax exemption for real-estate that is used exclusively for public religious worship, as a public school, for charitable purposes, or for purposes conducive to social development in Singapore.

In the United States, property tax rules are determined by the States. Land and buildings of churches are generally exempt, although some States limit the amount of eligible land (such as one acre). Land and buildings of other non-profits are also generally exempt, although this exemption may not apply to all types of non-profits. In Sweden, a PBO is exempt from real estate tax if the real estate is mainly used in activities promoting the worthy purpose.

3.6.2. Miscellaneous tax benefits for philanthropic entities

Lastly, there are a number of unique tax benefits that some countries offer philanthropic entities in their tax jurisdiction. In Norway, philanthropic entities are exempt from employers' SSCs on wage costs related to their worthy purpose activity. This exemption is limited to total wage costs below a total of NOK 800 000, and NOK 80 000 per employee. Australia and New Zealand both impose a fringe benefits tax (FBT) but provide preferential tax treatment to philanthropic entities (see Box 3.3)

In Portugal, PBOs are exempt from taxes on vehicles if they are used to pursue their philanthropic activities. In the Netherlands, PBOs (including churches) are, under certain conditions, eligible to repayment of half of the energy tax they pay. In France a PBO which owns a television set on January 1 of the tax year is liable for the contribution to public broadcasting. However, organisations hosting people are generally exempt. It Italy, philanthropic entities are exempt from the stamp duty and license duty, normally charged for the certification of documents and for the authorisation of administrative procedures. The United States has recently introduced some additional taxes on income tax-exempt entities (see Box 3.4).

Box 3.3. Fringe Benefit Tax and philanthropic entities

Australia

In Australia, some PBOs are exempt and other tax-exempt entities pay a reduced rate of fringe benefit tax (FBT). The Australian States also impose payroll tax based on the total size of the payroll. Exemptions are available to charities where the employees are engaged solely in the philanthropic activities of the charity.

New Zealand

In New Zealand, charities generally do not have to pay FBT on benefits provided to employees while they are carrying out the entity's charitable activities. For example, if an employee uses the entity's car while doing charitable work, there will not be any FBT due on any private benefit they receive. The one exception is where the employee is provided with a credit card or similar facility for private use and the value exceeds NZD 300. This will be liable for FBT. If the charity operates a business that is unrelated to the philanthropic purpose, FBT will be payable on any benefits provided to employees. New Zealand does not impose payroll tax.

Box 3.4. Implications of the Tax Cuts and Jobs Act (TCJA) for philanthropic entities

Overview

Signed into law 22 December 2017, the TCJA is considered the biggest overhaul of the US tax system in more than thirty years. It includes corporate and individual tax changes, which have implications for giving and philanthropic entities.

Excise tax on net investment income of foundations

The law imposes a 1.39% excise tax on the net investment income of most domestic tax-exempt private funds, including private operating foundations. The tax itself has applied since 1969, but the rate was previously 2% (or 1% in some years if certain requirements were met) until the TCJA made it a flat 1.39%.

An exemption (unaltered by the TCJA) from the excise tax may apply to an operating foundation if:

- it has been publicly supported for the last ten years;
- Its governing body consists of individuals fewer than 25% of whom are "disqualified individuals";
- It has no officer who is a "disqualified individual".

A disqualified individual refers to

- a substantial contributor; or
- an owner of more than 20% of the total combined voting power of a corporation, the profits of a partnership, or the beneficial interest of a trust which contributes to the PBO; or
- a member of the family of any individual described in (1) or (2).

Excise tax on excessive executive remuneration of exempt organisations

The law imposes a 21% excise tax (based on the top corporate tax rate) on remuneration in excess of USD 1 000 000 per year paid by tax-exempt organisations. The tax applies to the highest paid employees of a tax-exempt organisation. The tax also applies to termination payments.

Source: Internal Revenue Service (IRS) website and OECD Taxation and Philanthropy Questionnaire.

3.7. Abuse of tax incentives for philanthropic entities

3.7.1. Examples of tax abuse

Abuse of tax incentives for philanthropy occurs when the preferred tax status of a fund or PBO is abused either by the entity itself, or by taxpayers and donors, or third parties, such as fraudsters who pose as philanthropic entities or tax return preparers who falsify tax returns to defraud the government (OECD, 2009[4]). The abuse of tax incentives, and the diversion of monies intended for public purposes, discussed in this chapter focuses on the entities themselves. Common types of abuse include:

- Excessive salaries and compensation for board members and employees of PBOs and funds;
- Diverting funds intended for public purposes to private benefit, e.g. misusing the entity's funds for personal expenses such as cars, office spaces, or the employment of unqualified family members;
- A for-profit business poses as a PBO to benefit from the tax relief;
- Investment by a philanthropic entity in corporations owned or controlled by employees of the entity
- Liquidation of a PBO and distribution to individuals, eluding tax liability
- Salaried employees concealed as volunteer workers (and non-declaration of salary or wages);
- An entity not registered for VAT that is undertaking taxable activities.

In Canada, arrangements involving transactions between philanthropic entities and non-arm's length individuals and entities are an ongoing concern. This can include transactions involving investments by a charity in corporations owned by individuals controlling the charity or low or zero interest loans to such individuals or corporations. Often such amounts are at significant risk of not being repaid. Another form of non-arm's length transaction is the above-fair-market value contracts for services between charities and individuals or corporations that control the charity. This includes above fair-market value salaries paid to those involved, payment of personal expenses and other fringe benefits. In Colombia abusive schemes have included the setting-up of fictional philanthropic entities to take advantage of tax benefits, such as those provided for in the Special Tax Regime for Non-Profit Entities. For example, company-M may donate money to PBO-X, which is an entity that enjoys preferential tax treatment. Company-M therefore obtains a benefit consisting of a 25% tax credit of the value donated while PBO-X allocates the received donations towards programs in which company-M is a contractor, thereby receiving the initially donated value as income. To avoid such schemes some countries have, among other policies, strict donor-benefit rules discussed in Chapter 4.

In a 2009 OECD report on the abuse of charities for money-laundering and tax evasion, a number of countries identified tax evasion schemes related to philanthropic entities. Canada, the Czech Republic, and the United States reported that they have tracked schemes in which a philanthropic entity is set up so it receives approval for issuing donation receipts, but does not engage in the worthy purpose activities and instead the individuals who set up the entity use the fund for their personal benefit (OECD, 2009[4]). According to the report, the Canadian tax authority has noticed that charities and tax return preparers who previously have been identified as being involved in false receipting continue to issue the false receipts. At the time, the 2009 report found that suspected fraudulent alteration and creation of receipts has become more prevalent due to advancements in printing technology. Most suspicious activities seemed to involve tax return preparers and the use of electronic services.

3.7.2. Risk of terrorist financing

Another important finding of the 2009 OECD report is that although terrorist abuse of the philanthropic sector is rare, it does occur and there are vulnerabilities and risks that countries should keep track of. In the United States, the designation, prosecution and investigation of philanthropic entities has shown that terrorist abuse of philanthropic entities exists.

The Australian Charities and Not-for-profits commission (ACNC, 2020[5]) has published some of the ways in which terrorist organisations can misuse philanthropic entities to raise and distribute funds for their activities:

- A resident PBO may have an overseas partner organisation that uses its funds to finance terrorism.
- Terrorist organisations may use a philanthropic entity's assets (e.g., vehicles, storage, etc.).
- Terrorist organisations may attempt to use a philanthropic entity's name and status to raise funds without the entity's knowledge.
- Terrorist organisations may attempt to infiltrate a philanthropic entity to redirect money to fund terrorist purposes.
- A terrorist organisation may set up and register a philanthropic entity and hide its true purpose.

3.7.3. Detection of tax abuse related to philanthropic entities

To prevent abuse of tax concessions for philanthropic entities (including tax evasion and terrorist financing schemes), countries need to ensure that the administrative requirements (such as the application process, or annual reporting in some cases) enable the oversight body to identify and track suspicious entities and activities. However, the philanthropic entities have a role to play in limiting abuse too. As discussed in this section, some schemes occur without the entity's knowledge. Therefore it is important that the entities themselves regularly conduct internal audits and investigations, and engage in due diligence before financing certain projects or partnering with another organisation.

For the government oversight body, in-depth audits during an application or renewal of status can help detect cases of abuse. In Belgium, the tax administration also verifies if the entity has followed the directives with respect to tax receipt preparation and issuance, even if an entity has already been certified in the past (OECD, 2009[4]).

In a number of countries, tax authorities investigate cases of tax abuse in the philanthropic sector in partnership with other law enforcement agencies. Exchanging good practices as well as information with tax administrations and law enforcement agencies helps countries better detect and track tax abuse schemes involving philanthropic entities.

Keeping the public and especially donors aware of schemes involving philanthropic entities is also important. According to the 2009 OECD report on the abuse of charities, countries such as Canada and the United States have introduced awareness campaigns to alert the public about the risks associated with the abuse of charities (OECD, 2009[4]). Canada and the United States have put out tax alerts on their websites about donation schemes (such as a tax shelters) and the abuse by intermediaries (such as tax return preparers) with respect to charitable donations. In Canada, taxpayers can search the online charities listing and have access to the list of the registered charities, newly registered charities, charities whose status have been revoked and suspended, and which charities have been permanently annulled or have been fined. The public can also review the annual information returns filed by registered charities.

3.7.4. Rules on remuneration and total spending on employment

Philanthropic entities, generally meet a non-distribution requirement while the entity is in existence. An issue that can arise is whether the payment of salaries to employees breaches this notion of 'non-distribution'. Generally, the requirement does not prevent the payment of 'reasonable' remuneration for services (or the provision of goods). Some countries may impose restrictions in this regard, while others may be less prescriptive. Disclosure requirements may lessen the opportunities for excessive inurement.

To ensure that the untaxed income and received donations from philanthropic entities are not used for the personal gain of people associated with the entity, some countries have strict rules on remuneration and the total spending on employment. In Canada, for example, board members of PBOs are entitled to reasonable remuneration for the services they provide. This includes attendance fees and reimbursement of expenses, but does not generally include a salary simply for being a board member. The members of the board of trustees (or the board of directors) in Switzerland work on a voluntary basis and are generally only entitled to compensation of their effective expenses and cash expenses. For special services of individual members of the board of trustees (board members) it is allowed that an adequate compensation is paid.

In Colombia, the budget destined to compensate, remunerate or finance any disbursement, in money or in kind, for purposes of payroll, fees or commissions to the persons who hold managerial and directive positions of a philanthropic entity, may not exceed 30% of the total annual expenditure of the entity. If such payments exceed this limitation, the entity will be excluded from the Special Tax Regime.

Board members and trustees of PBOs in Ireland cannot accept a salary specifically for acting as a charity trustee, or receive other benefits for acting as such. However, they may be reimbursed for reasonable expenses, which they incur in carrying out their duties. Similarly, in Australia board members are generally unpaid but can be reimbursed for expenses.

In Sweden, board members of the PBO are entitled to remuneration. The only condition is that the PBO must use the main part of the income for a worthy purpose. In the Netherlands, PBOs can have volunteers, who may receive a limited compensation for their work. If the compensation is in line with the market, the volunteer will be seen as an employee and the normal rules for employees are applicable. In South Africa, employees and board members of philanthropic entities are entitled to remuneration, which is taxed as their personal income. Further, 75% of all donations received by a philanthropic entity in South Africa must be distributed for worthy purpose annually. Therefore, 25% is available to remunerate employees and others involved in the entity and for other expenses. The United States levies a 21% tax on excessive (over USD 1 000 000) remuneration for the five highest paid employees of exempt organisations (see Box 3.4 for more details).

References

ACNC (2020), *Governance Toolkit: Financial Abuse*, https://www.acnc.gov.au/for-charities/manage-your-charity/governance-hub/governance-toolkit/governance-toolkit-financial. [5]

Henry, K. et al. (2009), *Australia's Future Tax System*, https://treasury.gov.au/review/the-australias-future-tax-system-review. [2]

OECD (2019), *Tax Administration 2019: Comparative Information on OECD and other Advanced and Emerging Economies*, OECD Publishing, Paris, https://dx.doi.org/10.1787/74d162b6-en. [1]

OECD (2009), *Report on abuse of charities for money-laundering and tax evasion*, http://oecd.org/dataoecd/30/20/42232037.pdf. [4]

Tax Working Group (2019), *Future of Tax: Final Report*, Tax Working Group, https://taxworkinggroup.govt.nz/resources/future-tax-final-report-vol-i. [3]

Notes

[1] Value Added Tax (VAT) and the equivalent Goods and Services Tax (GST) in some jurisdictions area are referred to as "VAT" in this report.

[2] In the Brussels-Capital Region, for example, a reduced rate of 7% is applied for bequests (movable and immovable assets).

4 The tax treatment of giving

This chapter provides an overview of the tax treatment of donors and philanthropic giving across OECD member and selected participating countries. The first two sections of the chapter discuss the tax design of incentives for giving by individuals and countries' tax incentives for corporate giving. The last section highlights the potential risk of tax avoidance and evasion and the anti-abuse policies countries have put in place as a result.

4.1. Introduction

4.1.1. Characteristics of philanthropic giving

Philanthropic giving is the act of voluntarily transferring private resources to qualified philanthropic entities without receiving, or expecting to receive, anything of equal value in return. Both natural and legal persons can engage in philanthropic giving. Any benefit to the donor that arises from the gift must be within the statutory limits that apply. A number of countries (e.g. Australia, Austria, Canada, the United Kingdom, and the United States) have rules in place to accommodate the above fair market value purchase of goods and services from a philanthropic entity. Examples of such forms of philanthropic giving may include the purchase of tickets to a fundraising event (in the case of individuals) or the sponsoring of funds and PBOs in return for advertisement (in the case of corporations).

Philanthropic giving is a significant source of funding for funds and PBOs. All of the countries surveyed provide some form of tax incentives to encourage philanthropic giving. The generosity and design of the incentives varies. Countries may choose to encourage only some forms of giving or offer more support to some donors based on their income or wealth, or whether they are individuals or corporations.

The design of tax incentives for philanthropic giving depends on four characteristics of the transfer: (1) who is giving; (2) how is it given; (3) what is the gift; and (4) who is the recipient? As shown in Figure 4.1, giving can occur at an individual or corporate level, which has implications on motives as well as the tax used to incentivise this behaviour. At the individual level, we differentiate between donations during one's lifetime and testamentary giving on death. At the corporate level, we differentiate between donations and sponsorship payments to philanthropic entities, which may be considered part of the donor's business expenses. The gifts (or donations) themselves can be in the form of cash, or non-monetary assets (e.g. real estate, stocks, cultural assets, and in some cases even blood or organ donations). Finally, the type of recipient is important as it determines the philanthropic nature of the gift. This chapter will compare and contrast how countries use their tax systems to incentivise giving and how those incentives are designed to apply to the different forms of philanthropic giving.

Figure 4.1. Different tax implications depending on the characteristics of philanthropic giving

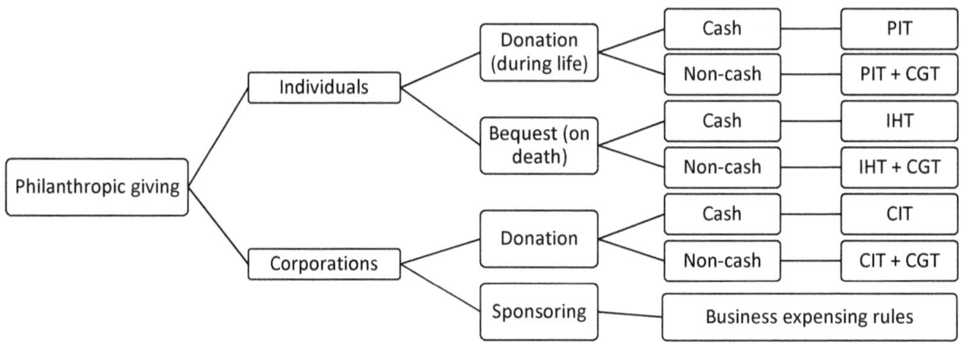

Note: This shows the most likely tax implications of philanthropic giving to funds and PBOs. Giving to individuals directly, in most cases, does not qualify as philanthropic and could instead lead to inheritance, estate or gift tax liabilities. Abbreviations: personal income tax (PIT); capital gains tax (CGT); Inheritance tax (IHT); corporate income tax (CIT).

4.1.2. Eligibility for tax incentives

For philanthropic giving, of any kind, to be eligible for tax incentives, the recipient must be an eligible (i.e. recognised) fund or PBO. None of the countries surveyed (see Box 4.1 for unique exceptions) offer tax subsidies to gifts made directly to individuals in need without passing through a fund or PBO. Moreover, such transfers may trigger estate, inheritance or gift tax liabilities. Gifts made to funds or PBOs that are earmarked for specific individuals usually do not benefit from tax incentives either. There are a number of reasons countries may want funds and PBOs to act as intermediaries between the donors and the final beneficiaries of philanthropy. Ensuring that each individual gift is distributed in a way that meets the not-for-profit, worthy purpose, and public benefit criteria would create a large administrative burden for governments and donors. As a result, it is more efficient to make funds and PBOs responsible for meeting the conditions necessary for philanthropic giving to be tax incentivised.

Box 4.1. Exceptions to the rules on giving to individuals directly

Chilean law concerning national emergencies

In Chile, philanthropic gifts to individuals directly (i.e. without passing through a fund or PBO) are exempt from any tax affecting them, and are deductible from the corporate income tax base, if they are given during a national emergency.

The Virginia Beach Strong Act in the United States

The Virginia Beach Strong Act states that a cash contribution made for the relief of the families of the dead or wounded victims of the mass shooting in Virginia Beach, Virginia, on May 31, 2019, shall be treated as a philanthropic donation despite being for the exclusive benefit of such families.

4.1.3. Key findings

The key findings of this chapter are that:

- The majority of countries surveyed, offer tax deductions to incentivise individual and corporate philanthropic giving. Other countries offer tax credits instead, and in some cases, donations are matched or facilitated through an allocation scheme. Furthermore, deductions are more common for corporate tax incentives than personal income tax incentives.
- Countries generally limit the value of their tax deduction or credit to a share of taxable or total income; a share of the income tax liability; a fixed value; a combination of ceilings; or limit the size of the donation itself.
- In countries with no tradition of philanthropic giving, an allocation scheme can create awareness among taxpayers, financially support funds and PBOs, and develop stronger ties between the general public and philanthropic entities.
- Countries that levy inheritance or estate taxes generally provide preferential tax relief for philanthropic bequests. In countries with an inheritance tax, the funds or PBOs receiving the bequest is liable for the tax and thus are the ones that receive the tax relief. In countries with an estate tax, on the other hand, the tax liability as well as the corresponding tax relief is with the estate of the deceased.
- The majority of countries that incentivise cash donations of individuals, also incentivise non-monetary donations. Countries may require appraisals if the value of a non-monetary donation exceeds a threshold, have different valuation rules for different types of assets, not require valuations or review valuations through audits.
- Corporate payments to philanthropic entities in return for advertising are considered business expenses in most countries, if they have a sufficient nexus with producing business income. However, these payments may have tax implications for the PBOs receiving them.
- Common types of tax avoidance and evasion issues with tax relief for philanthropic giving include: eligible philanthropic entities that wilfully participate in a tax evasion scheme to benefit their donors; falsified donation receipts prepared by the philanthropic entity, tax preparers or donors; payments for goods and services disguised as donations; overvalued gifts; and donations of assets in which the donor retains an interest in.

This chapter proceeds as follows. Section 4.2 summarises countries' tax policies that are intended to incentivise philanthropic giving by individuals. Within this section, the individual incentive schemes of countries are discussed in detail, followed by an analysis of tax rules for non-monetary donations by individuals. Section 4.3 provides an overview of tax policies incentivising philanthropic giving by corporations. This section covers the design of countries' tax incentives, as well as the tax rules concerning the sponsoring of the philanthropic entity in return for advertising. Finally, section 4.4 discusses the risks of tax avoidance and abuse that are related to the tax policies discussed in this chapter.

4.2. Philanthropic giving by individuals

In most of the countries surveyed, individual taxpayers that give to a qualifying fund or PBO during their lifetime receive some form of tax incentive. Philanthropic giving of individuals can occur during life, in the form of donations, or on death, in the form of philanthropic bequests. Donations by individuals are encouraged, directly or indirectly, through personal income and/or capital gains tax incentives. Almost all countries surveyed have tax incentives for individuals that donate during their lifetime to qualified funds or PBOs. In the absence of such an incentive, individual taxpayers that give would do so entirely from their post-tax income and with no change to their personal income tax liability or size of their gift (this is the case in Malta).

The design of tax incentives for individual donors differs across countries and depends on the nature of the gift. A philanthropic donation can be in the form of cash or non-cash, frequently referred to as non-monetary or in-kind donations. Non-monetary donations may include:

- real and intellectual property;
- stock or shares;
- trading stock;
- cultural assets;
- other personal property;
- services (volunteering); or
- blood and organ donations.

None of these forms of donating are always eligible for tax-subsidies. Countries may choose to limit their tax incentives to cash donations only (e.g., Austria, Finland, Israel, New Zealand, Norway and Sweden), or severely restrict the size and nature of non-monetary donations. Non-monetary donations also raise valuation concerns, which may have capital gains tax implications.

This section provides an overview of countries' tax treatment of donations made by individuals and is organised as follows: an overview of the design of the tax policies meant to support and incentivise philanthropy (deductions, credits, matching schemes, and allocation schemes), followed by a discussion of tax incentives for philanthropic bequests. Lastly, this section covers the tax policies for in-kind donations with a particular focus on the applicable valuation rules, as well as the potential capital gains tax implications.

4.2.1. Tax incentives for cash donations by individuals

In the large majority of countries surveyed, donations are deductible. Other countries offer tax credits and in some cases, donations are matched or facilitated through an allocation scheme. Although allocation schemes are not tax incentives, they are included in this discussion as they are part of the toolbox of tax policies intended to support philanthropy and are administered through the tax system. Table 4.1 shows that donations are deductible in 22 of the countries surveyed. Tax deductions effectively subtract the donation, or a portion of the donation, from the personal income tax (PIT) base before the tax liability is computed, thereby reducing the taxable amount before calculating the tax. Deductions that are tied to progressive tax brackets can become regressive since the value of tax deductions increases with marginal tax rates. In the context of deductible donations this means that in countries with a progressive personal income tax, the cost of giving is lower for the wealthy.

Another aspect to consider is whether countries have a comprehensive or schedular income tax system. In the case of the latter, the gross income, deductions, and credits are determined separately for each type of income (e.g., labour and capital income). Since rates may vary from type to type, the impact of the incentive may also. For example, countries with a dual income tax system may have a progressive tax rate for labour income, but a flat rate for capital income. As a result, a deduction would only be regressive if it is allowed against labour income.

Twelve countries incentivise donations through tax credits. A tax credit is an amount subtracted directly from the tax liability, after the liability has been computed. Unlike tax deductions, the value of tax credits is equal for all taxpayers (as long as their tax liability is equal to or larger than the value of the credit). If the value of the credit is larger than the tax liability of an individual, the credit would have to be refundable for the taxpayer to benefit fully from the incentive (this is the case in New Zealand for example). One country (Japan) offers donors a choice between a tax deduction and credit.

Table 4.1. Tax incentives for donations by individuals

Country	Deduction	Credit	Matching	Allocation	Other
Argentina	X				
Australia	X				
Austria	X				
Bulgaria	X				
Czech Republic	X				
Estonia	X				
Finland	X				
Germany	X				
India	X				
Indonesia	X				
Italy	X	X		X	
Japan	X	X			
Latvia	X				
Luxembourg	X				
Mexico	X				
Netherlands	X				
Norway	X		X		
Singapore	X		X		
Slovenia	X			X	
South Africa	X				
Switzerland	X				
United States	X				X[2]
Belgium		X			
Canada		X			
Chile		X			
Colombia		X			
France		X			
Greece		X			
Israel		X			
New Zealand		X[1]			
Portugal		X		X	
Sweden		X			
Ireland			X		
United Kingdom			X		
Hungary				X	
Lithuania				X	
Romania				X	
Slovak Republic				X	
Malta					X[3]

Note:
1. The tax credit is wholly refundable.
2. Some states have tax credits for certain donations.
3. In cases of shares and immovable property donations to a qualifying PBO, such transfers would not be subject to tax.
Source: OECD Taxation and Philanthropy Questionnaire and Ministry of Finance websites

The United Kingdom, Ireland, Norway, and Singapore have a matching scheme, where government tops up donations at a given rate so that the entity receiving the donation is able to claim the tax relief. In the United Kingdom and Ireland the matched amount is linked to the personal income tax rate of the donor.

Romania, Slovenia, Portugal, Hungary, Lithuania, and the Slovak Republic use a tax allocation scheme to support philanthropic entities. In countries with an allocation scheme, the tax administration allows taxpayers to designate a fixed percentage or amount of their income tax to a fund or PBO directly through their tax return. In itself, such a scheme is neither a tax incentive nor an act of giving. As discussed at the beginning of this chapter, philanthropic giving involves the voluntary transfer of private resources, and the money directed at funds and PBOs through a pure allocation scheme is public. Nevertheless, some have argued that allocation schemes can be used to help develop a culture of philanthropic giving in countries where there is no tradition of philanthropy (Bullain, 2004[1]). On the other hand, such a scheme may curb philanthropic giving as individuals will be less inclined to use their private resources to support funds and PBOs if they can do so with public resources (Bullain, 2004[1]).

4.2.2. Tax deductions

In countries with tax deductions, a donation (or a portion of it) is deductible from the personal income tax (PIT) base up to a limit that may be a fixed value and/ or expressed as a share of taxable or total income. To limit the size of the deduction, countries can: limit the share of the donation that is deductible (e.g. 50% of the donation is deducted from the PIT base); limit the size of the deduction to a share of taxable or total income (e.g. up to 20% of the PIT base); or limit the size of the deduction to a fixed value (e.g. up to EUR 1000). Table 4.2 shows that countries use any combination of tax deduction ceilings with different levels of generosity.

Decisions over what ceilings to use have policy implications on what income groups the tax subsidies target and what size of donations they most incentivise. For example, if the ceiling is a rather low share of total income but allows for a high fixed limit, high-income taxpayers will still receive a marginal benefit for large donations. If on the other hand, the ceiling is set to a high share of total income but the fixed limit on the deduction is low, the marginal benefit for any donation exceeding the fixed value limit will be zero. In Germany, for instance, deductions are simply capped at 20% of 'total income'[1], while in Estonia deductions are capped at 50% of 'taxable income' but may not exceed EUR 1 200.

Limiting the deduction to a share of taxable or total income

Table 4.2 shows that a number of countries (Argentina, Austria, Bulgaria, Switzerland, Germany, Indonesia, Italy, Mexico, the Netherlands, Slovenia, the United States, and South Africa) have ceilings that are only tied to income (as opposed to those limited to a fixed value). In these countries, the marginal cost of giving for large donations is lower for wealthy individuals regardless of the personal income tax rate, as higher income raises the deduction ceiling. Of course the fact that most countries have progressive personal income taxes leads to the cost of giving being even lower for those in higher tax brackets but this effect is independent of whether or not the ceiling is a function of total income or a fixed value.

Of the above mentioned countries, Argentina, Indonesia, Italy and Slovenia have the lowest ceilings. In Argentina, individuals can deduct donations up to 5% of 'annual earnings' of Argentinian source. In Indonesia, donations of up to 5% of current net income are deductible from the personal income tax base and for a taxpayer to be eligible for the deductible deduction, they must have net fiscal income (not a loss) based on the income tax return of the previous year, and the donation may not cause a loss in the current year. In Italy, individual taxpayers can choose between a deduction and a tax credit. Higher marginal tax rate taxpayers have a greater incentive to opt for deductions. Additionally, the gift may not be made through cash payments (i.e. it must be made through bank transfers, digital payments, etc.) in order to reduce the risk of abuse and tax evasion. For the tax deduction, individuals can deduct donations up to 10% of their taxable income. In Slovenia, a taxpayer with business and professional income can deduct donations but wage earners are incentivised through an allocation scheme. A taxpayer with business and professional income may claim a deduction for donations for humanitarian purposes, disabled persons assistance, social assistance, charitable, scientific, educational, health, sporting, cultural, ecological, religious and generally useful purposes. The deduction can be up to 0.3% of the taxpayer's 'taxable revenue' in the tax period. Additionally, a taxpayer may claim a deduction of up to an added 0.2% of the taxpayer's taxable revenue in the tax period concerned, for donations to cultural purposes and voluntary societies established for the protection against natural disasters. Donations for these purposes (culture and disaster relief) can be spread over three tax periods. As a general rule the sum of all tax incentives (not just those for philanthropic giving) cannot exceed 63% of the tax base.

Table 4.2. Limitations to personal income tax deductions

Country	Share of the donation that is deductible	Ceiling	Floor
Argentina	100%	5% of annual earnings	
Australia	100%	A deduction for a gift or contribution cannot add to or create a tax loss.	AUD 2
Austria	100%	10% of total income	
Bulgaria	100%	65% of taxable income (after the deduction)	
Czech Republic	100%	15% of taxable income	2% of the tax base or CZK 1 000
Estonia	100%	EUR 1 200 and 50% of the taxable income	
Finland	100%	EUR 500 000	EUR 850
Germany	100%	20% of total amount of income	
India	50% - 100%	10% of Gross Total Income	
Indonesia	100%	5% from current net income	
Italy	100%	10% of the taxable income.	
Japan	100%	40% of total income	JPY 2 000
Latvia	100%	EUR 600 and 50% of the annual taxable income	
Luxembourg	100%	EUR 1 000 000 or 20% of net income	EUR 120
Mexico	100%	For donations to private institution: 7% of last year's cumulative income. For donations to governmental institutions: 4% of last year's cumulative income.	
Netherlands	100%	10% of the total income.	1% of total income and over EUR 60.
Norway	100%	NOK 50 000	NOK 500
Singapore	250%	No limits	
Slovenia	100%	0.5% of taxable revenue	
South Africa	100%	10% of taxable income	
Switzerland	100%	20% of taxable income	CHF 100
United States	100%	60% or 30% of adjusted gross income depending on the beneficiary	

Source: OECD Taxation and Philanthropy Questionnaire and Ministry of Finance websites

In Bulgaria, Mexico, the Netherlands, and Slovenia the deduction rules vary across worthy purposes. In Bulgaria the limitations of deduction varies depending on the worthy purposes that the recipient fund or PBO is engaged in. Donations are deductible from the annual personal income tax base up to a total ceiling of 65% of the tax base after the deduction. For individual donations, the ceilings further differ depending on the beneficiary:

- Up to 5% of the annual tax base, where donations are in favour of:
    - healthcare and medical-treatment establishments;

  - social services for residential care, as well as of the Social Assistance Agency and of the Social Protection Fund under the Minister of Labour and Social Policy;
  - public nurseries, kindergartens, schools, higher schools or academies;
  - budgetary organisations, within the meaning given by the Accountancy Act;
  - any religious denominations registered in the country;
  - any specialised enterprises or cooperatives of persons with disabilities;
  - the Bulgarian Red Cross;
  - cultural institutes and community centres;
  - PBOs with the exception of any organisations supporting culture;
  - the Bulgaria Energy Efficiency and Renewable Sources Fund;
  - therapeutic communities for the treatment of drug-addicted persons;
  - the United Nations Children's Fund (UNICEF);
- Up to 15% of the annual tax base, where donations are in favour of culture;
- Up to 50% of the annual tax base, where donations are in favour of:
  - the National Health Insurance Fund: for activities related to the medical treatment of children.

In Mexico, the deduction limits vary depending on the nature of the receiving entity. Donations to private philanthropic entities are only deductible for an amount that does not exceed 7% of the 'cumulative income' earned by the taxpayer in the year immediately preceding the deduction. Mexico also incentivises donations to local government entities. Donations in favour of the Federation, the Federal Entities, the Municipalities, or their decentralized organisations, are only deductible in an amount that does not exceed 4% of the taxpayer's cumulative income in the previous year (donations to local government entities or institutions are outside the scope of this report and therefore not covered in more detail elsewhere). The sum of donations to private philanthropic entities and governments entities must not exceed 7% of the 'cumulative income' earned by the taxpayer in the year immediately preceding the deduction.

In the Netherlands donations are deductible if the amount of the donation is at least 1% (minimum EUR 60) and up to 10% of the donor's total income. A donation that is pledged for at least 5 years in a written statement (by a notary) can be deductible without the threshold and ceiling. For donations to a cultural PBO, there is a multiplier of 1.25 times the gift (up to a maximum of EUR 1 250). There are no rollover provisions and gifts are only deductible in the year they were given. Sole traders and unincorporated entities can deduct donations as business expenses as long as they do so for the purpose of producing income. Otherwise, the payment to philanthropic entities is deductible as a donation.

In the Czech Republic, donations to municipalities or qualifying philanthropic entities are deductible from the personal income tax base up to a ceiling of 15% of taxable income adjusted for deductible expenses. For the donation to qualify, it must be greater than the lesser of 2% of taxable income or CZK 1 000.

Austria, Australia, Germany, and the United States provide a deduction for donations to a broad range of philanthropic entities but also have rules to regulate donations for which the donor receives a benefit (donor-benefit rules). In Austria, cash donations of individuals are deductible from the personal income tax base in the year the money was donated. The only restriction is that the deduction may not exceed 10% of the total income. Donations cannot be carried over to a subsequent year. Austria also has very specific donor-benefit rules, for example, in relation to a fundraising event. Donors that give to funds and PBOs by purchasing an overpriced good or service, may deduct the amount paid that exceeds the fair market value of the good or service purchased. In a fundraising auction, where one individual donates a good and the other purchases it, the donor of the good may deduct its fair market value. The buyer of the good may in return deduct the amount paid in excess of the fair market value of the good.

In Australia, donations of more than AUD 2, are deductible from the personal income tax base. There is no specific upper limit on the value of a donation that may be deducted. The only limit is that deductions for donations cannot create or add to a tax loss. However, taxpayers can spread a donation over up to five income years. Furthermore, Australia differentiates between a gift for which the donor receives no benefit at all and a contribution for which the donor does receive a benefit. When the donor does receive a benefit (e.g. purchasing a ticket for a philanthropic fundraising event), the transaction is only tax deductible if the benefit to the donor is no more than AUD 150 and 20% of the value of the donation.

In the United States, deductions by individuals to philanthropic entities are generally limited to 60%[2] of 'adjusted gross income', although donations to private foundations are limited to 30% of adjusted gross income. Donations in excess of these limits can be carried over to up to 5 years. For taxpayers to benefit from the deductible deduction, they must itemise their deductions and cannot take the standard deduction (see Box 4.2). In the case of an above fair market value purchase of goods and services from a qualified fund or PBO (e.g. philanthropic fundraiser tickets), the excess payment (difference between the payment and the fair market value of the good or service) can be considered a philanthropic contribution and is tax deductible. However, for the excess amount to qualify, the individual must pay it with the intent of making a charitable contribution (i.e. the individual must be aware that they are paying more than the fair market value of the good or service).

In Germany, donations are considered special expenses and are deductible from the personal income tax base. The deduction is limited to 20% of 'total income' (or 4% of the sum of the total turnover and wages and salaries paid during the calendar year). Membership fees to entities that promote sports, certain cultural or heritage activities as well as customs and traditions are not deductible. Similarly, Germany has strict donor-benefit rules so that, unlike in the United States or Australia, the above fair market value purchase of goods and services from a fund or PBO (e.g. fundraiser tickets) is not tax deductible.

In Japan, the amount of a qualifying donation exceeding JPN 2 000 is deductible from donors' income up to 40% of total income. A donation qualifies for the tax incentive if it is made to public interest incorporated associations, public interest incorporated foundations and other corporations or groups that carry out business for the public benefit, which meet the requirements discussed in Chapter 3. Japan is a unique case because it allows donors to choose between a tax deduction and a tax credit (for some donations). The design of the tax credit is discussed in the next section.

In Switzerland, donations over CHF 100 are deductible up to 20% of 'taxable income' for federal income tax purposes. For cantonal (i.e. regional) income tax purposes, the thresholds are sometimes different. The majority of Swiss cantons have adopted the federal threshold and minimum donation amount. Some cantons, however, have eliminated the minimum donation amount or given its regional council the authority to wave the 20% threshold on a case by case basis if there is found to be 'a considerable public interest' in the relevant purpose. In South Africa, donations for the purposes of healthcare, conservation, education, and welfare activities, are deductible from the personal income tax base up to a limit of 10% of 'taxable income' (rollover provisions apply).

Limiting the deduction to a fixed value and/or a share of income

Countries with a fixed value limit (Estonia, Finland, and Norway) keep the size of the deduction under a certain maximum regardless of how high a donor's income is. This means that in these countries individuals with lower incomes can deduct a higher proportion of their income for philanthropic giving than those with high incomes. In Finland, donations between EUR 850 and EUR 500 000 are deductible from taxable income. Only donations for the purpose of promoting science, or art given to a publicly financed university, can qualify for the tax deduction. The ceiling is significantly lower in Norway, where the donation must be between NOK 500 and NOK 50 000 (~ EUR 4 500) to qualify for the tax deduction.

Furthermore, the design of the tax deduction in Estonia, Latvia, and Finland shows that there are regional similarities. In Estonia, donations of up to EUR 1 200 and 50% of the taxable income may be deducted. In

Latvia, donations can be deducted as part of the total eligible expenses including the acquisition of education and the use of health and medical treatment services. Total deductions are limited to 50% of the annual taxable income, and no more than EUR 600. So the deduction limit is set to the same share of total income in both Latvia and Estonia, but the fixed value limit is double the size in Estonia.

India is a unique case where the donations are limited if they are made in cash. All donations above INR 2 000 made in cash are not deductible and must be made by cheque or wire transfer. In India, 100% of the donation is deductible if it is given to certain funds (e.g. Prime Minister National Relief Fund) only 50% of the donation is deductible if it is given to most other philanthropic entities. In most cases, the deduction is capped at 10% of the gross total income (after all other eligible tax exemptions and deductions).

In Luxembourg, tax deductible donations must be at least EUR 120 and may not exceed 20% of the donor's total net income, or EUR 1 000 000. Donations that exceed these limits may be reported over the next 2 tax years. Additionally, the initial donation made by the founder of an eligible foundation or fund is also considered deductible donation.

Box 4.2. Implications of the Tax Cuts and Jobs Act (TCJA) for philanthropic giving

Signed into law on 22 December 2017, the TCJA is considered the biggest overhaul of the United States tax system in more than thirty years. It includes corporate and individual tax changes, which have implications for giving and philanthropic entities.

In the United States, taxpayers can choose between itemising their deductions on their income tax returns and claiming the standard deduction. Only taxpayers that itemise can deduct charitable contributions from their taxable income. Since the tax-subsidy for donations does not apply to those that claim the standard deduction, only itemisers have a tax incentive to give to philanthropic causes.

The TCJA just about doubled the standard deduction and capped the deduction for state and local taxes at USD 10 000. Since taxpayers only choose to itemise if the sum of their potential itemised deductions is larger than the standard deduction, this is likely to reduce the number of households claiming an itemized deduction especially among middle-income households.

Coupled with a slight decrease in PIT rates, the TCJA reduced the average tax subsidy for charitable giving considerably. In other words, the price of giving has increased and the overall design of the tax incentive has become even more focused on big donors.

Source: (Urban-Brookings Tax Policy Center, 2018[2]).

4.2.3. Tax credits

Belgium, Canada, Chile, Colombia, Greece, Israel, New Zealand, Portugal and Sweden all incentivise donations by individuals through tax credits. As discussed above, a tax credit is an amount subtracted directly from the tax liability, after the liability has been computed. Unlike a deduction, the value of a tax credit does not depend on the income tax rate paid by the donor and is, in itself, not regressive in countries with a progressive personal income tax.

To limit the size of tax credits countries may adjust the share of the donation that is creditable (e.g. 50% of the donation is creditable); limit the value of the credit to a share of taxable or total income (e.g. up to 20% of the PIT base); limit the value of the credit to a share of the total PIT liability (e.g. the credit cannot exceed 20% of the tax liability); limit the value of the credit to a fixed value (e.g. the credit cannot exceed EUR 1 000); or limit the size of the donation to a fixed value (e.g. up to EUR 1 000). Table 4.3 shows that countries use a combination of limitations to design their tax credits for philanthropic giving. The minimum amount necessary for a donation to qualify for the tax credit may be used to increase the efficiency of administrative costs and incentivise larger donations.

Table 4.3. Limitations to personal income tax credits

Country	Tax credit	Ceiling	Floor
Belgium	45%	Total amount of the donation may not exceed 10% of global net income nor EUR 375 350 per spouse	EUR 40 per institution
Canada	15% - 33%	Up to 75% of net income can be claimed (for cash donations)	
Chile	35-50%	Credits received for donations to charity, and education, culture and sport are limited at 20% of the amount of the donation subject to beneficial tax treatment or UTM 320 (approx. USD 20 558).	
Colombia	25%	Credit received is limited to 25% of the income tax liability (the excess may be carried over to the following year)	
France	66%	20% of taxable income	
Greece	20%	Total amount of the donation may not exceed 5% of taxable income	EUR 100
Israel	35%	The credit cannot exceed 30% of taxable income or NIS 9 000 000	
Italy	30% (35% for specific PBOs)	Up to EUR 30 000 of total giving	
Japan	40%	The donated amount cannot exceed 40% of total income and the value of the tax credit may not exceed 25% of the income tax liability.	JPY 2 000
New Zealand	33.33%	Total amount of the donation may not exceed 100% of taxable income.	NZD 5
Portugal	25%	The credit cannot exceed 15% of tax liability (no limit for donations to public institutions).	
Sweden	25%	The credit cannot exceed SEK 1 500	SEK 2 000 total donations and at least SEK 200 per individual donation

Source: OECD Taxation and Philanthropy Questionnaire and Ministry of Finance websites

Limiting the value of the credit to a share of taxable or total income

Canada offers tax credits for donations at the federal and provincial level. The federal tax credit is 15% on the first CAD 200 and 29% on donations above that amount, with the exception of individuals with taxable income exceeding the highest income tax bracket (which is indexed to annual inflation and approximately CAD 200 000), where the tax credit is 33% on all donations above the first CAD 200. Thus the value of the tax credit is larger for wealthier donors for all donations above CAD 200. Take, for example two donations of CAD 1 000 by donor A and donor B. Donor A has a taxable income above the highest income tax bracket (approximately CAD 200 000) and donor B does not. The monetary value of the tax credit for donor A and B is CAD 330 and CAD 290 respectively. Provinces tend to extend similar credits for provincial income tax at lower rates (e.g., Ontario provides a credit of 5.05% on the first $200 and 11.16% on donations above that). Generally, individuals are only able to claim up to 75% of their net income for the year but donations can be carried forwarded for 5 years. If the donor receives a benefit (e.g., the purchase of a ticket to a fundraising event), the fair market value of the benefit must be determined by the philanthropic entity (this is referred to as the 'split receipt' method) and deducted from the amount of the payment before the tax credit is applied. Furthermore, a donation is only eligible for tax relief if the value of the benefit received is less than 80% of the value of the donation. This is referred to as the 'intention to make a gift' threshold as gifts with a benefit to the donor above that amount are considered to have been made with no true intention of donating.

France provides a 66% tax credit for donations to philanthropic entities. The reduction applies within the limit of 20 % of taxable income. For donations to PBOs providing free meals, care or accommodation for people in need, the tax credit is 75% of a donation less than or equal to EUR 546. For the part of the donation that exceeds EUR 546, the tax credit is 66%. The 20 % of the taxable income limit remains constant. Additionally, France provides a reduction on the real estate wealth tax ("Impôt sur la fortune immobilière"). The reduction is 75 % of the amount of the donation with a cap at EUR 50 000.

In New Zealand, donors receive a fully refundable tax credit of 33.33% of the donation. Furthermore, the amount an individual can donate and claim a donation tax credit for is capped at 100% of their taxable income for the year the donation was made. The value of the tax credit is limited to 33.33% of the donor's taxable income. For a donation to qualify, it must be a gift of NZD 5 or more. The credits can be claimed by sole traders as well as individuals who are wage-earners.

In Japan, donors can select a 40% tax credit in place of the tax deduction for certain types of donations. However, the tax credit is only applied to the part of the donation that exceeds JPN 2 000. Furthermore, the donated amount cannot exceed 40% of total income and value of the credit cannot exceed 25% of the personal income tax liability.

Limiting the value of the credit to a share of the income tax liability

In Colombia and Portugal, the credit ceiling is tied to the tax liability instead of total taxable income. In Colombia, the tax credit is 25% of the value donated in the year or taxable period, limited to 25% of taxpayers' income tax liability of the year in which the donation was made. The excess may be offset against the income tax liability in the following tax year. For example, if an income taxpayer makes a donation of COP 150, such donation creates a credit of COP 37.5 (25% of COP 150). If the tax liability of the income tax payer is COP 80, the total amount of the credit that may be offset in the taxable year of the donation is COP 20 (25% of USD 80); the remaining COP 17.5 credit may be offset in the following tax year if it does not exceed 25% of the total income tax liability. In Portugal, the tax credit is set at 25% of the donation but limited to 15% of the tax liability which is ten percentage points lower than in Colombia.

Limiting the value of the credit to a fixed value

In Sweden, donors receive a 25% tax credit of up to SEK 1 500, corresponding to a maximum of SEK 6 000 a year in eligible donations. For the donation to be eligible for the credit it must be at least SEK 2 000 a year and SEK 200 at each giving occasion.

Limiting the value of the credit to a combination of ceilings

In Belgium, a 45% tax credit is granted for donations made to eligible philanthropic entities, provided the gifts amount to at least EUR 40 per beneficiary fund or PBO. The total amount of donations for which the tax credit is granted cannot exceed 10% of 'global net income' nor EUR 376 350 per spouse for a married couple.

In Chile, the size and limits of the tax credit depend on the worthy purpose of the entity receiving the donation. For donations to culture and sports, the tax credit can be 35% or 50%. Donations to social and public purposes and education, may receive a tax credit of 50%. The donation, however, is limited to 20% of the amount of the donation subject to beneficial tax treatment or 320 UTM (which is equal to about CLP 16 000 000 and EUR 18 000). For so called 'reconstruction donations', the tax credit is 40% and there are no limits to the size of the donation.

In Israel, the donor receives a tax credits equal to 35% of the eligible donations in the tax year. The value of the credit is limited 30% of the donor's yearly income or NIS 9 000 000.

Limiting the size of the donation

In Greece, donations are incentivised through a 20% tax credit provided that the sum of all donations exceeds EUR 100 during the tax year. The total amount of donations eligible for the tax credit cannot exceed 5% of taxable income and there are no carry over provisions. For individuals that have a business activity, donations can be considered business expenses without a limit or ceiling (as long as they comply with the business expensing rules).

Box 4.3. Tax measures to incentivise philanthropy in response to the Covid-19 pandemic

China

- In-kind donations to help combat COVID-19 are exempt from VAT and other consumption taxes. In addition, donations made by enterprises or individuals through qualified Public Benefit Organisations or government authorities can be fully deducted for corporate income tax and personal income tax purposes. Before the measure, Chinese taxpayers could only deduct part of their donation from their PIT base.

Chile

- Due to the Covid-19 crisis, a decree was issued by the Chilean government triggering the application of the tax benefits of Chilean law concerning national emergencies (see Box 4.1) to donations related with this catastrophe.

United States

- For 2020, up to USD 300 of monetary donations are deductible from the personal income tax base, whether or not the taxpayer itemises or takes the standard deduction (see Box 4.2).
- The United States also increased the limitations on deductions for charitable contributions by individuals who itemise, as well as corporations. For individuals, the 50% of adjusted gross income limitation is suspended for 2020. For corporations, the 10% limitation is increased to 25% of taxable income. This provision also increases the limitation on deductions for contributions of food inventory from 15% to 25%.

Italy

- Offered tax deductions of 30% for philanthropic donations linked to the COVID-19 emergency.

Belgium

- Companies donating medical material and equipment to hospitals do not have to pay VAT on these donations.

Iceland

- Persons and entities building, renovating or maintaining residential housing or vacation homes can seek reimbursement for 100% of the VAT incurred due to certain craftsman labour. The reimbursement rate has been increased from 60% to a 100% and now includes more types of labour, for example architects. This measure is further extended to PBOs such as charities and sports associations. These measures will remain in effect until end 2020.

Source: OECD Tax Policy Responses to COVID-19 database (http://www.oecd.org/tax/covid-19-tax-policy-and-other-measures.xlsm).

4.2.4. Matching schemes

In a matching scheme, the government tops up donations with a specific amount, which means that the fund or PBO receiving the donation is able to claim the tax incentive. The United Kingdom and Ireland both have matching schemes. The matching scheme in the United Kingdom is referred to as Gift Aid. The donation is treated as if the donor has had the basic tax rate (20%) deducted (i.e. a donation of GBP 1 000 is treated as GBP 1 250). The PBO or fund receiving the donation is then able to claim Gift Aid from the tax administration (HMRC in the United Kingdom) at the basic tax rate (see Table 4.4 for an illustration of Gift Aid). Higher rate taxpayers can claim the difference between the basic rate and the higher rate as personal tax relief.

The fiscal devolution of Wales and Scotland allows for differential tax rates across the United Kingdom. Nevertheless, Gift Aid claimed by charities regardless of their location within the United Kingdom is determined using the United Kingdom basic rate. On the other hand, the tax relief claimed by the Welsh or Scottish donor is determined using the difference between the United Kingdom basic rate and the Welsh or Scottish higher rate respectively.

Table 4.4. Example of Gift Aid in the United Kingdom

Income tax rate of the donor	Donation	Gift Aid claimed	PBO and fund receive	Personal tax relief
Basic (20%)	GBP 1 000	GBP 250	GBP 1 250	GBP 0
Higher rate (40%)	GBP 1 000	GBP 250	GBP 1 250	GBP 250

Note: (GBP 1000 / 80) * 100 = GBP 1 250.
Source: Government website (https://www.gov.uk).

In the United Kingdom, payments to funds and PBOs in return for goods or services (including the purchase of a ticket to a fundraising event or raffle) are not considered donations and cannot qualify for Gift Aid. However, specific rules apply to a charity auction where individuals are willing to pay substantially more than market value in order to support the philanthropic entity. For auctioned goods that have a retail price and are freely available, the benefit to the individual for Gift Aid purposes is considered to be the retail price. Any excess payment can be treated as a donation if the donor is aware of that the item's retail price and that it is freely available elsewhere (e.g., if an individual knowingly purchases a TV with a retail price of GBP 500 for GBP 700 at a charity auction, the excess GBP 200 pounds can qualify as a donation for Git Aid purposes). The value of goods that are not freely available and have no retail price (e.g., items belonging to celebrities) or services that are not usually available (e.g., babysitting for an evening) are considered to be worth the price that they are purchased for and therefore do not qualify for Gift Aid.

Ireland also has a matching scheme for incentivising charitable donations (called Charitable Donation Scheme). Philanthropic donations from an individual which are greater than EUR 250 per year, but do not exceed EUR 1 000 000 per year, attract tax relief. The relief may be claimed by the approved body to which the money is donated at a rate of 31%, or 10% if there is a connection between the donor and the organisation. The matching payment to an approved body cannot exceed the amount of tax that the donor has paid for that year. The donor cannot claim a refund of any tax that has been paid to the approved body.

In 2014, Norway introduced a matching scheme (also known as the gift reinforcement programme) in addition to the available deduction. The purpose of the program is to stimulate increased private sector funding for art and culture in the form of monetary donations. Recipients of donations receive an additional gift reinforcement sum, usually 25% of the donated amount. Applications for the receiving the reinforcement sum must be submitted to the Ministry of Culture.

4.2.5. Allocation schemes

In countries with no tradition of philanthropic giving, an allocation scheme (also referred to as 'percentage philanthropy' or 'tax percentage designation' scheme) can create awareness of philanthropy among taxpayers, financially support funds and PBOs, and develop stronger ties between the general public and philanthropic entities. Allocation schemes were introduced mainly in post-communist Europe during the transition period and reports have estimated that by 2016 these schemes have provided philanthropic entities in the region with around five billion in funding (Strečanský and Török, 2016[3]). Of the countries surveyed, Romania, Slovenia, Portugal, Hungary, Italy, Lithuania, and the Slovąk Republic have a tax allocation scheme to support their philanthropic entities. Hungary was the first country to introduce an allocation scheme in 1997, followed by Portugal in 2001, the Slovak Republic in 2002, Lithuania in 2003, Poland, and Romania in 2004, and Slovenia in 2007 (Bullain, 2004[1]).

Allocation schemes decentralise the decision-making process of allocating a certain percentage of income tax revenues to the taxpayers themselves. As discussed above, allocation schemes are not a form of philanthropic giving because they does not involve the transfer of private funds. Instead, taxpayers are able to indicate to the tax authorities what philanthropic entities or causes a set percentage of their income tax liability should be allocated to. The details of the scheme vary across countries, but typically taxpayers need to choose the philanthropic entity or worthy purpose from a list provided by the tax authority.

Some countries that have allocation schemes do not have incentives for individual philanthropic giving (e.g., Hungary, Lithuania, and the Slovak Republic), while others (e.g. Slovenia and Portugal) also offer tax incentives such as deductions or credits. This is worth noting because while allocation schemes can complement deductions, credits, or matching schemes, they should not be viewed as a replacement of this kind of tax relief for philanthropic giving because the scheme comes at zero cost to the taxpayer making the allocation. In Hungary, taxpayers can designate 1% of their personal income tax to an eligible PBO since 1997 and since 1998 they can designate an additional 1% to churches. In Lithuania, a taxpayer can designate up to a total of 1.2% of their personal income tax to eligible PBOs. In the Slovak Republic, individuals can allocate 2% of their income tax to a philanthropic entity and they can do so when submitting their tax return. If the taxpayer has volunteered for a 'worthy' purpose entity, for at least 40 hours during the tax year, the amount that can be allocated increases to 3% of the personal income tax liability. In Romania, individuals can allocate 2% or 3.5% of their personal income tax liability to philanthropic entities by submitting a form with the list of preferred recipients to the tax authority. The 2% share can be directed to philanthropic entities that are established and operate according to legal provisions, but also to religious units (including parishes). The share of 3.5% can be directed to PBOs and religious units that are also providers of social services. From 2021, the share will become 3.5% and can be directed to all PBOs and religious units that operate according to legal provisions.

What distinguishes Italy, Slovenia and Portugal is that they have tax deductions and credits to incentivise philanthropic giving, but have also implemented a tax allocation scheme. In Slovenia, taxpayers can allocate either 0.1%, 0.2%, 0.3%, 0.4% or 0.5% of their personal income tax to eligible funds and PBOs by submitting a form online, in person, or by mail at any point before end of the year for which the personal income tax is assessed. In 2018, a total of about EUR 5 million was allocated to over 5 000 entities, in 2017 the total sum allocated this way was around EUR 4.6 million and in 2011 it was around EUR 3.8 million.[3]

In Portugal a taxpayer can allocate 0.5% of their personal income tax for religious or charitable purposes, to a church, religious community, or PBO. They can do so as part of their annual personal income tax declaration or through an online portal by April. In addition to the personal income tax allocation scheme, Portugal also introduced a VAT allocation scheme in 2019 (see Box 4.4 for a more detailed overview of how it works).

In Italy a large amount of the financing for the philanthropic sector comes from the "5 per mille" option, an allocation scheme which enables taxpayers to allocate the 0.5% of their PIT to public and private entities operating in cultural, educational, scientific and charitable fields. PBOs represent a relevant part of the entities entitled to receive these funds. In 2018 this kind of financing amounted to EUR 439.8 million for PBOs.

Box 4.4. The Portuguese VAT allocation scheme

In addition to being able to allocate a share of their personal income tax, individuals in Portugal can also direct a share of some of their VAT payments to the same entity that they specified for the allocation of their income tax.

Contrary to the allocation of personal income taxes, the VAT allocation scheme comes at a cost to the taxpayer and is therefore a form of philanthropic giving. In Portugal 15% of the VAT paid to car workshops, restaurants, accommodation services (e.g. hotels), hairdressers, beauty salons and veterinaries, and 100% of the VAT paid for social passes (i.e. public transportation) is tax deductible. The allocation scheme allows taxpayers to direct their VAT deductible VAT payments to a philanthropic entity and forgo the tax benefit themselves.

4.2.6. Philanthropic bequests

Countries that levy inheritance or estate taxes generally provide preferential tax relief for philanthropic bequests. In countries with an inheritance tax, the PBO or fund receiving the bequest is liable for the tax and thus entitled to receive any tax relief. In countries with an estate tax, on the other hand, the tax liability as well as the corresponding tax relief is with the estate of the deceased.

The Brussels-Capital region in Belgium, for example, has a reduced regional inheritance tax rate of 7% for bequests of moveable and immovable assets to accredited philanthropic entities (as opposed to the standard rate of 25%).

In France, bequests made to PBOs recognized as being of public utility (see Chapter 3) are subject to the inheritance tax rate provided for inheritances between siblings:

- 35 % up to EUR 24 430;
- 45 % above EUR 24 430.

For other PBOs which do not benefit from the public utility status, the tax rate is set at 60%. Nevertheless, some type of donations and bequests are exempted from the inheritance tax:

- endowment funds of a philanthropic, educational, scientific, social, humanitarian, sporting, family, cultural nature, or contributing to the enhancement of artistic heritage, the defence of the natural environment or the dissemination of culture , French language and scientific knowledge;
- endowment funds whose management is selfless and which transfer the income from donations to other non-profit organizations,

In Bulgaria, bequests to the Bulgarian Red Cross, registered religious denominations and community centres are exempt from inheritance tax. Funds and PBOs are also exempt from inheritance tax in the Netherlands, Slovenia and Finland.

In countries with an estate tax, the estate receives the exemption or other tax relief. In South Africa, for example, bequests to PBO's are exempt from estate tax. In the United States, philanthropic bequests are fully deductible from the estate tax base.

Norway, Canada and Australia do not have an inheritance or estate tax, but donations on death or in the year before can still qualify for tax deductions. In Canada, the tax credit for a donations made by an individual in the year of death (but prior to the date of death) can be claimed either on the deceased individual's final tax return or the return for the preceding year. Additionally, the limit of the tax credit for donations made in the year of death is raised to 100% of the deceased person's net income or the eligible amount of gifts made in the year of death (in addition to any eligible unclaimed portion of the amount of any gifts made in previous years). In Norway, testamentary donations (i.e. bequests) are deductible under the same conditions as donations made before death. If the conditions are fulfilled, philanthropic bequests are deducted from the estate when the tax for the estate of the relevant deceased person is calculated. In Australia, a gift on death is not subject to capital gains tax, if the gift would have been deductible if made during the donor's lifetime. In Japan, assets donated by the heir to a PBO, are not included in the taxable value of inheritance tax.

4.2.7. Non-monetary donations of individuals

In countries that extend tax incentives to non-monetary donations by individuals, the limitation rules or form of tax relief may differ from cash donations. Not all countries that incentivise philanthropic giving of individuals include non-monetary donations. Of the countries that do (Argentina, Australia, Belgium, Bulgaria, Canada, Chile, Colombia, Estonia, France, Germany, Greece, India, Indonesia, Ireland, Italy, Latvia, Mexico, the Netherlands, Portugal, Singapore, Slovenia, South Africa, Switzerland, and the United States), some have specific rules that are different from those for cash donations discussed above. Non-monetary, or in-kind donations, refer gifts such as property, services, and in some cases even blood and organ donations (see Box 4.5). Donations of property can include real and intellectual property; stocks or shares; trading stock; cultural assets; or other personal property. Donations of goods and services typically refer to the provision of the kind of goods and services that PBOs themselves provide to those in need (e.g. clothing, food, medicine, volunteering at a homeless shelter, etc.). Not all of these different forms of in-kind donations are eligible in all countries, but most allow for the donation of property. A disposal of property may also give rise to a capital gain in some countries.

In Australia, the same rules that apply to cash donations apply to donations of shares and items of trading stock. For donations of property other than shares, the gift must be valued at more than AUD 5,000 unless it is donated within 12 months of purchase. Shares listed on a stock exchange must be valued at less than AUD 5 000 and acquired within the last 12 months. A disposal of property to a philanthropic entity as a gift could give rise to a capital gain (or loss), but this may be offset, in whole or part, by the gift deduction. In Belgium, donations in the form of works of art are eligible to receive a tax credit, provided that the donations are made to state museums, public welfare centres or communities such as regions, provinces, and municipalities.

In Canada, the valuation rules and by extension limitations to tax incentives also depend on the nature of the donated assets. In Canada, generally speaking, non-monetary property can be donated and the donor is entitled to claim the charitable donation tax credit on the full fair-market value (FMV) of the donation. Dispositions of such property may be subject to capital gains tax. Generally, individuals are only able to claim a credit up to 75% of their net income for the year and may be carry forwarded for 5 years. However, gifts of ecologically sensitive land to certain qualified PBOs (not private foundations) are not limited to a percentage of net income and may be carried forward for up to 10 years. Gifts of certified cultural property are not limited to a percentage of net income.

In Italy, the monetary value of the donation is evaluated according to the open market value of the asset. If the giving is higher than EUR 30 000, the donor has to provide with a technical report certifying the estimated value of the given asset. Donations of primary goods, such as food, drugs and hygienic products, are not taxable for income tax purposes and are exempt from VAT.

Box 4.5. Tax incentives for volunteering and blood and organ donations exist in only a few countries

Tax incentives for donations of services

Tax incentives for donations of services are difficult to design since PBOs often have both employees and volunteers and distinguishing between the two can be challenging.

Germany, for instance, extends preferential tax treatment to income from civic engagements and volunteering. Income from a 'side-line' activity paid to individuals by a PBO is tax-exempt up to EUR 720 per year. For certain side-line activities (trainer, instructor, childcare work, support work, artistic activity, part-time care of an old, sick or disabled person), the tax exemption is EUR 2 400 per year.

In the United States, volunteers cannot deduct the value of their services for income tax purposes. Expenses incurred as a result of the volunteering may however be deductible. For expenses to qualify for tax relief they must be unreimbursed, directly connected with the volunteering, expenses that only occurred because of the services given, and not personal, living or family expenses.

In the Netherlands, volunteers can deduct expenses of up to EUR 1 500 per year (and not more than EUR 150 per month) without having to itemise. Expenses above EUR 1 500 have to be itemised and justified. If unjustified, any reimbursements that individuals receive for these expenses are treated as income and taxed accordingly.

The Slovak Republic's allocation scheme indirectly incentivises volunteering because it enables taxpayers that have volunteered to designate one percentage point more of their income tax to a philanthropic entity of their choice (see section 4.2.3 for more information).

Incentives for blood and organ donations are less frequent

In Ireland, compensation received by living donors of kidneys for transplantation are exempt from income tax and not included in computing the PIT rate.

In some states of the United States, organ donations are eligible for certain tax deductions. In New York state, for example, a taxpayer that, while living, donates one or more of their human organs for human organ transplantation can deduct up to USD 10 000 from their PIT base for any expenses incurred. The deductible expenses are limited to travel expenses, lodging expenses, and lost wages.

In the Czech Republic, blood donations are valued at CZK 3 000 per donation and can be deducted from the donor's PIT base. The donation of bone marrow is also deductible from the personal income tax base and valued at CZK 20 000.

In the United States, contributions of certain 'long-term capital gain property' is deductible but generally limited to 30% of adjusted gross income (AGI). Qualified farmers and ranchers (over 50% of gross income from farming) can deduct up to 100% of AGI, less any other contribution deductions, for donations of qualified real property provided that the property remains generally available for agriculture or livestock production. In addition, deductions for certain contributions are limited to the donor's basis in the property.

Valuation rules of non-monetary donations

For non-monetary donations to receive any form of tax relief the value of the gift has to be determined. Regardless of whether it is a deduction, credit or matching scheme, the valuation of a non-monetary gift determines the amount that can be deducted, credited, or matched. The undervaluation of a gift will decrease the incentive power of the tax relief. If a gift is overvalued, on the other hand, the donation will increase the benefit to the donor and, in extreme cases, could exceed the actual value of the gift. The valuation of non-monetary donations is therefore essential for tax incentives for philanthropic giving to function efficiently. Generally, the fair market value (FMV) is used to calculate the respective tax subsides but the regulations concerning who is responsible for the valuation, and how the fair market value is determined, typically depends on the size of the gift and varies across countries. The different approaches are discussed below.

Regardless of whether the donor, beneficiary, or tax administration is responsible for determining the monetary value of a gift, the valuation process comes at a cost. In some cases it may be as simple as looking up the retail price of an item or the market value (e.g., of shares), but for real estate, used goods, or artwork, the process tends to be more time and resource intensive. Therefore countries tend to make the probable value of a good a determining factor of whether or not it needs to go through a more extensive valuation process. Small non-monetary donations (such as gifts of used clothing) are not worth getting appraised by an expert and may therefore not qualify for tax relief.

Require appraisals if the value is likely to exceed a threshold

In Australia, property valued at over AUD 5 000 (other than shares in a listed company) must be valued by the revenue authority i.e. the Australian Taxation Office and the cost of the valuation must be paid by the donor. Additionally, the cost of the valuation may be claimed as a deduction if the sole purpose of the valuation was to determine the value of a gift.

In Canada, it is the responsibility of the PBO to ensure that donations are properly valued at their fair market value (FMV). If the FMV of the property is less than CAD 1 000, a member of the registered PBO, or another individual, with sufficient knowledge of the property may determine its value. If, on the other hand, the FMV is greater than CAD 1 000, the valuation or appraisal will generally be carried out by a professional third-party appraiser. If it is appraised, the name and address of the appraiser must be included on the official donation receipt. In the case of donations of ecologically sensitive land and donations of certified cultural property, special rules apply with respect to valuation. Generally, there are rules that provide, respectively, the Minister of Environment and the Canadian Cultural Property Export Review Board, with the responsibility of determining the FMV of the donation.

Valuation rules depend on the nature of the asset

In Colombia, the valuation rules depend on the nature of the asset. The value of gold and other precious metals is the commercial value of such goods. The value of motor vehicles is the commercial appraisal established annually by the Ministry of Transportation; the value of shares, contributions and other rights in companies is determined in the donors' tax basis of these assets. The value of real or immovable property is the one registered in the donor´s last tax return, according to special tax rules.

In Mexico, the value of donations of land or shares is equal to the Original Investment Amount (MOI), updated for the effects of inflation, generated from the date at which the land or shares were acquired until the month immediately prior to the donation. In the case of fixed assets, the value of the donation should be the updated Original Investment Amount. For other real estate the amount of the donation is valued by updating the amount paid to acquire the good for the period of the month in which it was acquired up to the month of the donation for inflation. In the event that merchandise/trading stock is donated it would not be deductible since it was already considered within the cost of sales for tax deduction purposes.

The valuation of real estate for tax purposes in Germany, depends on whether the property is developed. The value of undeveloped real estate is determined and published by the committee of land valuation experts responsible for the local area. In the case of developed property, the value is calculated using the comparative value method, the rental value method or the material value method depending on the situation.

- The comparative value method is generally used to value detached and semi-detached houses as well as residential apartments and non-residential rooms forming part of larger properties. The value of the property is determined by comparison with the prices of similar properties.
- The rental value method is used to value property rented for residential purposes, as well as mixed-use and business property, for which it is possible to determine the customary amount of rent paid on the local market. The value of the property is calculated by determining the value of the land in the same way as for undeveloped property and adding a value representing the yield from the building.
- The material value method is used for real estate, for which neither the comparative value nor the rental value method is practical. Under this method, the value of the property is determined on the basis of the standard construction costs for the building and for other facilities together with the value of the land. If the taxpayer provides evidence substantiating a lower market value, this is to be recognised instead.

In the United States, donations of property (except publicly traded stock) above USD 5 000 must have a qualified appraisal. The appraisal must be signed by a qualified appraiser using generally accepted appraisal standards and, in most cases, the receipt of the donation must be acknowledged by the receiving entity. For donations of artwork over USD 20 000 and any donations valued over USD 500 000, signed copies of the appraisal must be filed with the tax return in which the deduction is claimed. Donations of artwork to a philanthropic entity are subject to review by art advisory committee. In general, a deduction is not allowed if the donor retains any interest in the property, or if the donation is of a partial interest in property. The primary exception is that a contribution of a conservation easement is deductible even though it is a contribution of a partial interest. The valuation of the easement is based on the loss of value due to the easement restrictions determined by a qualified appraiser.

In France, securities (e.g., stocks, bonds) are valued according to the last price known on the stock market (closing price the day before the donation) and the value of real estate (e.g., individual houses, apartments, forests, etc.) is estimated according to its market value.

In the Netherlands, the value of listed shares and bonds is based on the stock market price. For other assets the value is based on the FMV, which has to be determined before the donation is made.

No appraisals are required and valuation may be reviewed through audits

In some countries the appraisal of donated assets is not required, but the donor's valuation may be audited, in which case the indicated price of the asset has to be confirmed. This is the case in Chile, Estonia, and Ireland. In Chile, as a general rule, appraisal of non-monetary donations should be made according to special provisions of the inheritance and gift tax law. Special appraisal rules may apply in some cases. In Indonesia, the value of a non-monetary donation is determined according to historical value, book value, or the retail cost of other goods sold. In the case of in-kind donations such as the construction of infrastructure, the value is determined using the actual construction cost necessary to build the donated infrastructure.

Capital gains tax relief

Donations of assets that have increased in value may have capital gains tax implications in countries that levy a capital gains tax (CGT). If, for example, an individual donates property to a PBO that they purchased for EUR 50 000 but is now valued at EUR 100 000, a capital gain will be realised. In a country where donations are exempt from capital gains tax, the individual may benefit from the tax incentive schemes, but may also not have to pay the capital gains tax they would have otherwise had to pay once they had either sold or disposed of the asset.

Canada provides a full capital gains exemption for donations of certain types of property (in addition to such donations receiving the charitable donation tax credit). Specifically:

- Gifts of publicly-traded shares and stock options may be eligible for an inclusion rate of zero on any capital gain realised, subject to certain conditions. The capital gains tax on donations of shares in private companies, on the other hand, does apply and is not subject to CGT relief.
- Gifts of ecologically sensitive land to certain qualified funds (not private foundations) are eligible for an inclusion rate of zero on any capital gain realised, subject to certain conditions.
- Gifts of certified cultural property are also not subject to capital gains tax, subject to certain conditions.

Ireland exempts from capital gains tax the disposal of a work of art that has previously been loaned to an approved gallery or museum or to the Irish Heritage Trust, for a period of 10 years or more (6 years or more for loans made before 2 February 2006) and has been on display to the public. To qualify for this relief, a work of art must have a value of at least EUR 31 740 at the time it is loaned to the gallery. For information on the capital gains tax relief for the donation of shares, see Box 4.6.

Box 4.6. Irish capital gains tax (CGT) relief

Donation of property

Capital gains tax (CGT) relief is available for donors (both individual and corporate) of tangible assets, such as real property. A donation of property will be deemed to have been made at the value it had on the date the property was acquired by the donor. This is an exception to the normal rule requiring the disposal consideration to be treated for tax purposes as the market value at disposal. The donor will therefore be treated as having made neither a gain nor a loss on the disposal and will not be subject to capital gains tax.

Donation of shares

If an individual donor in Ireland, makes a donation of shares which have increased in value since the date on which they were acquired by the donor, the disposal would give rise to a CGT liability. The donor can claim CGT relief on this disposal, but the PBO would then not be able to claim the income tax relief (described in Box 3.2). If the donor chooses not to claim the CGT relief, then the PBO will receive the FMV of the shares plus the relief of 31% (or 10% if there is a connection between the donor and the organisation).

The charity will have no CGT liability on any subsequent sale of the shares provided the proceeds on the sale are applied for its charitable purposes. The donor, however, may (subject to their personal exemption on capital gains of EUR 1 270 per year) be liable for capital gains tax at 33% on the difference between the value of the shares transferred and the original cost of the shares.

A company making a donation of shares to PBO may choose between claiming corporation tax relief at 12.5% and deducting the donation as a trading expense, or claiming CGT relief, whichever is higher. If corporation tax relief is claimed then the company will be liable for CGT on the disposal and the charity will not be able to claim a repayment.

In the United States, no capital gains tax is imposed on donations of appreciated property, provided that the one-year holding period requirement is met.

In Australia, a gift of property, including shares, may trigger a capital gain or loss event. This is treated separately, i.e. the taxpayer may claim a deduction for the gift and must also record a capital gain or loss as applicable. Such a gain or loss is treated normally, increasing or decreasing the tax liability as applicable. However, a donor is exempt from paying CGT on donations of property to PBOs under the Cultural Gifts Program and donations of exempt personal use assets to PBOs (and will also be able to claim a deduction for the value of the gift). Testamentary gifts are not subject to CGT provided the gift would have been deductible if made during the individual's lifetime.

In Norway, a non-monetary donation to a philanthropic entity is not considered an event of realisation/divestment for tax purposes. Therefore, potential capital gains arising from donations, do not trigger capital gains tax in the hands of the donor. This is also the case in Argentina and Israel. In Indonesia, non-monetary donations are exempt from capital gains tax if they are given to a religious body, educational or other social entity including a foundation, or cooperative. In Colombia, Estonia, Latvia, Portugal South Africa, and Switzerland, donations in the form of assets are not exempt from capital gains tax.

4.3. Philanthropic giving by corporations

Of the countries analysed in this report, all except for Sweden incentivise corporate philanthropic giving to qualifying funds or PBOs. Corporate giving can occur in the form of donations or sponsorship payments. However, for corporate giving to be considered philanthropic it must comply with the country's donor-benefit rules. Since sponsoring payments to funds and PBOs are in return for publicity that generates a benefit to the donor, it will only be considered philanthropic giving if the benefit is within the statutory limits that apply. Corporate donations are encouraged through corporate income and/ or capital gains tax incentives. In the absence of such an incentive, corporate taxpayers that donate to philanthropic entities would do so from their post-tax profits and receive no tax benefit. In some countries, the donation would be considered an expense unrelated to economic activity and therefore remain part of the corporation's taxable income.

4.3.1. Tax incentives for donations by corporations

Tax incentives for donations by corporations include tax deductions, credits, and matching schemes. Additionally, this section also discusses allocation schemes, on the same basis as for individuals. Unlike the incentives for individuals, businesses can also use business expensing rules, which are linked to deductions, to incentivise corporate sponsoring of philanthropic entities. Table 4.5 shows that corporate donations are deductible in 29 countries.

Compared to the information in Table 4.1, Table 4.5 shows that deductions are more common for corporate tax incentives than personal income tax incentives. For instance, three countries that have personal income tax credits to incentivise individual giving (Belgium, Canada, and New Zealand), encourage corporate giving through deductions instead. A possible explanation for this difference is that countries view corporate donations as business expenses and thus simply allow them to deduct the gift through the same mechanism that other business expenses are deducted. Another contributing factor for the difference between corporate and individual tax incentives is that countries use personal income tax credits to avoid the regressive effect of tax deductions when rates are progressive. Since corporate income tax rates are typically flat, tax credits are no longer necessary to avoid the regressive effect (this is not the case in the Netherland and discussed in more detail below).

Six countries incentivise donations using tax credits, three of which (Chile, Latvia, and Portugal) also offer deductions. Corporate tax credits allow corporations to subtract a share of the value of their donation from their income tax liability, after the liability has been computed. In a number of countries, corporations can choose whether they want to make use of the deduction or the credit depending on which incentive would benefit them more.

Table 4.5. Tax incentives for donations by corporations

X denotes the tax incentive for corporations; O denotes the tax incentive for individuals (if different from that of corporations).

Country	Deduction	Credit	Matching	Allocation	Other
Argentina	X				
Australia	X				
Austria	X				
Belgium	X	O			
Bulgaria	X				
Canada	X	O			
Chile	X	X			
Czech Republic	X				
Estonia	X				
Finland	X				
Germany	X				
Greece	X				
Hungary	X			O	
India	X				
Indonesia	X				
Ireland	X		O		
Italy	X	O		O	
Japan	X				
Latvia	X	X			
Lithuania	X			O	
Luxembourg	X				
Malta	X				O
Mexico	X				
Netherlands	X				
New Zealand	X	O			
Norway	X		X		
Portugal	X	X		O	
Romania	X			O	
Singapore	X				
Slovenia	X			O	
South Africa	X				
Switzerland	X				
United Kingdom	X		O		
United States	X				
Colombia		X			
France		X			
Israel		X			
Slovak Republic				X	
Sweden		O			X[1]

Note:

1. No tax incentive for donations by corporations

Source: OECD Taxation and Philanthropy Questionnaire

Norway is the only country with a matching scheme for corporate giving and the Slovak Republic is the only country with an allocation scheme. The advantages of allocation schemes – such as their ability to foster a culture of giving by increasing the awareness of the general public – relate mainly to donations of individuals. Thus a potential explanation of the difference in the frequency of allocation schemes between incentives for individuals compared to corporations, is that aside from directing public funds to philanthropic entities (which can be done through grants) their effect on the visibility of the philanthropic sector is not as powerful when the scheme is applied to corporations.

The design of tax incentives for corporate donors differs across countries and depends on the nature of the gift. A philanthropic donation can be in the form of cash or non-cash, frequently referred to as non-monetary or in-kind donations. In the case of corporations such gifts may include

- real and intellectual property, stocks, and cultural assets;
- the provision of goods (e.g., a medical equipment producer donating its wheelchairs);
- or the provision of services (e.g., a construction company building infrastructure).

As with non-monetary donations of individuals, countries have rules regulating the valuation of gifts. Section 4.2.7. (above) provides an overview of these valuation rules and unless countries have specific regulations for corporate donations the valuation rules are not repeated in this section of the report.

4.3.2. Limitations for tax incentives to corporate donors

Tax deductions and credits for corporate donations are tied to the corporate income tax and may be limited to: a share of total revenue; a share of total taxable income; a share of the sum of total turnover and wages and salaries paid; a share of the corporate income tax liability, a share of the gift itself, a monetary value; or a combination of these tax relief ceilings. Furthermore, unlike individuals, corporations can deduct business expenses, and thus the sponsoring of philanthropic entities, as well as donating, may partly be encouraged through normal business expensing rules.

Countries can use a combination of limits to their deductions and credits with different levels of generosity. In some cases those limits depend on the worthy purpose of the receiving fund or PBO (e.g., Bulgaria, Chile, Hungary, and Slovenia). Other countries may offer the taxpayer a choice of limits or even type of tax-subsidy (e.g., Germany and Latvia). A number of countries limit their tax relief to a fixed monetary value in addition to a ceiling defined as a share of, for example, total revenue or taxable income (e.g. India, Belgium, and Lithuania).

Offering similar incentives for individual and corporate donors

In Argentina, Australia, Austria, Bulgaria, Colombia, the Czech Republic, India, Indonesia, Luxembourg, Norway, Singapore, Slovenia, and Switzerland, the same or similar treatment applies to donations by individuals and corporations (thus see section 4.2.3. and 4.2.5. for more details). The difference between tax reliefs for corporate donations is that the tax credits or deductions apply to the corporate instead of the personal income tax. The floors, ceilings, and type of tax subsidy remain the same. In Argentina, corporations can deduct donations up to a limit of 5% of annual earnings. In Australia, donations are deductible from the corporate income tax base with no upper limit as long as the deduction does not create a negative tax liability (and the donation can be spread over 5 years). In Austria, donations by corporations are deductible but cannot exceed 10% of total profit. Contrary to donations made by individuals, however, corporate donations receive preferential tax treatment for both cash and in-kind donations. In Colombia, corporations that make donations to philanthropic entities receive a tax credit of 25%, limited to 25% of the corporation's income tax. In the Czech Republic, corporations can deduct cash and in-kind donations up to a ceiling of 10% of the corporate income tax base if the value of the donation is above CZK 2 000. In India 100% of the donation is deductible if it is given to certain funds (e.g. Prime Minister National Relief Fund) but only 50% of the donation is deductible if it is given to most other philanthropic entities. In most cases, the deduction is capped at 10% of the gross total income (after all other eligible tax exemptions and deductions). In Indonesia donations are deductible from the corporate income tax base up to a limit of 5% taxable income. In Luxembourg, the tax deduction cannot exceed EUR 1 000 000 or 20% of total net income, where total net income consists of the revenue remaining after deducting expenses incurred for the purpose of acquiring, ensuring and maintaining revenue. In Norway, corporate donations up to NOK

50 000 are deductible. Singapore provides a 250% tax deduction on certain types of donations, such as cash donations, gift of shares and works of art given to qualifying philanthropic entities. In South Africa donations can qualify for a tax deduction of up to 10% of taxable income. In Slovenia, a corporation can deduct donations up to 0.5% of their taxable revenue. Deductions for donations to worthy purposes such as social assistance science, and religion are limited to 0.3% and deductions for donations for culture and disaster relief are capped at 0.5% of their taxable revenue. In Switzerland, donations are deductible up to 20% of the corporation's taxable income.

In Bulgaria the ceiling of the tax deduction varies depending on the worthy purpose and the percentages are similar to those for individual donors. Donations are deductible from the corporate income tax base (annual accounting profit) up to a total ceiling of 65% of the tax base. The ceilings differ depending on the beneficiary as follows:

- Up to 10% of annual accounting profit where the expenses on donations are incurred in favour of::
  - healthcare and medical-treatment establishments;
  - social services for residential care, as well as of the Social Assistance Agency and of the Social Protection Fund under the Minister of Labour and Social Policy;
  - homes for medical and social care for children;
  - public nurseries, kindergartens, schools, higher schools or academies;
  - public-financed enterprises within the meaning given by the Accountancy Act;
  - religious denominations registered in the country;
  - specialised enterprises or cooperatives of persons with disabilities or the persons with disabilities as well as their technical aids;
  - victims of disasters, or of the families thereof;
  - the Bulgarian Red Cross;
  - socially disadvantaged persons including children with disabilities or parentless children;
  - cultural institutes and community centres;
  - PBOs with the exception of any organisations supporting culture;
  - the Bulgaria Energy Efficiency and Renewable Sources Fund;
  - therapeutic communities for the treatment of drug-addicted persons;
  - the United Nations Children's Fund (UNICEF)
  - social companies listed in the Register of Social Companies, for the conduct of their social activities and/or for attainment of their social goals
- Up to 15% of the accounting profit for the assistance provided gratuitously under the terms and according to the procedure established by the Financial Support for Culture Act;
- Up to 50% of the accounting profit where the expenses on donations are incurred in favour of:
  - the National Health Insurance Fund: for activities related to the medical treatment of children which are financed by transfers from the budget of the Ministry of Health, and of the Assisted Reproduction Centre.
- Any expenses for donations of computers and computer peripheral equipment, which are manufactured within one year prior to the date of the donation, and donated to Bulgarian schools, including higher schools, shall be recognized for tax purposes.

Any expenses for donations of computers and computer peripheral equipment, which are manufactured within one year prior to the date of the donation, and donated to Bulgarian schools, including higher schools, shall be recognized for tax purposes.

Finland, Ireland, Mexico, the Netherlands, Germany, France and Israel, have the same tax incentive for corporate donors as they do for individual donors, but their limits differ significantly from the personal income tax incentives. In Finland, corporations can deduct cash donations to publicly funded universities between EUR 850 and EUR 250 000 euros for the purpose of promoting science, art or the Finnish cultural heritage. Additionally, cash donations between EUR 850 and EUR 50 000 are also deductible if they are made for the purpose of promoting science, art or Finnish cultural heritage and given to associations, foundations or other institutions on the condition that they have been nominated by the tax administration and that their purpose is promoting art, science, or the maintenance of Finnish cultural heritage.

In Ireland, a corporation which donates over EUR 250 to an approved philanthropic entity may claim a deduction for the donation as if it were a trading expense or an expense of management for the accounting period in which it is paid. For the donation to be tax deductible it must not confer any benefit, either directly or indirectly, on the donor or any person connected with the donor, and it must not be conditional on, or associated with, any arrangement involving the acquisition of property by the approved philanthropic entity. Capital gains tax relief is available for donors of tangible assets, such as real property (for more information on the donation of shares see Box 4.6). The capital gains tax relief for donations of works of art is the same for individuals and corporations and is discussed in Section 4.2.7.

Corporations in Mexico can deduct donations to private institutions up to 7% of taxable profit obtained in the previous tax year. For donations in favour of the Federation, Federal Entities, Municipalities, or their decentralized agencies, the deductible amount cannot exceed 4% of fiscal profits. The sum of both must not exceed 7% of taxable profits.

In the Netherlands, corporate donations are deductible up to a limit of 50% of fiscal profit to a maximum of EUR 100 000. Additionally the deductibility of donations cannot lead to a loss and excess donations cannot be spread over multiple years. Donations to PBOs with a cultural worthy purpose are marked-up and can be deducted at 1.5 times the value of the gift with maximum EUR 2 500. Because the Netherlands has a progressive corporate income tax rate (16.5% for profits up to EUR 200 000 and 25% for profits above € 200 000) the value of the deduction is higher for corporations with profits over EUR 200 000.

In Germany, donations are deductible up to 20% of taxable income (before the deduction) or 4% of the sum of the total turnover and wages and salaries paid (this is similar to the design of the corporate tax incentive for giving in Latvia, summarised in Box 4.7. Carry-over provisions apply and donations can be considered business expenses. If goods are donated, the corporation can choose between the common value approach and the book value approach (see section on valuation rules for more details on the approaches).

France provides corporate donors a 60% tax credit for the share of the donation up to EUR 2 million and a 40% tax credit for amount over EUR 2 million. For organizations providing free meals, care or accommodation for people in need the tax credit is 60 % of the total amount of donation. The annual cap of the tax reduction is EUR 20 000 or 5 % (5 per thousand) of annual turnover excluding tax (ceiling applied to all payments made). If the ceiling is exceeded, it is possible to carry the excess over the next 5 years.

In Israel, corporations that donate to an eligible philanthropic entity can benefit from a 30% tax credit. For the donation to qualify for the credit it must be between USD 50 and USD 2.5 Million. The deduction cannot exceed 30% of gross income and excess donations cannot be spread over more than one year. Furthermore, donations cannot be considered a business expense and capital gains tax applies when a non-monetary donation is made.

In Italy, corporations can deduct philanthropic gifts from their taxable income in the same way as individuals. However, they cannot opt for tax credits.

Offering tax credits to individual donors and tax deductions to corporate donors

Belgium, Canada, and New Zealand offer tax credits to individual donors and tax deductions to corporate donors. In Belgium, corporate donations to accredited philanthropic entities are deductible up to 5% of the taxable profit or 500,000 euros. In Canada, donations are deductible up to a limit of 75% of the corporation's taxable income. The limit is increased by 25% of the amount of taxable capital gains arising from donations of appreciated capital property and 25% of any capital cost allowance recapture arising from donations of depreciable capital property. The net income percentage limit does not apply to certain gifts of cultural property or ecologically sensitive land. As with individuals, gifts of publicly traded shares and stock options, ecologically sensitive land, and certified cultural property may be eligible for an inclusion rate of zero on any capital gain realised. Donations in excess of the limit may be carried forward up to 5 years with the exception of gifts of ecologically sensitive land, which may be carried forward up to 10 years. In New Zealand, corporations can claim tax deductions for all donations made to an approved funds and PBOs providing the deduction does not exceed their total annual net income. For a donation to qualify for the deduction it must be a gift of NZD 5 or more of cash. Gifts of property are not eligible for the tax deduction and excess donations cannot be spread over multiple years.

Japan provided individual donors with a choice between a deduction and a credit. Corporate donors, on the other hand, may only benefit from a tax deduction. To determine the deduction limit of general donations, Japan uses the following formula: *[(Amount of capital at the end of the fiscal year × Number of months in the current fiscal year / 12 × 2.5 / 1 000) + (income in the current fiscal year × 2.5 / 100)] × 1/4*. The limit of donations to PBOs with a special status is determined through this formula: *[(Amount of capital at the end of the fiscal year x number of months in the current fiscal year / 12 x 3.75 / 1 000) + (income in the current fiscal year x 6.25 / 100)] x 1/2*. The deductible limit is calculated in each fiscal year when the donation is made. It is not possible to carry over the deductible limit amount which is not used.

Offering both tax credits and deductions

Chile, Latvia and Portugal, offer both tax credits and tax deductions to corporate donors. Corporate donors in Latvia are able to choose from three tax relief options to receive a tax benefit from their donation (see Box 4.7 for more information). The options are a deduction with a limit tied to profits, a deduction with a limit tied to total gross work remuneration, and finally a tax credit tied to the tax on income from dividends. In Portugal, corporate donations can be deducted from the tax base by up to 8/1000 of total turnover. Depending on the worthy purpose, the donations receive a mark-up of 120% to 150% of their total value for deduction purposes. For example, if a corporation makes a donation of EUR 1 000 to a PBO with an educational purpose, the corporation will be able to deduct EUR 1 200 from their taxable income.

In Chile, certain corporate donations can benefit from a 50% tax credit and a tax deduction equal to the remaining amount. Others can benefit from a full deduction as a tax incentive. National emergencies' donations and donations made under municipal law are deductible from the tax base. Donations for reconstruction are eligible for a 50% tax credit and the remaining is deductible. Cultural donations are eligible for a 50% tax credit caped at the lower value of 2% of the tax base or a fixed amount and the remaining is deductible. Donations to charities are eligible for a 50% tax credit which is caped to a fixed amount and the remaining is deductible. Cultural donations are eligible for a 50% tax credit caped at the lower of 2% of the tax base or a fixed amount and the remaining is deductible. Donations for sporting associations are eligible for a 50% or 35% tax credit which is capped at 2% of the tax base or a fixed amount and the remaining amount is deductible. Donations to philanthropic educational entities qualify for a 50% tax credit and the remaining amount is deductible with different limits according to the type of educational entity. Additionally, in the majority of cases a general limit on the amount of the donation applies corresponding to 5% of the taxable base (special limits apply to entities in a tax loss position and other cases).

Box 4.7. Tax incentives for corporate giving in Latvia

The three relief options

Corporations that have made an eligible donation to an eligible philanthropic entity are entitled to choose one of the following three tax relief options:

- Tax deduction: Deduct the donated amount from the corporate income tax base, where the value of the deduction is limited to 5% of the profits from the previous reporting year (after the calculated taxes);
- Tax deduction: Deduct the donated amount from the corporate income tax base, where the value of the deduction is limited to 2% of the total gross work remuneration (e.g. wages paid) calculated for employees in the previous reporting year;
- Tax credit: Reduce the corporate income tax liability but only on income from dividends by 85% of the donations, where the value of the credit does not exceed 30% of the income tax on income from dividends.

The conditions for a donation to be eligible for the tax relief

A corporate donation is only eligible for the three tax relief options if the following conditions are met:

- The donation is not directed at a specific recipient who is related to the donor, an employee of the donor or a family member of an employee of the donor;
- The recipient of the donation does not perform activities of a compensatory nature that are related to having received the gift (e.g. advertising, invitations to high-value entertainments).
- The total amount of tax debt of the donor on the first day of the taxation period does not exceed EUR 150.
- The beneficiary of the donation has not publicised the donor's brand. This could be the case if the name of the beneficiary of the donation has an obvious link to the donor's brand (e.g., *Company A* donates money to the *Company A Foundation*). If the recipient publicises a list of all the donors, the name of each individual donor must not exceed 1/20th of the text area.

Offering allocation schemes to individuals but not to corporations

Of the six countries that have an allocation scheme for individual taxpayers (Hungary, Lithuania, Portugal, Romania, the Slovak Republic, and Slovenia) the Slovak Republic is the only country that has an allocation scheme for corporations. In the Slovak Republic, corporations can attribute 1% or 2% of their income tax to an approved non-profit entity. The minimum amount that can be allocated is EUR 8. In Lithuania, corporations are allowed to deduct twice the total amount of donations (except for donations in cash exceeding EUR 9 750 each to a qualifying philanthropic entity in a tax year). The total deduction amount cannot exceed 40% of the corporation's taxable income during the tax year. In Hungary, a set share of corporate donations are deducted from pre-tax profits as a business expense. If a corporation donates to a PBO, it can deduct 20% of the total value of the donation. If the donation is made under a long-term agreement, the corporation can deduct 40%. Additionally, 50% of donations to the Hungarian Fund for Clean-up and Salvage, the National Culture Fund or the Agricultural Compensation Fund are deductible.

4.3.3. Sponsoring philanthropy in return for advertisement

This report distinguishes between two kinds of sponsorship payments to philanthropic entities: (1) corporations purchase publicity and advertising from philanthropic entities for the fair market value of those services; and (2) corporations donate to philanthropic entities and the fair market value of the publicity and advertisement they receive as a result is below the value of the donation and in line with the country's donor-benefit rules. In most countries (e.g., Belgium, Latvia, Mexico, the Netherlands, New Zealand, Norway, the Slovak Republic, Sweden, and the United States), the first form of sponsoring is fully deductible. In some cases, advertising contracts tend to be required to ensure that the PBO does in fact provide publicity for the corporation. In Belgium, donations are capped at 5% of taxable profits or EUR 500 000 but sponsoring is fully deductible. In France, on the other hand, all payments towards philanthropic entities are considered donations. However, there must an advertisement contract in which the PBO is obliged to ensure the visibility of the brand or its products. In New Zealand and Australia, a payment to a PBO could be considered a business expense and is deductible under the general rules if the payment is incurred in deriving assessable income. Thus a sponsorship payment to a PBO may be deductible under the general rules for business expenses if the sponsorship is likely to increase the business's taxable income. In the United States, contributions that are directly related to the taxpayer's trade or business that are made with a reasonable expectation of a financial return commensurate with the amount paid may be deductible as a business expense. The deduction for a business expense is not limited to the 10% of adjusted gross income that the charitable deduction is limited to.

Although payments can be considered business expenses in many countries (as long as they have a sufficient nexus with earning income), these payments may have implications for the PBOs receiving them. The income from activities different to those related to the worthy purposes for which they were granted PBO status for, may be regarded as commercial activity and limited accordingly. In Mexico, for example, income from advertising activity is regarded as commercial and cannot exceed 10% of the PBOs income if it wants to be able to receive tax-incentivised donations. PBOs receiving sponsorship payments rather than donations may impose a set of obligations on the PBOs, which they may not be able to fulfil or that may trigger an increase in their tax liability. The income tax rules for PBOs are discussed in more detail in a separate chapter of this report.

When sponsoring is part of philanthropic giving, corporations may give more than they receive in publicity. For example, if a business in Canada receives special recognition for its donation, or if it receives more than minimal recognition (for example, banners or advertising of products), this is considered philanthropic sponsorship, and donor-benefit rules may apply. In some countries, the payment may not be eligible for tax relief (e.g., see Latvia's strict donor-benefit rules discussed in Box 4.7). In Canada, the fair market value of the publicity given to the corporate donor, is subtracted from the amount of the donation for tax deductibility purposes. When the value cannot be calculated, the charity cannot issue the business an official donation receipt and the business may be entitled to claim the payment as a deduction against income as an advertising expense (i.e. not necessarily a form of philanthropic giving).

4.4. Tax avoidance and evasion risks

4.4.1. Abuse of tax incentives for philanthropic giving

The abuse of tax incentives for philanthropy occurs when the sanctioned government status of a fund or PBO is abused either by the entity itself, by taxpayers and donors, or third parties, such as fraudsters who pose as philanthropic entities or tax return preparers who falsify tax returns to defraud the government (OECD, 2009[4]). The abuse of the tax incentives discussed in this chapter do not just lead to losses in tax revenue but erode the public's trust in the philanthropic sector as a whole. Common types of tax avoidance and evasion issues with tax relief for philanthropic giving include: philanthropic entities that wilfully participate in a tax evasion scheme to benefit its donors (see Box 4.8 for an example); falsified donation receipts prepared by the philanthropic entity, tax preparers or donors; payments for goods and services disguised as donations; overvalued gifts; and donations of assets in which the donor retains an interest.

Box 4.8. The Cup Trust Case in the United Kingdom

Background

In 2009 the Charity Commission for England and Wales registered the Cup Trust as a charity, with a company based in the British Virgin Islands as its only trustee. Of the GBP 176 000 000 that the Cup Trust received in so-called donations, it claimed GBP 46 000 000 in Gift Aid and only gave GBP 55 000 to philanthropic causes.

Overview of the scheme

The Cup Trust charity was found to be involved in a circular transaction scheme with the objective of receiving Gift Aid from the government and obtaining personal tax relief for individuals. The infographic below shows a simplified version of how the scheme was designed to work in a 24-hour transaction. In summary, the Cup Trust charity took up a loan with which it bought a government bond worth GBP 50 000. Cup Trust then proceeded to sell the bond to a third-party intermediary for GBP 5, under the condition that it would either receive a donation of GBP 50 005 within 24 hours or the legal title to the bond would be returned to the charity. A tax-paying individual would then purchase the bond from the third-party intermediary for GBP 5, sell the bond for its full market value of GBP 50 000 and donate the sum of GBP 50 005 back to Cup Trust, with the intention of receiving personal tax relief for the full GBP 50 005. The Cup Trust then used the donation to pay back the loan, which was interest free as long as it was paid within 24 hours. The intention was then to claim Gift Aid on the donation it received.

One 24-hour transaction

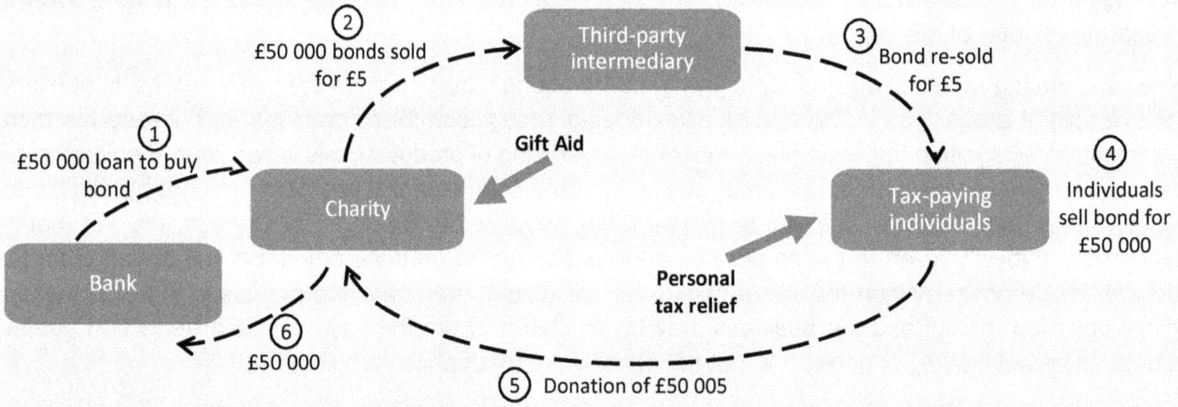

Lessons on how to prevent such schemes

- Regular exchange of information about philanthropic entities of common concern between a registering authority and the tax administration to help focus limited resources on suspicious entities and track tax avoidance and evasion schemes in the philanthropic sector.
- Due diligence by registering authorities to check whether there is a clear public benefit to an entities purpose before granting them the preferential tax status.
- The importance of regulation of philanthropic entities is important to safeguarding access to tax concessions. Need to improve accountability and transparency through reporting requirements and make better use of data from different agencies.

Note: The infographic is a simplification of the scheme using the transaction of one government bond.

Source: https://www.gov.uk/government/publications/the-cup-trust-charity-commission-inquiry-results/the-cup-trust-inquiry-results-formerly-a-registered-charity

Overvaluation of non-monetary gifts

Lax valuation rules and lack of oversight can lead to overvaluation schemes. Overvaluation schemes refer to cases in which taxpayers, for example, buy property at a low price and donate it at a much higher value (often with supportive valuations) thereby generating excess benefits when claiming the charitable donation tax relief. These schemes often utilize foreign entities (foreign PBOs and offshore trusts in tax havens) to obscure, but also legitimise, the transaction. In Canada, this was a significant problem in the 2000s. As a result, the country passed legislation and increased audit resources to address valuations of donations, which appears to have curbed the problem. Colombia and Germany too, have experienced schemes in which the value of the donations were artificially inflated to increase the tax benefit.

In the United States, the valuation of donated property has long been an issue. Over time, requirements for appraisals and other requirements have been made stricter by legislation or regulation when abuses were found. One example is the valuations of donations of used vehicles, which was frequently abused. To curb the overvaluation of used vehicles, legislation required appraisals for vehicles valued over USD 500 and forms required to be submitted to the revenue required information about the year, model and vehicle identification number for auditing purposes.

The falsification or sale of donation receipts

A lack of oversight and targeted tax audits has, in some countries, led to the sale or falsification of donation receipts. The sale of receipts involving PBOs, and tax preparers selling donation receipts for a fraction of the value indicated on the receipt, has resulted in an excess tax benefit when claiming the tax incentive. In Canada, this was a particular issue in the late 1990s and early 2000s.

In-kind donations deducted as business expenses

In some countries, in-kind donations have falsely been deducted as business expenses. This occurs in Indonesia, where in-kind donations are not deductible. In some cases, businesses will deduct an in-kind donation as a business expense and financial assistance is often misused as a personal expense.

Payments for goods and services disguised as gifts

Individual donors may, together with the entity involved, want to disguise a payment for goods or services as a donation. Common examples of these schemes involve charities that receive donations and then use the funds to provide a scholarship to a donor's child or pay tuition at a private school attended by a donor's child. This was identified as an issue by Canada as well as New Zealand (see Box 4.9).

4.4.2. Anti-abuse policies

To ensure that the tax expenditures used to encourage philanthropic giving is efficient, it is important for countries to tackle tax avoidance and evasion schemes related to philanthropic giving, and implement regulations and policies in response to these schemes. On the other hand, excessive rules and requirements can significantly increase the administrative burden to the tax administration/regulatory authority, as well as philanthropic entities and their respective donors. Thus countries report that the use of targeted audits, increased fines and legal consequences, better use of data, as well as clear tax rules have been effective anti-abuse policies.

The majority of anti-abuse policies, however, are in the form of regulations and transparency and reporting requirements for funds and PBOs discussed in chapter five. This is because, a key anti-abuse policy is that the recipients of philanthropic giving must be accredited philanthropic entities. This allows the tax administration to focus its resources on these entities and shifts the worthy purpose and public benefit requirement on to the funds and PBOs that receive the donation. The registration process for entities to qualify as funds and PBOs that are eligible to receive tax subsidies donations is intended also to legitimise philanthropic entities, which in return can foster public trust and financial support for the sector as a whole. This suggests that a key part of a regime that provides tax concessions for philanthropy is a robust system of approval and regulation of philanthropic entities.

Box 4.9. Common avoidance and evasion schemes related to philanthropic giving in New Zealand

Avoidance schemes

- Beneficiary and donors treat payments for goods and/or services as gifts (e.g. private school fees). Such a scheme would allow the 'donor' to receive the goods or services and claim 33% of the price paid as a tax credit on their personal income tax.
- In New Zealand, tax relief for individual donors is limited to gifts of cash. Thus some donors make cash 'gifts' to philanthropic organisations on the understanding that the organisation uses those funds to buy an asset owned by the donor (turning the effective gift of an asset into a gift of cash for tax purposes).
- Donors pay cash 'gifts' to a related charity on the understanding that it is immediately loaned back to the donor, or an associate, for use in its ongoing business activities (the donor claims a tax concession whilst the charity may effectively never have use of the funds).

Evasion schemes

- Fraudulent alteration or manufacturing of donation receipts.
- Using other people's ID to make a fraudulent donation claims.

References

Bullain, N. (2004), "Explaining Percentage Philanthropy: Legal Nature, Rationales, Impacts", *International Journal of Not-for-Profit Law*, Vol. 6/4, https://www.icnl.org/resources/research/ijnl/explaining-percentage-philanthropy-legal-nature-rationales-impacts. [1]

OECD (2009), *Report on abuse of charities for money-laundering and tax evasion*, http://oecd.org/dataoecd/30/20/42232037.pdf. [4]

Strečanský, B. and M. Török (2016), *Assessment of the Impact of the Percentage Tax Designations: Past, Present, Future*, ERSTE Foundation, http://www.erstestiftung.org/en/publication/percentage-tax-designations/. [3]

Urban-Brookings Tax Policy Center (2018), *How did the Tax Cuts and Jobs Act affect incentives for charitable*, https://www.taxpolicycenter.org/briefing-book. [2]

Notes

[1] In the German income tax code, the "total amount of income" (Gesamtbetrag der Einkünfte) is a precisely defined intermediate amount during the assessment process. It roughly refers to taxable income minus related business expenses or entrepreneurial costs, reduced by some special allowances for single parents and retirees.

[2] The TCJA created a 60% contribution limit for gifts of cash until 2026.

[3] Data published by the Slovenian Ministry of Finance. http://edavki.durs.si.

5 The tax treatment of cross-border philanthropy

This chapter examines the tax treatment of cross-border philanthropy. It first considers tax incentives for cross-border giving: both donations and bequests; and also considers how gift and inheritance taxes apply and how capital gains tax might apply where the gift is non-cash. It then considers the tax treatment of philanthropic entities that operate across borders, examining whether tax relief is extended to foreign philanthropic entities operating domestically, and the tax treatment of domestic PBOs operating across borders. Finally, it considers the tax treatment of international grant-making by funds.

5.1. Introduction

This Chapter considers the approach countries adopt in relation to cross-border philanthropy and tax. Cross-border philanthropy can occur where a person (and individual or corporation) makes a gift to an entity in another jurisdiction ('direct philanthropy'). Cross-border philanthropy can also occur where a domestic entity operates in another in another jurisdiction or where a foreign entity operates domestically ('indirect philanthropy'). This Chapter considers the tax treatment of both cross-border giving and cross-border operations by philanthropic entities.

The Chapter considers the extent to which countries provide tax incentives (deductions, rebates or matching) for giving to foreign philanthropic entities, either inter vivos gifts or gifts made on death (bequests). It also considers whether other taxes apply to the making of the gift i.e. gift taxes, inheritance taxes or, if it involves a transfer of property, capital gains taxes. Apart from the position in the European Union (EU) (that extends to countries in the European Economic Area (EEA)), that is governed by rulings of the European Court of Justice (ECJ), there is little tax support in other countries for cross-border giving. The position in the EU requires Member States to adopt a 'comparability' approach to ascertain whether a gift to a philanthropic entity in another Member State is entitled to tax relief. This may require a case-by-case approach to determine eligibility, and due to differences between Member States relating to tax relief, means that relief is not straightforward. There also appears to be less than complete adoption of the position in the ECJ rulings by all Members of the EU. Outside of the EU there are a few cases where there are limited tax incentives for cross-border giving. These limitations have led some philanthropic entities to establish 'work arounds' with entities in various jurisdictions, so that gifts can be made to domestic entities (that are eligible for tax relief) but are then passed on to entities in other countries.

This Chapter also considers whether tax relief is provided to entities that operate across borders – foreign philanthropic entities operating domestically, as well as domestic philanthropic entities operating, wholly or in part, outside the jurisdiction. Apart from the position in the EU, most countries do not provide tax relief for foreign philanthropic entities. The position in the EU is governed by ECJ rulings requiring Member States to adopt a 'comparability' test to determine the eligibility of an entity in another Member State for tax relief, and once again the position is complex. Beyond the EU, there are a few examples of other countries providing tax relief for foreign philanthropic entities on a case-by-case basis. The inability of foreign entities to qualify for tax relief has meant that many entities that operate internationally establish local entities that are eligible for tax relief. Many, but not all, countries provide tax relief to domestic entities that operate abroad, particularly where the activities are related to humanitarian relief or development assistance.

This Chapter proceeds as follows: Part 5.2 considers tax incentives for giving: donations and bequests; and also considers how gift and inheritance taxes apply and also how capital gains tax might apply where the gift is non-cash. Part 5.3 considers the tax treatment of philanthropic entities that operate across borders. This Part considers whether tax relief is extended to foreign philanthropic entities operating within the country, including any conditions that must be met for that tax relief. It then considers domestic PBOs, including domestic PBOs that are branches of international philanthropic entities, operating across borders. It also considers the tax treatment of the making of international grants by funds (grant-making).

5.2. Cross-border giving

Despite fairly widespread use of incentives for domestic philanthropy, the landscape for a more global approach to philanthropy remains fairly guarded. The issues that arise relate to:

- incentives for individuals and corporations for the making of a cross-border donation;
- incentives relating to cross-border bequests; and
- other tax treatment of cross-border donations or bequests e.g. exemptions from gift taxes; inheritance taxes and, where property is disposed of, capital gains tax.

5.2.1. Incentives for cross-border donations

This section gives an overview of the tax incentives for cross-border donations. The focus of the section are the tax incentives that countries may or may not extend to corporate or individual donors that give to a foreign PBO operating abroad. For the majority of countries, cross-border donations are not incentivised as a general principal (see Table 5.1). However, certain specific situations allow for a subsidy, if the foreign entity meets a set of domestic and/or international requirements. This section will cover three different scenarios: donations within the EU/EEA; donations between countries with bilateral tax agreements; and countries with other specific regimes.

Table 5.1. Tax incentives for cross-border donations

Country	Country incentivises cross-border donations
Argentina	No
Australia	No
Austria	Yes, if EU/EEA[1] and countries where administrative cooperation exists
Belgium	Yes, if EU/EEA
Bulgaria	Yes, if EU/EEA
Canada	No, except under DTA
Chile	No
Colombia	No
Czech Republic	Yes, if EU/EEA
Estonia	Yes, if EU/EEA
Finland	Yes, if EU/EEA and entity registered
France	Yes, if EU/EEA
Germany	Yes, if EU/EEA and some connection to Germany
Greece	Yes, if EU/EEA
Hungary	Yes, if EU/EEA (only corporate donors)
India	No
Indonesia	No
Ireland	Yes, if EU/EEA and entity registered
Israel	No, except under DTA
Italy	Yes, if EU/EEA
Japan	No
Latvia	Yes, if EU/EEA and DTA
Lithuania	Yes, if EU/EEA
Luxembourg	Yes, if EU/EEA
Malta	Yes, if EU/EEA and entity registered
Mexico	No, except under DTA
Netherlands	Yes, if entity registered
New Zealand	No, except for specific cases
Norway	Yes, if EU/EEA
Portugal	No (does not comply with ECJ rulings)
Romania	No (does not comply with ECJ rulings)
Singapore	No
Slovak Republic	No (no relief for domestic donations)
Slovenia	Yes, if EU/EEA
South Africa	No
Sweden	Yes, if EU/EEA and entity registered
Switzerland	No[2]
United Kingdom	Yes, if EU/EEA[3]
United States	No, except under DTA

Note:
1. EU' refers to countries that are Members of the European Union. They are Austria, Belgium, Bulgaria, Croatia, Republic of Cyprus, Czech Republic, Denmark, Estonia, Finland, France, Germany, Greece, Hungary, Ireland, Italy, Latvia, Lithuania, Luxembourg, Malta, Netherlands, Poland, Portugal, Romania, the Slovak Republic, Slovenia, Spain and Sweden. 'EEA' refers to the European Economic Area and includes EU countries and also Iceland, Liechtenstein and Norway. It allows them to be part of the EU's single market.
2. In general, as Switzerland is not in the EU, it is not subject to decisions by the ECJ. It may be that Switzerland can benefit from the ECJ ruling for incoming donations based on the principle of free movement of capital that prohibits restrictions on the free movement of capital not only between Member States but also between Member States and third states. Oberson notes that the question whether the same treatment can apply in the other direction, i.e. gift from Switzerland to an institution established in an EU Member State, is less clear: (Oberson, 2015[1]).
3. This may change post-BREXIT.
Source: OECD Taxation and Philanthropy Questionnaire

Apart from the position in the European Union, which applies to all members of the European Economic Agreement (EEA), the general position is that the relief available for donations to domestic philanthropic entities is not available for donations to foreign entities. Most countries limit the tax relief to donations to entities that are 'in', 'formed in', or 'established in' the jurisdiction or have some other connection to the jurisdiction. The nature of the connection required is important in determining whether tax relief is available and is discussed further below. Generally, the rules are the same whether the donor is an individual or a corporation, although Hungary only provides tax relief to corporations and Sweden only provides tax relief to individuals.

There are three situations where tax relief is available for donations to foreign entities: the first involves the Member States of the EU (and EEA) that are subject to rulings of the ECJ. The ECJ has developed a general non-discrimination principle relating to philanthropic giving (see Box 5.1). Second, some countries have bilateral agreements that permit cross-border tax relief. Third, some countries have a process for recognising foreign PBOs in limited circumstances and allowing tax relief for donations to those entities.

EU law

The EU Treaties provide for the free movement of capital between Member States and freedom of establishment. European Community law therefore requires Member States not to discriminate against a gift to a PBO in another Member State. This does not mean a gift to a foreign PBO will automatically benefit from the same treatment as a domestic PBO, it means that the nationality of a PBO is not sufficient to justify a difference of treatment. The ECJ in *Hein Persche v Finanzamt Ludenscheid* [2008] Case 318/07 (14 October 2008) (*Persche's* case), stated that European Community law does not require Member States to automatically acknowledge a foreign charity status when granting tax relief to donations. However, where a taxpayer in one State (in that case Germany) makes a donation to an entity that has philanthropic status in its own State (in that case Portugal), the State of the taxpayer cannot deny the right of equal tax treatment solely because the recipient entity is not resident in its territory. In that case, Mr Persche, a German resident, claimed a deduction from personal income tax for an in-kind donation of bed and bath linen, walking frames, and other equipment. The donation was made in favour of a Portuguese PBO working on a number of social issues including providing care homes for the elderly. The ECJ did not go so far as to require Member States to provide mutual recognition of philanthropic entities, but rather required Member States to accord tax benefits when there was 'comparability', and in this case Germany had not considered whether the Portuguese PBO satisfied such a test. Following this, and other ECJ cases, the burden is on the taxpayer to prove that the entity would be entitled to tax relief in the Member State in question but for its establishment elsewhere; and if the taxpayer can prove this the authority must consider the evidence presented.

Almost all Member States have amended their legislation and/or procedures to recognise donations to comparable or similar entities in other Member States. A number of Member States assess comparability on a case-by-case basis which is often a time-consuming and costly exercise for taxpayers, including the requirement to provide translations of relevant documents. This approach typically requires individual donors to obtain approval, often from a regional authority, in each case; no record is retained, and no precedent is established. This is the case in Belgium, Bulgaria, Czech Republic, Estonia, Germany, Hungary, Latvia, Lithuania and the Slovak Republic, although in Belgium it is possible to obtain a Ruling that the foreign entity is comparable from the central authority. Other Member States require the philanthropic entity to demonstrate comparability and/or be registered in that State as well as in their home jurisdiction. This is the case in Austria, Finland, Ireland, Malta, Netherlands, Norway and Sweden. This approach has the advantage that once registered, other donors can rely on the registered status to support the tax relief. However, due to the difficulties of establishing comparability, very few entities are registered under this approach.

Determining whether a gift to a foreign entity is comparable is problematic because of the diversity of approaches to the question of tax relief for donations in the Member States. Differences between the jurisdictions that might be relevant include whether the gift is money or in-kind (Finland and Portugal only provide tax relief for cash donations) and whether the donor is an individual or corporation (as noted above, Hungary only provides relief for corporations and Sweden only provides relief for individuals). There may also be differences related to the eligibility of the entity: whether it is a PBO or a fund and the nature of its purposes (Austria, Germany, Finland, Malta and Romania have more limited purposes), how monies are disbursed including on overheads (Austria, Belgium, Estonia, Latvia and Lithuania all restrict the expenditure on 'overheads' in different ways). There are also differences relating to directors' remuneration (most countries prohibit payments to board members, but Sweden does not), whether the entity engages in activities abroad (Germany imposes restrictions) and on timely disbursement of funds (Portugal and Sweden impose specific time limits while others require the monies to be expended in a 'reasonable period').

Some Member States impose additional requirements on foreign entities. For example, Latvia only provides relief in relation to Member States with which it has a Double Tax Agreement. The German tax legislation also requires that the activities of all philanthropic entities 'either have to support individuals which have their permanent residence in Germany, or the activities could benefit Germany's reputation'.

The Netherlands is the most open of the countries responding. The Netherlands makes no distinction between domestic and foreign entities, whether from the EU/EEA or elsewhere. Providing the entity can satisfy the requirements of the tax law, they are entitled to be registered and donors can claim deductions. These entities must be comparable and satisfy other requirements such as integrity requirements, to demonstrate that those involved with the entity are 'fit and proper persons'.

Finally, it should be noted that some Member States (Portugal, Romania and the Slovak Republic) do not comply with the ECJ rulings.

Bilateral agreements

The second situation in which a donation may obtain tax relief when made to a foreign PBO is where there has been a bilateral agreement between countries to provide such relief. This is the case for the United States that has such agreements with Canada, Mexico and Israel. A similar provision applies in the treaties between the Netherlands and Barbados and between Mexico and Barbados.

The US-Canada tax treaty (1980) provides for limited cross-border deductions in certain circumstances. Article XXI allows US donors to deduct gifts to Canadian 'registered charities', subject to US percentage limitations, *but the deduction can only be offset against Canadian-source income.* The treaty also allows US donors a deduction against their US-source income for donations to Canadian colleges and universities attended by the donor or a member of the donor's family (again, subject to US percentage limitations). The treaty also provides for reciprocal charitable credit for gifts by Canadian residents to US tax exempt organisations that could qualify in Canada as 'registered charities' if they were Canadian organisations *but the deduction can only be claimed against US-source income*, (subject to Canadian percentage limitations). Gifts to US colleges or universities attended by the donor or a member of the donor's family are creditable against Canadian-source income (again, subject to Canadian percentage limitations).

A further issue is whether the Canadian charity will be treated as a private foundation or a public charity under US law – as these types of entities have different percentage limits i.e. the deductible donation is limited to a maximum of 50% of the donor's adjusted gross income for public charities or 30% for private foundations. A Protocol to the US-Canada treaty recognises that Canadian law governing tax exempt status is materially equivalent to US law governing charities. Under the Protocol, the public charity status of a Canadian entity is now recognised by the United States, without a separate determination by the IRS or a requirement to lodge financial information by the Canadian entity, and vice versa.

The US-Mexico tax treaty (1992), also contains provisions allowing deductions for cross-border charitable gifts. Article XXII of the treaty allows income tax deductions to US donors for contributions to Mexican charities. The deductions are allowed *only with respect to Mexican-source* income and are subject to US percentage limitations. Mexican donors are allowed reciprocal deductions *only against US-source income* (subject to Mexican percentage limitations) for contributions to US charities. The responsibility for determining public charity status resides with the taxing authority of the nation in which the charity is organised. Although the deduction is limited to particular sources of income, the status of the foreign charity is recognised.

The US-Israel tax treaty (1995), Article 15-A, permits US donors to deduct contributions to Israeli charities *against their Israeli-source income*, but only if the Israeli charity would have qualified for tax exemption under US law had it been established there (a comparability test). The deduction is capped at 25% of Israeli-source 'adjusted gross' income for individual donors and 25% of *Israeli-source taxable income* for corporate donors. Israeli donors are permitted a reciprocal deduction against *US-source income* for contributions to US charities that would qualify for tax exemption under Israeli law if organised there. The deduction is limited to 25% of US-source taxable income.

Another example of bilateral relief can be found in The Netherlands- Barbados Tax Treaty (2006), and in the Mexico-Barbados Income Tax Treaty (2008). Article 22 of The Netherlands-Barbados Treaty provides that a contribution by a resident of State A to a charity in State B is deductible in State A where the competent authority of State A agrees that the entity qualifies as a charity in State A (i.e. it satisfies a comparability test). The Mexico-Barbados Treaty provides that a resident of State A can claim a deduction for a contribution to an entity that is a qualifying charity in State B. The competent authority in State A can consult with the competent authority in State B to ensure that the entity is qualified in State B (that is, there is mutual recognition).

The inclusion of a provision on charitable donations seems to be part of the tax treaty policy of Barbados. A similar provision on donations to charitable institutions is included in article 21 of the Barbados-Seychelles Income and Capital Tax Treaty (2007), Article 22 of the Barbados-Mauritius Income Tax Treaty (2004), and Article 23 of the Barbados-Ghana Income Tax Treaty (2008).

Specific recognition

There are also a few examples of countries that have a process for providing tax relief for gifts to approved foreign PBOs in limited circumstances, namely Canada and New Zealand. In Canada, a tax credit is available (to an individual) for a gift to a 'qualified donee'. This generally means a registered charity, that is, a charity that is created in and resident in Canada. However, a foreign entity can become a qualified donee if it is:

- a university outside Canada, the student body of which ordinarily includes students from Canada, that has applied for registration by the Minister, or
- a foreign charity that has applied to the Minister for registration. The Minister may register, in consultation with the Minister of Finance, a foreign charity for a 24-month period that includes the time at which Her Majesty in right of Canada has made a gift to the foreign charity, if the Minister is satisfied that the foreign charity is:

  (i) carrying on relief activities in response to a disaster;

  (ii) providing urgent humanitarian aid; or

  (iii) carrying on activities in the national interest of Canada.

  There are currently only 4 approved foreign charities.

New Zealand also has a process for foreign PBOs to become approved donees. In such a case, an application is made to the Minister through the Inland Revenue Department (IRD) for approval and inclusion on a list in Schedule 32 of the *Income Tax Act 2007* (NZ). The criterion for approval is that the money received must go towards at least one of these things:

- relieving poverty, hunger, sickness, damages from war or natural disaster;
- the economy of developing countries recognised by the United Nations; or
- raising the educational standards of a developing country recognised by the United Nations.

Charities are specifically excluded from being listed if they form to foster or administer any religion, cult or political creed. There are currently approximately 120 listed charities.

The non-recognition of a foreign philanthropic entity does not preclude a foreign entity establishing an entity or branch in the other jurisdiction. Where an entity is set up in one country but will perform some or all of its activities in another country, the issue will be whether a domestic entity is allowed to undertake activities abroad. This is considered in Part 5.3.2.

Finally, it should be noted that in those countries such as the Slovak Republic, that do not provide tax relief for donations to domestic PBOs, such relief does not apply to cross-border donations.

Box 5.1. Cross-border philanthropy in the European Union regulatory framework

Emergence of a non-discrimination principle

Historically, EU Member States did not grant tax privileges to foreign PBOs. Indeed, the general rule was that tax incentives were restricted to domestic PBOs and donors giving to domestic PBOs. However, this regulatory framework was overhauled by a series of judgements by the European Court of Justice (ECJ).

Between 2005 and 2011, these judgements developed a general non-discrimination principle as regards to tax law in the area of public-benefit activities. It has set the below-mentioned rules for Member States.

Design of the non-discrimination principle

It is at the discretion of Member States whether or not they wish to provide tax privileges for PBOs and their donors (1). Similarly, Member States are in principle free in determining the relevant conditions and requirements. Among admissible conditions, Member States may theoretically limit the beneficiary circle of PBOs' activities to domestic citizens or persons living within the domestic territory (2). There is also no obligation of automatically granting a PBO status to an entity recognised as a PBO in another country (3)

However, limits to the Member States regulatory powers are established by the fundamental freedoms of the Treaty on the Functioning of the EU. Indeed, Member States may not exclude a foreign EU-based PBOs and their donors from eligibility for tax privileges if they fulfil all requirements for domestic PBOs (4). Moreover, it is not permitted that a Member State requires a PBO to undertake its philanthropic activities solely in its jurisdiction in order to benefit from a preferential tax treatment (unless there are compelling objective reasons for this). For example, Member States may not restrict tax benefits for donations strictly to domestic universities or laboratories (5)

Member States should carry out a comparability test to determine whether a foreign EU-based PBO meets the requirements of national tax law. Such tests are to be carried out by the national authorities and courts of the Member State concerned. (6). While conducting the comparability test, Member States may ask that a foreign EU-based PBO provides any document useful for the carrying out of the test (7).

Note: (1) ECJ, 27. 1. 2009 - C-318/07 (Hein Persche/Finanzamt Lüdenscheid). (2) ECJ, Stauffer, paras. 37f., 57, Missionswerk, para. 30 (3) ECJ Stauffer, para. 39; Persche, para. 48. (4) ECJ, Persche, para. 46, Missionswerk, paras. 30-31. (5) ECJ, Laboratoires Fournier, para. 23; or Commission/Austria, paras. 35-38 (6) ECJ, Persche, para. 49, Missionswerk, paras. 33-34. (7) ECJ, Persche, paras. 53-58.

5.2.2. Incentives for cross-border bequests

This section summarises the tax treatment of bequests to foreign PBOs (also referred to as cross-border bequests). Although a number of countries did not provide information on this issue, Table 5.2 suggests that countries that grant tax incentives to domestic philanthropic bequests also incentivise cross-border bequests to PBOs, although exceptions exist. These are predominantly members of the EU, and the responses indicate that the same comparability requirements that apply for donations would apply to bequests.

Table 5.2. Tax incentives for cross-border bequests

Country	Countries incentivise domestic and cross-border philanthropic bequests
Australia	No (but CGT relief available)
Austria	Yes
Belgium	Yes
Bulgaria	Yes if EC/EEA
Canada	Yes (limited)
France	Yes, if EU/EEA
Japan	Yes
Netherlands	Yes
Norway	Yes
Slovenia	Yes
United Kingdom	Yes (limited)
United States	Yes

Source: OECD Taxation and Philanthropy

Canada states that in limited circumstances a cross-border bequest is possible. This would apply where the bequest is to a foreign universities or foreign charities approved under the *Income Tax Act 2007* (Can) (discussed above) or where the US-Canada tax treaty provides comparable tax relief.

The survey asked whether different rules applied for bequests to funds rather than PBOs. There were no differences indicated.

5.2.3. Gift tax, inheritance tax and capital gains tax

This section provides an overview of other taxes that countries may levy upon cross-border giving. The taxes covered are gift taxes, inheritance/estate taxes and capital gains taxes. Although the approaches differ across countries, the majority of countries do not levy taxes on cross-border giving (see Table 5.3). Finally, this section provides examples of countries that do levy the before listed taxes on cross-border giving.

Many countries (22) do not levy gift taxes or inheritance taxes. In some countries that do not levy such taxes, a disposal of property could give rise to capital gains tax (5) or stamp duty (1).

The US provides an exemption from gift duty (s 2522(a) of the *Internal Revenue Code*) and from inheritance tax (s 2055(a) of the *Internal Revenue Code*) for donations and bequests that could apply to gifts to foreign PBOs.

European countries that do impose such taxes generally noted that an exemption may be available to other Member States, presumably on the basis of comparability. This is supported by the case of *Missionswerk Werner Heukelbach eV v Belgium* [2011] Case 25/2010,10 February 2011 (*Missionwerk* case). Missionswerk was a religious association and PBO registered in Germany. Mrs R, a Belgian citizen, who had lived her whole life in Belgium, died in 2004 in Belgium, having left her estate to Missionswerk. The

Belgian regional tax authority applied inheritance tax at a rate of 80% on the amount Missionswerk was to receive. Missionswerk sought to have the reduced tax rate of 7% applied instead, which was the rate applied for legacies to resident PBOs. The Belgian tax authority rejected the request for the application of the reduced tax rate on the grounds that it was only to be applied to foreign EU-based PBOs in cases where the testator had lived or worked in the country in which the foreign entity was based. The ECJ ruled that legacies are protected under the free movement of capital and that a restriction on tax incentives would be permissible only in the case that the German PBO was not comparable to a Belgian PBO. The *Missionwerk* case means that revenue authorities in Member States are at least obliged to apply the comparability test – the practical difficulties of applying the comparability test, including that some States assess comparability on a case-by-case basis, have been discussed above.

Table 5.3. Cross-border giving and gift taxes, inheritance tax, and capital gains tax (CGT)

Country	Gift Tax	Inheritance tax	Exemption	Other taxes
Argentina	No	No		
Australia	No	No		disposals of assets may be subject to CGT
Austria	No	No		
Belgium	No	Yes	may be exempt including within EU/EEA	
Bulgaria	Yes	Yes	may be exempt including within EU/EEA	
Canada	No	No		disposals of assets may be subject to CGT
Chile	Yes	Yes		
Colombia	No	No		disposals of assets may be subject to CGT
Czech Republic	No	No		
Estonia	No	No		
Finland	Yes	Yes	may be exempt including within EU/EEA	
France	Yes	Yes	may be exempt including within EU/EEA	
Germany	Yes	Yes	may be exempt including within EU/EEA	
Greece	Yes	Yes	lower rate for PBOs, including within EU/EEA	
Hungary	Yes	Yes		
Indonesia	No	No		
Ireland	No	Yes	may be exempt including within EU/EEA	
Israel	No	No		disposal of assets may be subject to CGT
Italy	Yes	Yes	May be exempt including within EU/EEA	
Japan	No	No		
Latvia	No	No		
Lithuania	No	No		
Malta	No	No		may be stamp duty
Mexico	No	No		
Netherlands	Yes	Yes	may be exempt if entity registered	
New Zealand	No	No		
Norway	No	No		
Portugal	No	No		
Romania	No	No		
Singapore	No	No		
Slovak Republic	No	No		disposals of assets may be subject to CGT
Slovenia	Yes	Yes	may be exempt including within EU/EEA	
South Africa	Yes	Yes		
Sweden	No	No		
Switzerland	Yes	Yes		
United Kingdom	No	Yes	may be exempt within EU/EEA	
United States	Yes	Yes	exemptions available	

Source: OECD Taxation and Philanthropy Questionnaire

Three countries appear have a gift tax or inheritance tax that might be imposed on the making of a donation or bequest to a foreign PBO: Switzerland, Greece, and South Africa. In Switzerland, in most cantons, gifts and bequests by Swiss residents in favour of foreign resident PBOs are subject to gift and inheritance taxes, unless a 'reciprocity declaration is concluded with the country where the foreign charity is registered. Almost all Swiss cantons have so-called reciprocity declarations with France, and some of them with the US, Germany and Israel. Greece taxes bequests and donations to philanthropic entities at a lower rate, including where the entity is within the EU/EEA. In South Africa, the bequest is taxed in the hands of the recipient, so a foreign recipient may be beyond the reach of the domestic taxing authorities.

In countries that do not impose gift tax or inheritance tax, a donation or bequest that takes the form of a disposal of property may be subject to CGT. This is the case in Australia, Canada, Colombia, Israel and the Slovak Republic. Malta indicated that stamp duty may be payable on the disposal.

5.3. Cross-border treatment of PBOs and funds

This section considers the tax treatment of philanthropic entities that operate across borders. This includes the tax treatment of foreign philanthropic entities engaging in activities in another country. It also includes domestic PBOs carrying out activities in other countries and funds transferring assets or, more commonly, making grants to PBOs or other entities in other countries. Although most countries do not provide tax preferences for foreign philanthropic entities, many countries do permit domestic tax-preferred entities to operate abroad in various situations.

5.3.1. Tax treatment of foreign PBOs

This section analyses the tax treatment of foreign PBOs that engage in activities domestically. An entity that was granted a PBO status in one country may engage in activities in another jurisdiction, which raises numerous tax questions related to the treatment of income arising from domestic sources. The section focuses on the following issues: the extension of the PBO status granted abroad, the test applied by domestic jurisdictions allowing for a preferential treatment of domestic income received by the foreign entity and the taxation of these incomes in cases where the foreign entity fails to meet domestic requirements

Table 5.4 shows whether countries provide preferential tax treatment to foreign PBOs operating domestically. Most European countries treat comparable philanthropic entities within EU/EEA in the same way as domestic entities. The requirement to accord comparable treatment arises from the ruling of the ECJ in *Centro di Musicologia Walter Stauffer v Finanzamt München für Körperschaften* [2006] Case-386/04, 14 September 2006 (*Stauffer's* case). In that case, an Italian philanthropic entity awarded scholarships to young people from Switzerland, particularly those from Bern, to pursue studies in music. The entity owned a building in Germany from which it obtained rental income. Under German tax law this type of income was exempt from corporate tax for domestic philanthropic entities. However, the exemption was said to not be available to foreign philanthropic entities. The ECJ stated that European Community law does not require Member States to automatically acknowledge a foreign charity status. However, where an entity that has philanthropic status in its own State (in that case Italy), also satisfies the requirements in another State (in that case Germany), the Member State cannot deny that entity the right of equal tax treatment solely because it is not resident in its territory. The operation of the comparability test to cross-border donations and cross-border bequests has already been noted. Philanthropic entities deriving income in another Member State will need to satisfy the revenue authorities in the source jurisdiction as to comparability and this can be complex and costly. Three Member States, Ireland, Malta and The Netherlands, require registration of the relevant foreign PBO. The Netherlands is the most generous of all countries as it permits entities from any country to register provided it meets the eligibility requirements in the legislation. Belgium allows the foreign PBO to assess whether it is exempt from corporate tax on one of two criteria. The first criterion is that the PBO does not carry out operations of a for-profit nature. The exemption based on this criterion can be claimed by both domestic and foreign PBOs. The second criterion (which may enable a wider exemption) is that the PBO belongs to one of the privileged sectors enumerated by Article 181 of the *Income Tax Code* (for instance, education). However, this basis for exemption is only applicable to domestic PBOs.

A large number of countries (16) indicated that they did not provide tax concessions to foreign PBOs, including some Member States of the EU.

Table 5.4. Preferential tax treatment of foreign PBOs

Country	Country provides preferential tax treatment to foreign PBO
Argentina	No
Australia	Generally no, but may obtain approval
Austria	Yes, if within EU/EEA and countries where administrative cooperation exists
Belgium	Yes, if within EU/EEA but only for one of two alternative grounds
Bulgaria	Yes
Canada	Foreign charities are not exempt; foreign NPOs may be
Chile	No
Colombia	No
Czech Republic	Yes, if within EU/EEA
Estonia	No
Finland	Yes, if within EU/EEA
France	Yes, if within EU/EEA
Germany	Yes, if within EU/EEA
Greece	Yes, if within EU/EEA
Hungary	Yes, if within EU/EEA
India	No
Indonesia	Some foreign PBOs may be recognised
Ireland	Yes, if within EU/EEA but must be registered
Israel	No
Italy	Yes, within EU/EEA
Japan	No
Latvia	No
Lithuania	Yes, if within EU/EEA
Luxembourg	Yes, if within EU/EEA
Malta	Yes, if within EU/EEA but must be registered
Mexico	No
Netherlands	Yes, must be registered
New Zealand	Generally no, but may obtain approval
Norway	Yes, if within EU/EEA
Portugal	No
Romania	No
Singapore	No
Slovak Republic	No
Slovenia	Yes, if within EU/EEA
South Africa	No
Sweden	Yes, if within EU/EEA
Switzerland	No
United Kingdom	Yes, if within EU/EEA
United States	No

Source: OECD Questionnaire on Taxation and Philanthropy

The remaining countries had some limited arrangements for recognition of foreign PBOs. For example, Indonesia has an arrangement that involves some foreign PBOs being granted a permit by the Central Government (see Box 5.2). Canada allows a foreign PBO to qualify as a 'non-profit organisation' if it meets the conditions under the legislation, specifically that it is not a charity and that it is organised and operated for social welfare, civic improvement, pleasure, sport, recreation, or any other purpose except profit. If it qualifies as a non-profit organisation its income will generally not be subject to tax but unlike a registered charity, it is not eligible to receive tax preferred donations. In Australia, a small number of foreign PBOs are approved by regulation as income tax exempt (but not as deductible gift recipients). The New Zealand revenue has the ability to approve foreign entities as tax charities, which means that they can become approved donees (see Part 5.2.1) and also eligible for tax exempt status. It is however necessary to have a strong connection with New Zealand, meet the requirements for registered charities, apart from residency and demonstrate that they are eligible for charity tax concessions in their home jurisdiction. This approval and inclusion on a list in Schedule 32 of the Income Tax Act 2007 means the foreign entity will be able to derive non-business income (i.e. passive investment income) and not be subject to income tax. They will, however, be subject to income tax on any business income in New Zealand if all of their charitable purposes are carried out overseas. As noted above there are currently approximately 120 listed foreign charities.

South Africa notes that foreign PBOs may establish 'branches' and the United States, allows the establishment of entities that are closely aligned with foreign PBOs e.g. as 'friends of' a foreign PBO (these types of entities are discussed in Part 5.3.2).

To the extent that a foreign PBO does not qualify as a tax-exempt entity, it would likely be taxed as a corporation. As a result of these limitations, many philanthropic entities establish separate entities in each jurisdiction to take advantage of the tax concessions available to domestic entities (see Part 5.3.2).

Box 5.2. Foreign PBOs operating in Indonesia

In Indonesia, a PBO status issued by another country will be verified by relevant ministries before the PBO gets an approval to operate in Indonesia. Foreign PBOs must obtain a **principal permit** and an **operational permit** from the Central Government

Obtaining of principal permit

- The country issuing the PBO status has diplomatic relations with Indonesia
- The PBO has a non-profit principle and worthy purpose

Obtaining an operational permit

- The PBO needs a principle permit from the central government
- It also need a written agreement with relevant ministries/ government agencies according to its operational field.
- An annual work-plan with the relevant regional government is required

Source: Government Regulation No. 93 Year 2010

5.3.2. Tax treatment of PBOs that operate abroad

This section provides an overview of the tax rules concerning domestic PBOs engaging in activities abroad. Preferential tax treatment is usually granted to a PBO's domestic activity and thus PBOs with activities abroad may risk losing its preferential tax status. In most cases however, responding countries allow a domestic PBO to conduct activities abroad. Typically, this authorisation is reliant upon the respect of worthy purpose requirements imposed by the national legislation, usually similar to requirements imposed to domestic PBOs. This forces the imposition of strong documentation requirements for PBOs in order to respect the national criteria. Some countries allow these requirements to be lifted in certain specific cases, such as the occurrence of a natural disaster or humanitarian crises.

The question is, of course, concerned with what the tax provisions have to say about operating overseas. There may in addition be other requirements or restrictions on cross-border financial flows or activities. For example, most countries have regulations aimed at illicit financial flows and anti-money laundering, including following FATF recommendations about not permitting monies to be transferred to high-risk countries.[1] Many countries also have regulations aimed at foreign interference, including restrictions on contributions to political parties (Canada, United States) and in some cases restrictions on contributions to philanthropic entities (Hungary, India, and Israel). There may also be restrictions on fundraising, both domestically and internationally, that restrict the ability of philanthropic entities to operate abroad. For example, in Singapore, if funds are raised from the public, a permit is required, and the applicant has to apply at least 80% of the net proceeds of the funds raised within Singapore (and the donations will not be tax-deductible). The rule may be waived for private donations or for appeals in aid of providing immediate disaster relief. These non-tax restrictions may affect the ability of philanthropic donor or entities to transfer funds or engage in activities in other countries.

Most countries provide tax support to domestic PBOs to carry out activities in another country (see Table 5.5). Most countries indicated that the requirements for approval were the same for entities that carried out their activities abroad as those that operated domestically. Some countries indicated that there may be restrictions relating to purpose and some countries impose additional reporting requirements when PBOs operate abroad. It is also important to consider how philanthropic entities can permit donors to support overseas activities ('indirect philanthropy').

Purpose requirements

Countries that do allow domestic PBOs to engage in such activity typically require the PBO to meet the domestic worthy purpose requirement. For example, 17 countries indicated that the same purposes were relevant whether the entity would be operating domestically or overseas. In some other countries, the relevant purpose must be related to assistance for developing countries or to assistance following disasters. For example, the Slovak Republic notes that a donation for material humanitarian aid provided abroad is a deductible tax expense for the donor, if donated through the Ministry of Interior of the Slovak Republic (s 19(2)(u) of the *Income Tax Act* No 595/2003 as amended). Presumably such donations are tax exempt in the Slovak Republic. In Australia, a registered charity can establish a 'developing country relief fund' if the Foreign Affairs Minister has declared the country to be a 'developing country' and has approved the entity. There is also a provision for the Minister to recognise a 'disaster', including in countries other than developing countries, if the disaster develops rapidly and results in death, serious injury or other physical suffering of a large number of people, or in widespread damage to property or the natural environment. In India, if a charitable trust derives income from property held for a charitable purpose which 'tends to promote international welfare in which India is interested' and is applied to such purposes outside India, the income is exempt, subject to special approval processes.

In the case of natural disasters and humanitarian crises, some countries note special arrangements. For example, in Canada, the Canada Revenue Agency (CRA) has indicated that following a natural disaster, such as an earthquake or flood, many organisations want to provide immediate assistance and relief to those affected, and as a result, the CRA often receives applications from such organisations seeking to be registered. The CRA has indicated that it will typically assign priority to these applications. In Germany, in cases of natural disasters or humanitarian crisis the tax administration may publish a catastrophe decree ('Katastrophenerlass'). These decrees allow entities with preferential tax treatment to collect donations for worthy purposes not set out in their constitutions. In Indonesia, the government permits tax relief for natural disasters, although it is not clear whether the disaster must be within Indonesia or whether it could be in some other country (Government Regulation No. 93 Year 2010). In New Zealand, a domestic registered charity must apply 75% of its funds within New Zealand, allowing up to 25% to be devoted to charitable purposes outside New Zealand. The Inland Revenue Department (IRD) indicates that if the figure is below 75% in any year, the cumulative total of its funds applied over the current and preceding two years can be used for the purposes of determining whether a tax credit or deduction is available. This allows some year-on-year variation for exceptional years, for example in response to natural disasters: IRD Interpretation Statement 18/05. Importantly the 75% requirement does not apply to foreign charities listed under Sched 32 of the Income Tax Act 2007 (see Part 5.3.1).

Table 5.5. Domestic PBOs allowed to carry out activities abroad

Country	Country permits PBOs to carry out activities abroad
Argentina	Yes
Australia	Yes+
Austria	Yes
Belgium	Yes
Bulgaria	Yes
Canada	Yes+
Chile	Yes
Colombia	Yes
Estonia	Yes
Finland	Yes
France	Yes
Germany	Yes+
Greece	Yes
Hungary	Yes
India	Yes+
Indonesia	Yes+
Ireland	Yes
Israel	Yes
Italy	Yes+
Latvia	No
Lithuania	Yes
Luxembourg	Yes+
Malta	Yes
Mexico	No
Netherlands	Yes
New Zealand	Yes+
Norway	Yes
Portugal	Yes
Romania	No
Singapore	Yes+
Slovak Republic	Yes+
Slovenia	Yes
South Africa	Yes
Sweden	Yes
Switzerland	Yes+
United Kingdom	Yes
United States	Yes

Source: OECD Taxation and Philanthropy Questionnaire
Note: Yes+ indicates that there are additional requirements that must be satisfied or restrictions. These are discussed below.

Additional requirements

Another group of countries, namely Australia, Canada, New Zealand and Switzerland, require the domestic entity to meet the specified worthy purpose but also to satisfy additional reporting requirements (documentation, justification of activity, proof of control of the activity abroad etc.). For example, in Australia domestic entities will only be approved to engage in activities abroad, whether on their own or in partnership with in-country entities, if they can demonstrate that the entity's focus is on supporting development and/or humanitarian assistance activities in developing countries (under the Overseas Aid Gift Deduction scheme); that they have the capacity to manage and deliver overseas aid activities and that they have appropriate safeguards in place to manage risks associated with child protection and terrorism. Some other philanthropic entities that pursue activities abroad may be eligible for income tax exemption provided that the entity has a physical presence in Australia and 'pursues its objectives and incurs its expenditure principally in Australia'. This does not mean that the beneficiaries must be in Australia. The requirement in Canada that to be tax exempt, the PBO must carry on its activities itself, does not prevent the PBO from entering into contracts with local providers or appointing a local agent, but it is important that the domestic entity retains direction and control over any intermediaries. Switzerland notes that there must be suitable documentation for activities abroad.

In Luxembourg, a PBO can carry out activities abroad as long as it does not do so exclusively and its main activities are domestic. If the PBO has a non-government organisation status (which is authorised by the Ministry of Foreign and European Affairs), it is able to carry out activities abroad more extensively.

In Italy, domestic PBOs can carry out activities abroad only if related to humanitarian aid. If a PBO gives funds abroad, the allocation is allowed only for a humanitarian purpose. In such a case, the domestic entity has to comply with additional accounting requirements, with reference to the accountability of the foreign beneficiary entity/institution and with reference to how the funds will be spent.

A few countries, such as Singapore and Romania, indicated that they do not provide tax relief to domestic PBOs that engage in activities beyond the borders of the country, although it appears that they may permit certain international philanthropic entities such as the Red Cross, World Vision or Oxfam to operate with tax relief available.

Indirect philanthropy

The restrictions on tax relief for foreign philanthropic entities, but widespread acceptance of domestic entities operating overseas, means that donors wishing to support overseas causes need to find a suitable domestic entity to make donations to. From the perspective of the philanthropic entity, there are essentially two models available for entities to raise funds in one jurisdiction and spend money or carry out activities in another jurisdiction:

- the separate entity model; or
- use of an intermediary.

Separate entity model

An entity that seeks tax-preferred status in a particular jurisdiction, perhaps with a view to fundraising in that jurisdiction, but carrying out activities in another jurisdiction, may set up a domestic PBO. The entity will, of course need to comply with the tax and other requirements of that jurisdiction. There are two types of this model – the international PBO and the specific purpose PBO.

Many international organisations, sometimes referred to as International Non-Government Organisations (INGOs), establish separate entities in different countries e.g. Red Cross, CARE, Amnesty International, Greenpeace, World Vision, Oxfam and Médecins Sans Frontiere, because of the inability to make tax-preferred gifts to foreign PBOs or for a foreign PBO to obtain tax relief. For example, there are 192 national

Red Cross societies carrying out the work of the international Red Cross movement. The critical point is that the funds are to be used in a foreign country by a domestic entity as opposed to being donated to and used by a foreign entity.

Another type of cross-border PBO will typically relate to a particular purpose, perhaps an educational or arts-related purpose in another jurisdiction, but because of the inability of donors to obtain tax relief for cross border donations, the PBO will establish a separate entity in jurisdictions where potential donors may be located. For example, there are a number of entities in the US that support various museums and art galleries e.g. the Tate, Museo del Prado and the Rijksmuseum. There are also entities that support educational institutions, such as The University of Oxford – including in the US, Canada, Switzerland, Germany and Australia. In some countries the entity might be referred to as a 'branch' or 'affiliate' of the foreign entity, but will be treated as a separate domestic entity for tax purposes. Some entities will simply adopt a name that reflects the purpose e.g. the Oxford Australia Scholarship Fund. The US has a tradition of allowing US taxpayers to support overseas PBOs through a 'Friends of' PBO e.g. American Friends of Oxford University, and this nomenclature has now been adopted in Switzerland (Swiss Friends of Oxford) and Germany (German Friends of Oxford). South Africa permits a foreign organisation that is incorporated, formed or established in a country outside South Africa, which is exempt from income tax in that other country to obtain tax relief as a PBO. The critical point in each of these cases is that it is a domestic entity (and so subject to regulatory oversight) that will generate monies that will be passed onto the foreign entity in accordance with the stated purposes.

Use of intermediaries

An increasingly common phenomena is the use of intermediaries to transfer funds to a foreign PBO. A donor may be able to make a donation to a domestic PBO or fund that is authorised to make grants to foreign PBOs. It is likely that such entities will have to satisfy various requirements to be able to make grants overseas (see Part 5.3.3) and will need to have some oversight of the spending of the monies. Examples of intermediaries that operate in this way include the Charities Aid Foundation (CAF), Global Giving, Transnational Giving Europe and the King Baudouin Foundation.

Where a local intermediary is used to direct monies from donors to a nominated foreign PBO, the donation will get the benefit of domestic tax relief and the monies will be applied abroad in accordance with the donors' wishes. In some cases, the intermediary may allow the donor to have an account (sometimes called a 'Donor Advised Account') and have some say about how the monies are to be applied. The domestic PBO or fund agrees to act as a 'conduit' and pass on donations to nominated foreign PBOs. This will typically generate a fee for the entity acting as a conduit (which is likely to be treated as business income of the recipient intermediary). For example, Transnational Giving Europe charges a fee equivalent to 5% of the donation up to EUR 100 000 and 1% above this, capped at a maximum fee of EUR 15 000.

Some countries have restrictions on philanthropic entities acting as conduits. For example, in Canada a PBO is required to carry on its charitable activities itself. If the purpose of a PBO was to raise funds for another entity, the PBO would not be entitled to registration as a charity. A Canadian foundation can make grants to other entities, but the entity would need to be a qualified donee. However, a Canadian PBO may enter in contracts with foreign entities, provided that the domestic entity ensures that the funds are applied for philanthropic or charitable purposes by the foreign PBO. This imposes an obligation on the PBO to take 'reasonable steps' to ensure that the funds are applied appropriately.

In some countries, the earmarking of a contribution by a donor for a particular entity or project may impact on the tax relief. For example, In the United Kingdom, tax reliefs are not available if the charity makes payments overseas unless the charity takes reasonable steps to ensure that the funds remitted overseas are not only intended for use for a purpose that would qualify as a charitable purpose according to UK law, but that the funds are in fact so used. Simply passing on monies to another entity is unlikely to satisfy this requirement. In the US, a donor cannot deduct a contribution made to a qualifying philanthropic entity if the contribution is directed to go to a foreign PBO (or some other entity). However, it may be possible to express a preference, rather than a direction, as to how the monies are to be used. In the US, the qualified entity must approve the program as furthering its own exempt purposes and must keep control over the use of the contributed funds. Simply passing on monies would not suffice. However, where the foreign entity is an administrative arm of the qualified US entity, a deduction will be available.

5.3.3. International grant-making

This section provides an overview of rules concerning international grant-making. Indeed, donations of assets or grants to foreign PBOs by a fund can have tax implications. While some countries support this form of cross-border giving, others may withdraw the tax-preferred status if grants are made to foreign PBOs.

Some countries indicated that funds were able to make grants to PBOs in other countries without losing their tax preferred status. The relevant countries are Austria, Belgium, Bulgaria[2], Germany, Ireland, Malta, the Netherlands, Sweden and the US.

Although many countries have funds that make international grants, the US is home to some of the largest funds making such grants and accounts for a significant proportion of grants worldwide. According to a report by COF and Foundation Centre in 2018, 'The State of Global Giving by US Foundations', covering the period 2011-2015, private US foundations give around USD10 billion a year to organisations that work on social and environmental problems outside of the country, particularly in Africa, South Asia, and other low-income parts of the world. Since the early 2000s, international grant-making has increased from about 14 to about 30 percent of all foundation giving in the US, which itself has grown dramatically. Half of international giving comes from the Bill & Melinda Gates Foundation; the remainder is from other large foundations, which might be either independent, community, corporate or operating foundations. According to the report, the top 10 international grant-makers are:

1. Bill & Melinda Gates Foundation
2. The Susan Thompson Buffett Foundation
3. Ford Foundation
4. Foundation to Promote Open Society
5. The William and Flora Hewlett Foundation
6. Walton Family Foundation
7. The Rockefeller Foundation
8. The David and Lucile Packard Foundation
9. Open Society Institute
10. Silicon Valley Community Foundation

There are different types of recipients of these types of grants. Foundations may seek to build relationships with governments; or to support international NGOs or develop relationships with in-country NGOs (often referred to as 'local partners'). The Council on Foundations and the Foundation Centre found that about 88% of all international grants went to or through INGOs.

The US Internal Revenue Service (IRS) imposes some restrictions on international grant-making by private foundations (i.e. foundations that are tax exempt under the Code), to ensure that grant proceeds will be used by the foreign grantee for appropriate charitable purposes. Private foundations may demonstrate compliance with such requirements through one of two methods: 'expenditure responsibility' which requires a level of oversight by the grantor, or 'an equivalency determination' that requires the grant-maker to form opinion that the foreign organisation it wishes to support is essentially the equivalent of a US s 501(c)(3) public charity.

US public charities may also make international grants and are generally not subject to the same restrictions on international grant-making as private foundations. A public charity must ensure that the foreign recipient of its funds engages in activities that are consistent with the public charity's exempt purpose. This invariably means having a grant agreement in place requiring progress reporting and return of the funds if they are used for an improper purpose.

Other countries indicated that a fund may lose its tax-preferred status if grants are made to PBOs in other countries. For example, in Australia an approved fund (which may be a Private Ancillary Fund or a Public Ancillary Fund) can only make grants to PBOs in Australia (although those PBOs may undertake activities in other countries, see 5.3.2).

Similarly, in Canada, tax-preferred charitable foundations are only allowed to gift funds to 'qualified donees' which are generally only situated in Canada. Foundations that donate assets or make grants to PBOs in other countries may have their registration temporarily suspended or revoked or be subject to a monetary penalty. However, foundations are able to carry out activities through intermediaries. This means that foundations can transfer funds to PBOs in other countries, provided that they maintain sufficient direction and control over their resources such that the activity can be considered their own.

In New Zealand, as is the case for PBOs (see 5.3.2), funds will lose their donee status (so donors will not be eligible for tax concessions) if monies are not applied 'wholly or mainly to charitable, benevolent, philanthropic or cultural purposes within New Zealand'. This means that a maximum of 25% of funds could be applied to purposes outside NZ. These restrictions do not apply to foreign charities listed in Sched 32 of the Income Tax Act 2007 (see 5.3.1)

Colombia, Israel and Mexico indicated that funds that make grants abroad may lose their preferential tax treatment.

Notes

[1] The FATF recommendations in relation to non-profit entities are discussed in Chapter 2.

[2] The Bulgarian income tax legislation does not place any restrictions on making grants to PBOs in other countries.

6 Conclusions and policy options

This concluding chapter brings together the key insights from the report and discusses their tax policy implications. It highlights the importance of countries ensuring that the design of their tax incentives for philanthropic giving are consistent with their underlying policy goals. It also suggests that countries reassess the merits of providing tax exemptions for the commercial income of philanthropic entities, at least insofar as this income is unrelated to the entity's worthy purpose. More broadly, it finds scope for countries to both reduce the complexity and improve the oversight of their concessionary regimes for philanthropic entities and philanthropic giving. Finally, in light of the increasingly global nature of many policy challenges – such as environmental and public health concerns (including the COVID-19 pandemic) – it suggests countries reassess the restrictions commonly imposed on access to tax concessions for cross-border philanthropy.

6.1. Introduction

Philanthropy plays an important role in most countries, providing private support to a range of activities for the public good. This differentiates the sector from government initiatives (i.e., public action for the public good) and profit-based initiatives (i.e., private action for the private good). Almost all OECD countries provide some form of preferential tax treatment for philanthropy. Entities with a philanthropic status typically receive tax relief directly in relation to their activities, while both individual and corporate donors to these entities are typically able to receive tax incentives that lower the cost of giving.

This report has undertaken a detailed review of the tax treatment of philanthropic entities and philanthropic giving in 40 OECD member and participating countries. It has first examined the various arguments for and against the provision of preferential tax treatment for philanthropic entities and giving. It has then reviewed the tax treatment of philanthropic entities and giving in a domestic context, before then examining the cross-border taxation of philanthropy. This final chapter brings together the insights from this analysis and discusses their tax policy implications.

This chapter is structured as follows. Sections 6.2-6.5 summarise the key messages from the preceding chapters in the report. Section 6.6 then presents the resulting conclusions and discusses a range of policy options.

6.2. The case for preferential tax treatment for philanthropy

Chapter 2 summarised the various arguments for and against the use of tax concessions for philanthropic entities and philanthropic giving. This highlighted that there is no single generally accepted rationale for preferential tax treatment of philanthropic entities. Economic theory provides a limited rationale for providing tax concessions for philanthropy (potentially both for entities and giving) where there is under-provision of a public good or where there are positive externalities associated with the activity of the philanthropic entity. The under-provision of a public good rationale requires there to have been a combination of "market failure", "government failure" and "voluntary failure", in the sense that the private market, government, and voluntary sector are all unable to provide the welfare-maximising level of public good provision.

A related public good-based rationale put forward by legal scholars posits that tax favoured status (again potentially for both entities and giving) is justified on the basis that it provides a subsidy for the provision of public goods that would otherwise be required to be provided by the state (the "subsidy" rationale). Another often articulated argument is the "base defining" rationale which argues that the surplus of a philanthropic entity is different in nature to income and therefore beyond the scope of the income tax base. Additional arguments include that philanthropic giving, as well as the institutions it develops, strengthen civil society and decentralise decision-making, and are thus an important feature of a democratic society and worth supporting.

A number of arguments have been raised against the provision of tax preferences for philanthropic entities and/or giving. The cost of providing concessions is often highlighted as a concern. By reducing government revenue, tax concessions for philanthropy require other taxpayers to bear an increased tax burden (or alternatively result in less government expenditure on other policy priorities). Another argument, is that taxpayers are often relatively unresponsive to tax incentives for philanthropic giving, suggesting they may not be "treasury efficient" in the sense that they increase giving by less than the tax revenue lost. Empirical evidence on the elasticity of giving provides some support for this argument. However, it is important to note that a tax incentive could be treasury inefficient but still welfare improving if the benefit to society of the activity funded by the giving is sufficiently large. While grants could in this case be more effective, concerns of government grants crowding out private donations may in some instances still justify the use of tax incentives. A concern regarding exemption of commercial income of philanthropic entities is that this may create an unfair competitive advantage for philanthropic entities over for-profit businesses.

Two related concerns that are raised regarding tax incentives for giving are that they may be regressive and undemocratic. Tax incentives may be regressive in that higher income taxpayers benefit from a larger tax incentive than lower income taxpayers. This can be the case in both aggregate terms, but also in proportionate terms as a tax deduction will provide a greater benefit to higher income taxpayers if they are subject to higher marginal tax rates than lower income taxpayers. The democratic argument highlights the concern that, as a tax incentive effectively reallocates tax revenue towards the favoured philanthropic entity, higher income taxpayers that make greater donations benefit from a disproportionate influence in the determination of how tax revenue is spent. This may be of particular concern where the priorities of donors are not consistent with those of society in general. Greater control by the government over the range of entities for which donations are eligible for tax incentives may limit this concern to some extent.

Irrespective of these arguments, most countries do provide tax incentives for giving, and in general provide exemptions from some taxes for philanthropic entities. The next sections summarise the approaches countries have taken.

6.3. Taxation and philanthropic entities

In almost all of the countries analysed in this report, entities with a philanthropic status (funds and PBOs) can receive tax incentivised gifts from individuals and corporations, as well as receive tax relief directly in relation to their activities. The report finds that for an entity to receive a philanthropic status with the associated tax benefits, it must meet not-for-profit, worthy purpose, and public benefit requirements.

The not-for profit requirement does not prohibit a philanthropic entity from making a surplus, instead, it generally includes non-distribution requirements so that the surplus is not distributed as dividends or other benefits beyond the scope of the entity's worthy purpose. An issue that can arise is whether the payment of some salaries to employees breaches this notion of 'non-distribution'. This report finds that generally the requirement does not prevent the payment of 'reasonable' remuneration for services (or the provision of goods). Some countries may impose restrictions in this regard, while others may be less prescriptive.

With regard to the worthy purpose requirement, welfare, education, scientific research, and health care are deemed worthy purposes most frequently across countries. Countries generally stipulate that the benefit must be open to all, that the benefit can be restricted to groups with specific characteristics, or that the characteristics used to specify who can benefit must relate to the fulfilment of the entity's worthy purpose.

Additionally, to help assess whether entities meet these requirements, countries tend to impose a number of administrative requirements. Almost all countries surveyed in this report require philanthropic entities to undergo a specific application process to become eligible for preferential tax treatment. Countries typically follow one of three broad approaches in determining the administrative and oversight body. Under the first approach, the tax administration is responsible for oversight of the sector (including the accreditation process). The second approach is to assign the responsibility to both the tax administration and a competent authority such as an independent commission. Lastly, in some countries the accreditation and oversight responsibility lies entirely with another department and not the tax administration.

The report identifies two approaches for providing tax relief for the income of philanthropic entities: the first is to exempt all or specific income, and the second is to consider all forms of income taxable, but allow the entity to reduce its taxable income through current or future reinvestments towards the fulfilment of its worthy purpose. Countries following the first approach generally exclude non-commercial income (received gifts or grants) from the tax base. Approaches to dealing with commercial activities and the income generated from those activities, diverge. Countries, whose philanthropic entities are fully income tax exempt, restrict these entities from engaging in certain kinds of activities. On the other hand, countries that want philanthropic entities to pay taxes on some of their income generally differentiate between commercial income that is related and unrelated to the worthy purpose.

The report also finds that countries that offer preferential VAT treatment to philanthropic entities tend to exempt them from having to collect VAT on certain (or all) supplies. As such an exemption can create an input tax burden, some countries have implemented rules that enable philanthropic entities to reclaim a portion of their input tax.

Philanthropic entities may own real estate that they use to fulfil their social objectives, or they may own it as a source of income. The report finds that, in some countries, entities that use their real estate for their worthy purpose, such as the location of offices or philanthropic activities, may be exempt from property taxes.

A number of common types of abuse of the preferential tax treatment provided to philanthropic entities are identified in this report. For example, they include diverting funds intended for public purposes to private benefits, for-profit businesses posing as PBOs to benefit from the tax relief; philanthropic entities investing in corporations owned or controlled by employees or managers of the entity; salaried employees concealed as volunteer workers; or entities not registered for VAT that are undertaking taxable activities.

6.4. Taxation and philanthropic giving

In most of the countries surveyed, individual taxpayers that give to a qualifying fund or PBO receive some form of tax incentive. In the large majority of countries surveyed, donations are deductible. Other countries offer tax credits instead and, in some cases, the donations of individuals are matched or facilitated through an allocation scheme. In countries with a matching scheme, government tops up donations at a given rate so that the entity receiving the donation is able to claim the tax relief. In countries with an allocation scheme, the tax administration allows taxpayers to designate a fixed percentage or amount of their income tax to a fund or PBO directly through their tax return. Although allocation schemes are not tax incentives, they are included in this discussion as they are administered through the tax system and their objective is to support philanthropy. Unlike individual donors, companies can also claim deductions (under standard business expensing rules) for corporate sponsoring of philanthropic entities. As a result, the report finds that deductions are more common for incentives for corporate donors than for individual ones.

In countries with no tradition of philanthropic giving, an allocation scheme can create awareness among taxpayers, financially support funds and PBOs, and develop stronger ties between the general public and philanthropic entities. The report finds that allocation schemes were introduced mainly in eastern European countries and may thus be a part of a regional trend.

Countries' approaches to limiting the fiscal cost of their incentives vary. Countries that provide tax deductions, may cap the share of the donation that is deductible, cap the size of the deduction to a share of taxable or total income, cap the size of the deduction to a fixed value, or use a combination of these ceilings. Countries that provide a tax credit, may cap the value of their tax credit to a share of taxable or total income; a share of the income tax liability, a fixed value, a combination of ceilings, or cap the size of the donation that is creditable. To limit the cost of matching schemes, countries set the rate at which the relief may be claimed by the receiving philanthropic entity.

The report also finds that countries that levy inheritance or estate taxes generally provide preferential tax relief for philanthropic bequests. In countries with an inheritance tax, the PBO or fund receiving the bequest are liable for the tax and thus are the ones that receive the tax relief. In countries with an estate tax, on the other hand, the tax liability as well as the corresponding tax relief is with the estate of the deceased.

The majority of countries that incentivise cash donations of individuals also incentivise non-monetary donations. Nevertheless, some countries choose to limit their tax incentives to cash donations only, and some severely restrict the size and nature of non-monetary donations. With respect to countries that incentivise non-monetary donations, the report identifies a number of different approaches to designing valuation rules: some countries require appraisals if the value of a non-monetary donation exceeds a threshold, others have different valuation rules for different types of assets and a number of countries do not require appraisals and review valuations through audits.

Corporate sponsoring of philanthropic entities (i.e. payments in return for publicity or advertisement) is considered a business expense in most countries, as long as there is a sufficient nexus with earning income. However, the report finds that, in a number of countries, these payments may be considered commercial income of the philanthropic entities receiving them and thus have tax implications.

Common types of tax avoidance and evasion issues with tax relief for philanthropic giving include: falsified donation receipts prepared by the philanthropic entity, tax preparers or donors; payments for goods and services disguised as donations; overvalued gifts; and donations of assets in which the donor retains an interest. Given that a key anti-abuse policy is that the recipients of philanthropic giving must be accredited philanthropic entities, the majority of anti-abuse policies identified in the report are in the form of transparency and reporting requirements for funds and PBOs. This allows the tax administration to focus its resources on these entities and generally shifts the onus of demonstrating that the worthy purpose and public benefit requirements have been satisfied on to the philanthropic entities that receive the donations.

6.5. Taxation and cross-border philanthropy

The report has also examined the tax treatment of cross-border philanthropy. Cross-border philanthropy can occur where a person (an individual or a corporation) makes a gift to an entity in another jurisdiction ('direct philanthropy'). Cross-border philanthropy can also occur where a domestic philanthropic entity operates in another jurisdiction or where a foreign entity operates domestically ('indirect philanthropy').

The report finds that, beyond the European Union (EU), there is little tax support provided by countries for cross-border giving. Within the EU, Member States are governed by European Court of Justice (ECJ) rulings requiring Member States to adopt a 'comparability' approach to ascertain whether a gift to a philanthropic entity in another Member State is entitled to tax relief. This typically requires a case-by-case analysis to determine eligibility, and due to differences between Member States relating to tax relief, can result in considerable complexity and uncertainty. The report finds that the ECJ rulings have not been fully adopted by all Members of the EU. Beyond the EU, there are a small number of bilateral treaties (such as the US-Canada and US-Mexico treaties) where tax relief may be obtained for a donation in the partner country. There are also a small number of countries (e.g. Canada) that provide tax concessions for donations to certain approved foreign PBOs. The limitations imposed on tax support for cross-border giving have led some philanthropic entities to establish 'work arounds' with entities in various jurisdictions, so that gifts can be made to domestic entities (that are eligible for tax relief) but are then passed on to entities in other countries.

With regard to PBOs that operate across borders, most countries do not provide tax relief for foreign philanthropic entities. The position in the EU is again governed by ECJ rulings requiring Member States to adopt a 'comparability' test to determine the eligibility of an entity in another Member State for tax relief. Beyond the EU, there are a small number of countries that provide tax relief for foreign philanthropic entities on a case-by-case basis (e.g. Australia, Canada, Indonesia). The inability of foreign entities to qualify for tax relief has meant that many entities that operate internationally establish local entities that are eligible for tax relief.

Many, but not all, countries provide tax relief to domestic entities that operate abroad, particularly where the activities are related to humanitarian relief or development assistance. Typically, this authorisation is reliant upon the philanthropic entity respecting the worthy purpose requirements imposed by the national legislation, usually similar to the requirements imposed on domestic PBOs.

6.6. Policy options

While, as noted above, there are arguments both in favour of and against the use of tax incentives for philanthropy, in practice most governments judge them as worthwhile. This section draws on the preceding analysis to highlight a number of key issues that countries face in the design of their tax rules for philanthropic entities and philanthropic giving.

First, it is important that countries ensure that the design of their tax incentives for philanthropic giving are consistent with their underlying policy goals. Second, there is scope in many countries to reassess the design of tax concessions for philanthropic entities. More broadly, countries should also look to both reduce the complexity and improve the oversight of their concessionary regimes for philanthropic entities and philanthropic giving. Finally, there may be merit in countries reassessing the restrictions that are typically imposed on cross-border philanthropic activity. These issues are discussed in more detail below.

6.6.1. Ensuring the design of tax incentives for philanthropic giving meets policy goals

Designing tax incentives for philanthropic giving is complicated due to the need to balance a range of potential policy goals. While the overall aim of a tax incentive can be seen as maximising social welfare, determining how to achieve this is challenging and requires various value judgements to be made. Broadly speaking, trade-offs must be made between incentivising giving, limiting fiscal cost, and managing both the distributional and democratic (in terms of influence over how tax revenue is spent) impacts of the tax incentive. A range of design choices impact on these goals.

Choice of eligibility criteria

Most countries allow tax incentives for a broad range of worthy purposes. The choice of eligibility criteria offers policy makers a means of targeting the benefit of tax concessions. Narrower eligibility conditions will ensure tax concessions more tightly target activities that align with the priorities of policy makers, but may result in a lower level of total giving. In contrast, wider eligibility conditions will ensure that the philanthropic priorities of a wider range of taxpayers are eligible for concessionary treatment and may therefore lead to increased giving.

Countries that are particularly concerned about restricting support to those areas prioritised by government may wish to consider limiting the breadth of eligibility. For example, by restricting eligibility to activities that directly support those suffering from poverty, illness and disability. Ensuring that tax incentives are limited to a narrow scope of activities is likely to be a more effective means of targeting support than by imposing fiscal caps (see below).

Tax deductions vs tax credits

As noted above, the most popular tax incentive for philanthropic giving across the countries examined in this study is a tax deduction. However, for countries with a progressive personal income tax (PIT) system, a deduction will disproportionately benefit higher income taxpayers because the benefit of the deduction increases with the marginal tax rate of the giver. This may create distributional concerns in light of the broader goals of progressivity and redistribution associated with the progressive PIT systems adopted in most countries. Furthermore, it may also create concern regarding the increased degree of influence that high-income taxpayers are given in the determination of how tax revenue is spent (with richer households potentially favouring different types of philanthropic activities than poorer households), and the consistency of this with democratic principles. This, in turn, may exacerbate distributional concerns if higher income taxpayers not only benefit more in terms of the tax concession they receive, but also in terms of the benefit they derive from the type of activities the tax-incentivised giving funds. At the same time, providing a greater tax incentive to richer taxpayers is likely to result in greater increases in aggregate philanthropic giving both because the bulk of giving comes from higher income as compared to lower income taxpayers and they are also more responsive to tax incentives.

In contrast, countries particularly concerned about distributional impacts, may wish to consider moving to a tax credit. A tax credit will ensure that the same proportionate tax benefit is provided to taxpayers irrespective of their income level. Providing a credit that is lower than the deduction currently available to top-PIT rate taxpayers may reduce the incentive to give among high-income earners. Alternatively, matching the top-rate may come at some additional fiscal cost. This creates a trade-off that governments will need to balance. At a minimum, countries with deductions should reassess the merits of maintaining the deduction to ensure that the decision to maintain the deduction is based on a clear policy decision to provide a greater incentive to higher income taxpayers.

Fixed vs percentage-based fiscal caps

Restrictions on the size of tax incentives are common in light of countries' desire to restrict the fiscal cost of their tax incentives for giving. Some countries adopt caps on the size of the tax incentive set equal to a specific fixed currency amount, while others adopt caps based on a percentage of the donor's income or tax liability, and some adopt a combination of both.

The adoption of such caps do, however, have an impact on both the degree of incentive provided by the concession and their distributional impact. A fixed cap will result in no taxpayers above the cap receiving any additional incentive to give on their marginal earnings, thereby reducing the amount of giving. The extent of the restriction will depend on the level of the cap set. Such a cap may improve distributional outcomes as it will ensure that the maximum potential aggregate benefit available to both poor and rich households will be the same. It will also cap the influence of high-income taxpayers in the determination of how tax revenue is spent. However, the imposition of a relatively high cap may be binding on high-income taxpayers but not on low-income taxpayers and will still result in a greater concession being provided to high-income taxpayers in practice.

A percentage-based cap will instead equalise the maximum potential proportional benefit available to both poor and rich households. Richer households will still benefit more in aggregate terms, but not in proportional terms (with a proportionate cap more likely to be binding on lower income households than a high fixed cap). For a given fiscal cost, this may result in a greater increase in giving than a fixed cap due to the greater responsiveness of higher income taxpayers. As such, if a country aims to maximise total giving for a given fiscal cost then it should consider applying a percentage based cap, rather than a fixed cap. If instead distributional concerns are of high importance then consideration may be given to applying a fixed cap. An alternative option in balancing these goals may be to combine a percentage-based cap together with a generous fixed cap. Such an approach may be of particular merit for countries concerned about the disproportionate influence of high-income taxpayers in the determination of how tax revenue is spent.

Allocation schemes

A small number of countries apply allocation schemes, where taxpayers can designate a fixed percentage or amount of their income tax to a fund or PBO directly through their tax return. Allocation schemes can increase the visibility of the philanthropic sector and create a culture of giving in a country where there is no such a culture. However, allocation schemes do not provide a tax incentive to give and so are unlikely to have a significant impact on the level of giving. As such, the use of tax incentives should generally be preferred where the aim is to increase the level of giving.

6.6.2. Preferential tax treatment of philanthropic entities

As stated above, a common approach of countries that provide tax concessions to philanthropic entities, is to exempt all or specific income of these entities. Furthermore, a number of countries exempt philanthropic entities from having to collect VAT on certain (or all) supplies. This section discusses the challenges that may arise as a result of these concessions and provides policy options that may reduce complexities and distortions as well as increase compliance.

Commercial income of philanthropic entities

Philanthropic entities may have commercial and/or non-commercial income, but the distinction is not always clear or the same across countries. Generally, non-commercial income refers to income from philanthropic gifts (discussed in Chapter 4) and government grants, or (in the case of PBOs) grants from supporting funds. Broadly, commercial income is income derived from the supply of goods or services in return for some form of payment.

If there are no restrictions on the commercial activities a philanthropic entity can engage in and the income from those activities is fully tax exempt, it may give rise to competitive neutrality and revenue loss concerns. To avoid such concerns, the report identifies a number of policy options. A common approach is to only exempt income generated from commercial activities that are related to the philanthropic entity's worthy purpose. However, the definitions of related and unrelated commercial income vary widely across countries and such tax rules often result in significant complexity.

Other approaches are less complex, but may not fully exclude unrelated income from the preferential tax treatment. One approach is to only exempt income generated from commercial activities where it is reinvested towards the entity's worthy purpose in a timely fashion. To facilitate some flexibility on behalf of the entities, such a policy could potentially be subject to an exception or allowance for the creation of small reserves that may be necessary to support the ongoing pursuit or expansion of the philanthropic entity's activities that are directly connected to its worthy purpose. Another approach may be to limit the size of the expansion through a threshold beyond which income from commercial activities is taxed.

The competitive neutrality concerns associated with exempting the commercial income of philanthropic entities gives rise to an important issue that requires the attention of policy makers. For this reason, countries should reassess the merits of providing tax exemptions for the commercial income of PBOs, at least in so far as this income is unrelated to the entity's worthy purpose. However, in undertaking such a reassessment, countries will need to consider the added complexities associated with distinguishing between taxable (i.e. unrelated commercial income) and exempt income and weigh the additional compliance and administrative costs against the pursuit of competitive neutrality.

VAT

Exempting philanthropic entities, or their activities from VAT may also lead to competitive neutrality concerns between for-profit and philanthropic entities. Furthermore, policies intended to refund parts of the tax paid on inputs tend to be very complex. Therefore, countries that currently provide an exemption should consider fully subjecting philanthropic entities to the VAT. As is typically the case with for-profit businesses, a registration threshold could be applied to exclude small philanthropic entities for whom compliance costs are likely to be disproportionate relative to the VAT revenue collected.

6.6.3. Reduce complexity

Another challenge for designing tax incentives for philanthropy is to find a balance between tailoring policies to the wide range of philanthropic activities and limiting the complexity of the tax system. This report identifies three key areas that could benefit from reducing the complexity of the tax rules in a number of countries: eligibility requirements for different kinds of tax incentives, tax rules for non-monetary donations and the valuation processes, and payroll giving.

Overly complex tax rules risk increasing compliance costs and uncertainty. This, in turn, can lead to both accidental and deliberate tax compliance issues. Complex tax rules and the related compliance costs that ensue may also put low-income donors and smaller philanthropic entities at a disadvantage compared to high-income donors and larger philanthropic entities. This is because the compliance costs may be lower in relative terms for high-income donors and large entities, which may also be more likely to afford tax advice from experts. Therefore, limiting complexity where possible has the potential of making tax incentives for philanthropy more efficient, less regressive, and increase overall compliance.

Eligibility requirements for different kinds of tax incentives

The report finds that in most countries, entities with a recognised philanthropic status are able to receive tax-incentivised gifts from individuals and corporations, or receive tax relief directly in relation to their activities. For an entity to be eligible for these incentives, it must meet not-for-profit, worthy purpose, and public benefit requirements. To reduce complexity, countries should consider applying the same eligibility tests for both kinds of incentives.

Non-monetary donations

A philanthropic donation can be in cash or non-cash form, with the latter frequently referred to as non-monetary or in-kind donations. Non-monetary donations may include: real and intellectual property; corporate stock or shares; trading stock; cultural assets; other personal property; services (volunteering); or blood and organ donations. To apply a tax incentive to non-monetary donations, the gift must be assigned a value. The valuation rules and process increase compliance and administration costs for donors, government, and in some cases the receiving entities. The valuation of a non-monetary donation determines the value of the tax incentive for the donor, and thus creates an incentive for donors to inflate the value of their donation. As such, valuation rules for non-monetary donations are intended to limit the possibility of abuse. Furthermore, the value of assets can fluctuate significantly. To the extent that the value of assets is subjective, valuation rules need to establish a process through which the value is determined as objectively as possible. This, in turn, may require a professional assessment (e.g., the valuation of artwork), which increases the compliance cost to whoever is responsible for the valuation.

In light of the complexities around valuation and the associated compliance costs, imposing a minimum value threshold for a non-monetary donation to receive concessionary tax treatment, may be warranted. Furthermore, countries may consider reassessing the kinds of non-monetary donations eligible for the tax incentives. When considering what kind of non-monetary donations to incentivise, the benefit resulting from the donation being non-monetary (as opposed to cash), should be weighed against the additional cost associated with the required valuation process and risk of abuse.

On the other hand, determining the kinds of non-monetary donations that could more effectively be made through cash donations, may be challenging as future needs are uncertain. For example, the COVID-19 health crisis has shown how an unexpected shortage in personal protective equipment (PPE) created a demand for non-monetary donations of masks and other PPE products. Similar needs can arise where natural disasters occur and often the provision of goods and materials that are urgently needed, may be more helpful than the provision of cash donations.

Payroll giving

A number of countries have introduced payroll giving schemes. These schemes enable employees to elect to have donations to approved philanthropic entities deducted from their income by their employer, and for them to receive the relevant tax incentive (deduction or tax credit), within an extended pay-as-you-earn withholding tax system. Effectively, they shift the compliance costs associated with giving from employees to employers – who may be able to more efficiently bear this compliance burden. Such schemes may therefore be an administratively efficient way to increase the effectiveness of a tax incentive for giving.

6.6.4. Improve oversight

Improving oversight of the philanthropic sector is important for protecting public trust in the sector as well as ensuring that the tax concessions used to subsidise philanthropy are not abused through tax avoidance and evasion schemes. This section provides an overview of policy options that may help protect public trust, increase compliance, limit loopholes and ultimately improve oversight of the philanthropic sector and its activities.

Publicly available register of approved philanthropic entities

Public trust and confidence in the philanthropic sector is a key priority for government as well as the sector itself. In part due to philanthropy's reliance on private philanthropic giving, public trust is an essential component of financing the sector. Additionally, because philanthropy benefits from considerable tax support, public trust is also important in justifying and upholding the tax concessions used to subsidise philanthropic activities. A key way in which many countries improve transparency, certainty and accountability regarding what entities are eligible for receiving tax concessions as well as tax incentivised gifts, is to make publicly available a register of approved philanthropic entities. Countries that do not currently do so, should consider adopting such a publicly available register of approved philanthropic entities.

Such a policy may also help combat schemes in which fraudulent entities pretend to be eligible funds or PBOs in order to receive donations. Having a publicly available register would enable donors to cross-reference the information. Furthermore, a publicly available register invites public scrutiny, which may help to increase compliance and improve the detection of abuse.

Annual reporting requirements

A key challenge for oversight bodies (whether that is the tax administration, an independent commission or other department within the government) is to be able to collect the information needed to evaluate whether the philanthropic entities are complying with existing regulations and meeting the necessary requirements of organisations benefitting from preferential tax status. This report finds that in the majority of countries, entities have to go through an application process in order to qualify for the preferential tax status. Such a process, however, can only ensure that entities are compliant and meet the requirements at the time of their application (which frequently is at the start of their operations).

Imposing annual reporting requirements on funds and PBOs could improve oversight. This is because the oversight bodies are able to use the annual reports to keep track of philanthropic entities even after they have been granted preferential tax status. Such a policy may also help countries better identify errors or compliance issues early on, which may be beneficial for the entities as well. Furthermore, annual reports also have the potential to increase public trust, especially if some of the information in the report is made public. As annual reporting requirements may increase compliance costs, countries may wish to consider the adoption of a *de minimis* amount of revenue above which the reporting requirements would apply.

Combined oversight approach

The range of activities that philanthropic entities may engage in is typically very broad and thus it may be challenging for a tax administration to properly assess and oversee entities that are involved in fields that are not within the expertise of the tax administration. Additionally, it may be difficult for a revenue administration to justify the allocation of significant resources to the oversight of a largely untaxed philanthropic sector, resulting in a degree of under-supervision. To both improve the level of oversight in areas that require specific expertise, and alleviate the workload on the tax administration, countries should consider the adoption of a combined oversight approach. In a combined oversight approach, the tax administration and a competent ministry or commission with experts in a field related to the worthy purpose, would oversee the philanthropic entity and its activities.

Tax avoidance and evasion schemes

Abuse of incentives for philanthropic giving could deprive governments of much-needed revenues and risks undermining public trust in the government and the philanthropic sector. To reduce the risk of tax abuse, countries should consider a number of policy options:

- Maintaining a database of suspicious activities to help identify trends and develop expertise on tax abuse related to tax concessions for philanthropy. Collecting data on suspicious activities may also assist the oversight bodies to conduct more targeted audits and thus become more efficient.
- Exchanging good practices as well as information with tax administrations and law enforcement agencies may improve the efficiency of the oversight process as non-compliant actors in the philanthropic sector may already be on the radar of other law enforcement agencies. More specifically, exchanging information across law enforcement agencies may also strengthen the effort to ensure that organisations involved in illegal and inappropriate activities do not abuse the concessions afforded to the philanthropic sector to finance their activities.
- Implementing limits to fundraising expenditures may be an effective approach to restrict tax-exempt entities from overspending on fundraising events.
- Similarly, implementing rules that limit certain types of operating expenses of PBOs that are at an increased risk of being misused for the private benefit of people associated with the entity (e.g., vehicles, residential real estate, etc.) may limit schemes in which managers, employees, board members, or large donors use the assets of tax-exempt entities for their private benefit.
- Limiting the remuneration of staff, managers, and board members of PBOs may help ensure that the untaxed income and donations received by philanthropic entities are not used for the personal gain of people associated with the entity. Unreasonably high remuneration may also be an indication of a scheme to circumvent the non-distribution requirement of the not-for-profit status. Therefore, limiting the remuneration that people associated with the entity can receive could be an effective policy at ensuring the not-for-profit requirement is met.
- Screening non-resident PBOs and funds eligible for receiving tax-incentivised donations helps ensure that the requirements countries impose on resident entities that may receive tax-incentivised donations are also met abroad. Furthermore, screening non-resident PBOs is a key strategy of a number of countries to combat terrorist financing schemes involving philanthropic entities.
- Implementing clear and transparent procedures for authorities to deal with non-compliance quickly.

Rules for corporate and individual giving

As discussed in Chapter 4, corporate philanthropic giving can occur in the form of donations or sponsorship payments. Sponsoring funds and PBOs are payments in return for publicity and thus generate a benefit to the donor. This report has highlighted that in many countries, sponsorship or advertising payments (which have a sufficient nexus with earning income) are deductible under business expensing rules and not subject to the limitations placed on deductions for corporate donations. This in turn may create an incentive for managers or owners of businesses to support causes through business sponsorship payments instead of personal donations in order to circumvent the limits placed on the tax incentives for philanthropic giving in a number of countries. Therefore, countries should better align rules for corporate and individual giving to limit distortions and ambiguities. This may be achieved by, for example, implementing similar limits for tax incentives for corporate and individual donations.

To do so, tax rules should clearly differentiate between donating and sponsoring. This may be done by, for example, requiring a sponsorship contract that clearly specifies the publicity the corporation will receive. This, in turn, allows policy makers to only provide deductions for sponsorship equal to the market value of the publicity/advertisement received in return for the payment. The amount of the payment in excess of the fair market value should be treated as a donation and subject to the respective limits.

Clearly differentiating between donations and sponsorship may also have important tax consequences for the philanthropic entity receiving the donation or the sponsorship payment. Countries that tax the commercial income of philanthropic entities may consider advertising to be a commercial activity and tax the sponsorship payments accordingly (while the income from donations is generally exempt).

Data collection and tax expenditure reports

Part of improving oversight of the tax incentives provided for philanthropy is to be able to estimate the cost of these incentives. To do so, countries should collect data and estimate as well as publish tax expenditures used to subsidise philanthropy. Furthermore, tax expenditure data may also enable countries to conduct studies that evaluate the efficiency of their individual incentives.

6.6.5. Reassess the current restrictions for international giving

Concerns regarding the degree of benefit (or lack thereof) to the country providing the tax concession, as well as regarding a potential lack of oversight, have resulted in only a very limited degree of tax support for cross-border philanthropy. However, the global nature of many of the challenges facing the world emphasises the importance of countries taking a global rather than an insular perspective. In particular, responding to issues such as poverty, war and conflict, environmental concerns, medical research, and public health issues such as pandemics, may require countries and institutions to cooperate across borders. A number of countries now also see a role for cross-border philanthropy in limited circumstances such as the provision of development assistance, and in relation to conflict situations.

In this context, there is merit in countries reassessing whether there may be some instances where equivalent tax treatment should be provided to domestic and cross-border philanthropy. For example, countries may wish to consider ensuring that domestic PBOs operating overseas for certain health, environmental and development assistance purposes, or those providing direct humanitarian support in conflict situations, should receive equivalent tax treatment to those operating domestically.

To address concerns regarding oversight and risks of abuse of tax concessions, countries could impose equivalent requirements as apply in the domestic philanthropy context, or require additional checks before providing tax-favoured status. Given the difficulties associated with monitoring and ensuring the compliance of philanthropic entities operating overseas, it would seem appropriate that additional checks and mechanisms would be required to ensure that the tax support provided is being directed towards the entities' worthy purposes and that these entities are complying with all requirements that would be expected of entities operating domestically.

In the European Union, countries may wish to examine the possibility of explicitly incorporating the non-discrimination requirements of European Court of Justice (ECJ) rulings as they pertain to philanthropic entities into their domestic legislation. This may reduce uncertainty for both philanthropic entities and donors, and minimise compliance and administrative costs associated with the current case-by-case comparability analysis required under the ECJ rulings.

www.ingramcontent.com/pod-product-compliance
Lightning Source LLC
Chambersburg PA
CBHW061219240926
51846CB00006B/1276